JAY H.
BROWN

TRUTH IN GOVERNMENT

Restoring Pride and Prosperity in America

TRUTH IN GOVERNMENT
Restoring Pride and Prosperity in America

Freedom Publishing Company
2550 Crawford Avenue
Evanston, IL 60201
Phone (847)491-6775
Fax (847)491-6987

Publisher's Cataloging in Publication
(Prepared by Quality Books Inc.)

Brown, Jay H.
Truth in government : restoring pride and prosperity in America / Jay H. Brown.
p. cm.
Includes bibliographical references and index.
ISBN 0-9638152-3-7

1. United States--Politics and government. 2. Waste in government spending--United States. I. Title.

JK469.B76 1996 353
QBI96-20301

ACKNOWLEDGMENTS

* *

Thanks to my family who, like most hard-working, honest Americans, continues to support and pay taxes for the indiscretions of politicians at all levels. They inspired me to show the need for honesty in politics, which will lead to a more informed public, making the United States better than ever.

A special thanks goes to the individuals and organizations who attempt to honestly educate the public regarding the activities of our government. The list includes The Heritage Foundation, The Cato Institute, Citizens Against Government Waste, the Center for Public Integrity, Ross Perot, American Conservative Union, Martin Gross, Rush Limbaugh, Project Vote Smart, the Congressional Budget Office, the U.S. Chamber of Commerce, the Concord Coalition, the United States Government Printing Office, and many others.

I also wish to thank the leaders of our country, who made the research for this work not only possible, but easy. My only regret is that I couldn't include an extra 1,000 pages or so of waste, fraud and abuse that our politicians have so selfishly forced us, our children, and future generations to pay for.

This book is dedicated to the hard-working Americans who are paying over $2.5 trillion dollars in various forms of taxes each year. We deserve honest representation from our elected officials. We deserve the truth.

**"Blessed are the young,
for they shall inherit the national debt."**

Herbert Hoover

CONTENTS

"Those who corrupt the public mind are just as evil as those who steal from the public purse."

Adlai Stevenson

FOREWORD

There are some who question another person's patriotism, or love of country, when they criticize the government or the politicians who work for us. However, patriotism and love of country should not be measured by how readily we agree with our politicians, but by how much effort we put into trying to improve our country.

The purpose of *Truth In Government* is to provide workable solutions to some of the momentous problems facing the people of the United States today. These problems arise from our stifling government, in the form of choking taxes and smothering regulations and laws. If, once you see the examples outlined in this book, you agree that there are serious problems that must be addressed and corrected, then we may tackle the area of reform that will be the most productive – the way Congress works. How Congress works is the single most important explanation for the condition of our country.

Much of this book is devoted to showing examples of government waste, fraud, abuse, and arrogance in Washington. Awareness of this is essential because, even though there have been countless books and studies on this subject, much high-profile debate, and powerful organizations behind some reform groups, there has been only modest success at reform.

This book studies solutions that are achievable, but only if enough pressure is put on our "civil servants." *Truth In Government* goes a long way toward the reform necessary to fix this impaired nation, for the most significant and efficient reform will be one of education. The public needs to know what to look for in politicians and how to force them to tell the truth about their actions. The politicians must know that if they don't tell the truth they will suffer sure and severe consequences.

Why is it so difficult for our leaders to provide real, honest, meaningful, tangible reform? Simply because no matter what the reform, there is at least one special interest group that will suffer. Quickly. Try to think of an example of meaningful reform that doesn't negatively affect some group. Where do we find spending cuts that no one cares about? And politicians, who always have an eye on the polls and the ballot box, do not want to alienate any group. The more powerful the group, the less likely it is a politician will have the courage to make a change the group may oppose.

There's a lot of talk about reform at this time, but we have been promised changes for generations. Over the years, most of the changes we've seen have empowered politicians even more, resulting in less freedom for the public. The evidence shows that we need more than talk. We need serious reform. We need to reform our elected officials, our public servants, who talk a great game but haven't gotten to second base yet when it comes to working for us, the taxpayers.

But, you say, Congress has been stomping on the middle class for decades, and we haven't done anything about it. Correct! Congress has been stomping on the middle class, and the lower class and upper class as well. Fortunately for the politicians, however, they have a "machine" in place that puts a positive spin on anything they do and sways popular opinion in their direction.

But let's not get too involved yet. Suffice it to say that I will attempt, with your patience and open mind, to reveal to you in the simplest terms possible, the most pressing issues of the day. I will try to encourage you to help yourself by putting enough pressure on Washington to make the changes necessary to maintain the United States as the premier nation in the world, as we go into the second millennium. Only after these changes are made will we be able to restore public confidence in our elected officials, our government, and our country.

INTRODUCTION

"POLITRICS" AS USUAL

Would you like to find some simple solutions to fix the problems (heal the ills) that exist in the United States government? *Truth In Government* explains why the United States government hasn't worked for us for years, and why our country is in the trouble it's in. It offers surprisingly simple solutions to the problems in government that are keeping the United States from reaching its full potential.

Truth In Government is a partisan book - not to Democrats or Republicans - it is partisan to the citizens of the United States of America. It shows how and why we, the citizens, have lost control of our country, and how an elected few have brazenly changed the rules over the years to make themselves our bosses. *Truth In Government* shows not only how it happened, but how we can take our country back.

We have a unique opportunity to regain our country and restore the American Dream. But to do so means that we must unite as a people. Serious, meaningful reform will take place only if we can match the passion of the politicians, become informed about their actions, keep a watchful eye on them, and eliminate the temptations of politics that corrupt. Only then will we be able to make this country as strong, productive, and bountiful as it can be.

Over past decades, we have given our politicians relatively free reign to make laws and rules, and to run the country as they saw fit. And we discovered that, because we did not watch them closely enough, they used their power primarily for their own personal gain. As you read *Truth In Government,* you will see that the only way we will be able to reform and improve our government is to watch the politicians carefully. Using the ideas discussed in this revolutionary book, we can force Congress to represent us the way we deserve.

If political reform becomes a reality, the only losers will be the lawyers, lobbyists, and Washington insiders who have milked the system, and with it the American taxpayers, for decades. Without the reforms outlined in *Truth In Government*, these insiders will continue to have their way and control the way our government is run, while we continue to pay the bills.

"Big brother is watching" used to mean that the government was watching its citizens. But we are turning the tables on the government. Now, "Big brother is watching" will mean that we are watching the politicians to make sure they are representing our interests.

What Congress fears most is a well-informed public. The more informed citizens become, the more difficult it will be for Congress to manipulate them with their "politrics."

CHAPTER 1

TRUTH IN GOVERNMENT

These three little words may be the most powerful in the history of this nation. Why? Because, although the United States is without argument the most powerful and wealthy country in the world, we are just three words away from being even more powerful and affluent. The purpose of this book is to show the reader why we haven't reached our full potential as a nation, what the consequences have been, and how we can become the best nation we can be – now and for future generations.

Progress doesn't occur without imagination and the willingness and courage to change. I'd like you to use your imagination as you read about the problems and solutions offered in this book. Imagine discovering that you have been lied to by a friend. Would you feel betrayed? What if the lie was coming from an elected official, to whom you have entrusted the lofty authority to control your daily life as well as your pocketbook? Keep in mind that your elected officials have a tremendous amount of power and control over your life, present and future, and the lives of your family, grandchildren, and great-grandchildren.

Hopefully, as you read this book, something will move you to action. A nation needs the support and influence of its citizens if it is ever to reach its full potential. That will happen only if enough people develop a strong enough interest to become informed, and band together to defeat those people in government who are not working on their behalf. The American Dream is not, and should not be, the exclusive domain of the members of Congress. The American Dream is the belief that every citizen can reach his or her full potential in life. The more waste and debt Congress heaps upon the taxpayers, however, the farther we are from achieving our dreams.

This book's most difficult task is to get those people who are used to the entrenched government process, and who have religiously voted for a particular party for decades, to allow for the possibility that there may be a better way, and that serious reform may be necessary for this country to maximize its potential.

Over the years, and after hundreds of discussions with intelligent, clear-thinking individuals, I have found it excruciatingly frustrating to discover so many people who still blindly trust certain politicians, no matter what those politicians say or do. Sometimes I will ask, "What will it take for a politician to lose your support and trust? How many times does someone have to lie to you, intentionally and willfully deceive you, insult your intelligence, or undermine your trust, before you finally decide that you deserve better?"

Often, even catching a politician in a lie doesn't diminish the devotion of his supporters. Proof of fraud and negligent waste doesn't do the trick. Yet there must be some breaking point where even the most trusting and loyal individual will see a politician for what he really is. Have we become so hardened by current events, when jurors let murderers off the hook, that we feel that anything a politician does, short of murder, is acceptable?

An Analogy

After much thought, I determined that the best way to illustrate my idea was to use an analogy. Suppose you are the owner of a business and decide that, for health reasons, it is time to retire. You must still depend on your company's profitability to support you and your family, but need to hire someone to run the company, since you are no longer able to do so.

As you go through the resumes, you see you have a wide variety of choices. Will you choose someone who has business experience, or someone who has never run a business profitably before? Will you choose someone who has a track record of fiscal responsibility, or someone who has a record of frivolously spending his and other people's money? Will you choose someone who has specific ideas, or someone who speaks vaguely in "soundbites"? Will you choose someone who lies to you, or someone who speaks directly and gives you plenty of information with supporting documentation and references? Will you ask the applicant tough questions that will give you all the information you need, or will you make an uninformed decision based upon his appearance, his charisma, and his eloquence? Finally, if the applicant sounds good, will you take him at his word, or will you take the time to check out his answers to see if they are fact or fiction?

Going along with this analogy, you choose an applicant with whom you feel the most comfortable. He is charming, and he promises to do what is best for the company and its employees. He tells you he will make sure the company improves, that it will be the best company in its field, and that you, as owner, will prosper because of your decision to hire him. In effect, he says all the right things. With such confidence in his abilities and attracted by his winning personality, you have no choice but to hire Mr. Smith.

A few years pass and your health gets worse. You're still getting checks from your business to support you and your family, but you've been too busy worrying about your health to keep a close eye on the company. Then, one day, one of your advisors insists that you take the time to study how the business is doing. You call Mr. Smith, the president of the company, and tell him you're flying in for a meeting.

You meet with Mr. Smith at his office, and he tells you that things are going great. He says that although the economy took a slight downturn, and the industry took a beating, the company is on the right track and will soon be profitable again. He sees the worry in your eyes and insists that there is nothing to be concerned about. He tells you that within the next few years the company will not only be profitable again, but will be the leader in its field. He settles you down, and you leave his office feeling more confident about the future.

Before you get out the door, however, your company controller who has been with you for over 25 years takes you aside. He pulls you into his office and sits you down. "I didn't want to tell you this," Richard says, "but it's about time you find out about some things. Otherwise, I'm not being honest with you, and the business may not survive."

You turn white as Richard tells you the following.

Shortly after joining the company as president, Mr. Smith began making changes in how things were run. Had you been in better health and more involved, Richard insists, you would have been told. Because of your condition, there was no way to let you know what was happening until now. Some of the things that Richard tells you are:

• The company started losing money within a year after Mr. Smith took over.

• Despite the losses, Mr. Smith voted himself, and the people he hired to help him run the company, exorbitant raises over the years; much higher than the rate of inflation.

• Mr. Smith took a number of trips to exotic places overseas at company expense, even though there was no direct business benefit to the trips.

• Mr. Smith gave everyone in the company raises. Even the entry-level people were raised over 15% per year, since he decided that the wages being paid were not comfortable enough. The company paid twice what the rest of the industry paid for entry level-positions. This generosity earned Mr. Smith tremendous employee loyalty, and everyone at the company likes him.

• Your company made a number of "charitable contributions" to Mr. Smith's favorite organizations, even though it was losing money and piling up debt.

• Because of the losses that were accumulating, the company had to borrow money just to pay the bills for the first time in its history, and had developed a debt that required a payment of interest equaling 1/6 of all the company expenses.

• Despite the debt and the company's dim future, the extravagant spending continued at an unprecedented pace.

• Because of the high annual increase in company overhead, prices were raised, and the employees had to work longer hours and weekends to help lagging production. The company had cut research and development, among other growth areas, to help make up for the lack of funds. Instead of planning for the future, the company was finding it increasingly difficult to meet current obligations.

• And how was financing obtained to pay for the annual losses? By a combination of the good reputation that the company had when you, the owner, were running it, long-term relationships you had established, and finally by the fact that Richard had been told to make the profit-and-loss statement and balance sheet look better than they really were.

• Reports that had been sent to you over the years were sketchy at best, misleading, and never included the details you had just learned.

By the time Richard finished telling you this and much more, you looked like you had seen a ghost. At the very least, you felt deceived. Mr. Smith had not run the company in a fiscally responsible manner. He lied to you about its condition. He wasted much more money than the company could handle on any reasonable basis.

Your company had gone from being a profitable, stable leader in the industry to, despite all outward appearances that still looked rosy according to the biased company reports, a company that was drowning in its own losses and piled debt. Richard saw no way to make the payments on its overhead, let alone pay down some of the debt, which some of its lenders were requiring at this time.

Finally, now that you had all the facts, you had to decide whether to get rid of Mr. Smith, who had put you, your company, and all of your employees in this dangerous position, or go along with what Mr. Smith insisted, just moments earlier, were the stated goals of the company. What would you do?

How did this happen? In simplest terms, you had given Mr. Smith too much power and leeway, you didn't have the time or inclination to follow his actions closely, you were not kept well informed with all the necessary factual data, you didn't bother to ask the right questions, and there were not sufficient checks and balances put in place ahead of time. Mr. Smith made his own rules, ran the company as he saw fit, and deceived you and many others along the way as to the true condition of the company.

How is the above analogy different from what has happened with our federal government? The only real difference is that when Congress goes over budget, it can keep the government running by either raising our taxes or borrowing more money. Unlike businesses that don't have the luxury of raising prices upon demand or borrowing unlimited amounts of money, Congress has made a practice, mostly over the past 30 years, of spending more money than it takes in, to our detriment.

Remember, YOU are a part-owner of the largest business on Earth – the United States government. By not paying attention to those who are running the government, you are allowing your elected officials to devastate YOUR government and your country, not only for you, but for your children and future generations. It is this author's opinion that we should be keeping an eagle eye on what Congress is doing. It does matter to each of us what they do every day. It really does affect our lives. Our paying close attention is the first step towards getting better results. We must pay attention because we all have a vested interest in the economic viability of our nation.

We as taxpayers are asked to pay over $2.5 trillion to fund the federal and local governments each year. Don't we deserve, and shouldn't we demand, to be told the truth about our government? Furthermore, do those politicians who are not honest with us deserve to be in office and continue to have the opportunity to fleece the public?

Now, I'd like you to once again use your imagination.

What if your taxes were less, and you paid only two months' salary towards taxes every year instead of four or five months' salary?

EVERYONE – don't fall into the trap of believing that if you are in a low tax bracket, or pay no taxes, a more efficient and affluent government doesn't affect you. It certainly does. Did you know that individuals' federal income taxes represent less than half of the revenue the government takes in each year? Other sources of revenue include state and county taxes, sales tax, and corporate income tax. A more efficient government, needing significantly less revenue, would mean a tax savings for individuals by lowering personal income taxes. It would make it possible for corporations to pay less taxes as well. You understand that whatever a corporation pays in taxes is ultimately passed onto the consumer in higher prices. So, it follows that a corporate tax savings would result in a savings to the consumer (you) in reduced prices for products that you purchase every day.

Likewise, a government that runs efficiently could also reduce its sales tax and real estate tax; two other items that every consumer ultimately pays. Thus, even if you pay no income taxes at this time, an efficiently run government means dollars in your pocket in many ways.

What if you could trust your elected officials to tell you the truth and always act in your best interests, not their own, and you could believe them when they talk?

The frustration of many Americans is that politicians and the media continually insult the intelligence of the American people. So far, they've gotten away with it. I will show you that a massive fraud has been perpetrated on the citizens of the United States.

Two of the most vocal and high-profile critics of the way taxpayers are being treated by Washington are Ross Perot and Rush Limbaugh. They have brought the budget and many other important issues to the forefront of America's discussion and vocabulary, but they have only scratched the surface. This book digs deeper, simplifies the problems, and comes up with workable solutions that everyone can understand. Even politicians.

Among other things, I will illustrate why you are paying way too much in taxes, and explain by example the real truth about your taxes, the deficit and national debt, its consequences, and what should be done to correct the problems.

THE NATIONAL DEBT is an amazing anomaly. As hurtful as it is to every American, we have just let it continue to grow and get totally out of control. When you see a leaky faucet, don't you turn it off? Why don't we work as aggressively to fix the national debt as we do on many other less crucial problems of the day? You don't want to pay more for something than absolutely necessary. Why haven't we turned off this faucet? The answers follow.

The political process has, over the years, BROKEN our country almost beyond repair. An argument could be made that the political process has been responsible for almost every evil that has occurred within our society. It is my contention, which will be proven later, that because of the lack of discipline of Congress to regulate spending, the hard-working taxpayers have had to pay obscenely higher taxes.

What's the big deal about higher taxes, you may ask. High taxes result in less disposable/spendable income, which causes a greater need for two family incomes.

Often, without a parent at home, the moral fabric of the family dissipates, which in many cases leads to more troubled children. These children have less guidance and encouragement for school and studies, and may in turn be less likely to complete their education. With less direction from parents, children are more likely to get into trouble. These children may eventually have children of their own, born out of wedlock, which increases the welfare doles.

The increase in two-income households is largely responsible for the breakup of the family structure, i.e., divorce. This situation, in many cases, is the beginning of a dysfunctional family life which may lead the child(ren) to a discouraging and dim future.

Following the above model, this can lead to crime from the children, as well as the parents, who have a harder time supporting their family. The increased crime requires more tax dollars spent on the criminal justice system (police, lawyers, court, jails, judges, administrators, etc.) The jails turn into a network for criminals, and breed harder criminals who learn more about crime, drugs, etc., while they are imprisoned.

This may be a simplified version of one of the problems of higher taxes, but there is no doubt that the social fabric of society has crumbled, and there is little hope for improvement the way things are going.

Why would anyone pay for a Cadillac and be happy to receive a Honda Civic? This (paying taxes) is the only time one can document that so many are so willing to overpay for what they get in return. Why this apathy? It is simply a lack of knowledge of what is happening every day to their tax dollars that allows them to give up so freely!

THE TRUTH ABOUT YOUR TAX BURDEN

It is the goal of the author to show you how you can

save at least 25% of your money that goes to all forms of taxes each year – while not losing any essential government services.

The annual spending for the federal government is now over $1.5 trillion, with another trillion or so for local government, making a total of $2.5 trillion we are paying for all government services! This breaks down to an average tax bill of over $9,500 per person (based upon a current population of 263,000,000)* for every man, woman, and child in the country, or $38,000 for a family of four. However, keep in mind that many families pay no taxes. Thus, if you are an average taxpayer with a family of four, and recognizing that 30% of all people in the U.S. pay no taxes at all**, you must pay 30% more, or a total of more than $54,000 per year in taxes! Isn't it comforting to know that an average taxpaying family of four must pay $54,000 per year just to cover their "fair share"?

As if that's not enough, at the writing of this book, the national debt is almost $5 trillion dollars. This represents

*Note that this calculation assumes that individuals ultimately pay all taxes, and corporations pay none. The reasoning here is that corporate taxes, and all other forms of taxes, are ultimately paid for by the consumer when they purchase a product or service. Realize that the product would be cheaper if the taxes a corporation adds to the cost of the product were less. Therefore, the individual ultimately pays for all taxes, either directly or indirectly. Hence, the argument that corporations aren't paying enough in taxes is nothing but a political con, since the corporation usually finds ways to pass on any higher taxes to the consumer.

**Everyone pays some taxes as a consumer of goods and services (sales tax and their share of the corporate tax [reimbursement]), a renter (real estate tax reimbursement), etc. Our formula, for simplicity's sake, generalizes that for every individual or family who isn't paying income tax, those people in large number are receiving an equivalent amount of government transfers, be it subsidies, food stamps, medical care, welfare, or one or more of dozens of entitlements. Thus, for the convenience and simplicity of this model, we are assuming a zero break-point regarding the taxes paid, and the entitlements received, for that segment of the population.

almost $19,000 for every American. Again, the debt for a family of four would be $76,000. I'll bet you didn't know that you had that much debt to pay off. Regardless of the rationalization of the deficit by politicians or other so-called economists, is it fair that a child born today, before he has taken his first breath, is already in debt almost $20,000? If you think a newborn baby is crying because he was just spanked by the doctor, think again. He has just been informed that he's in debt almost $20,000. If this doesn't illustrate the irresponsibility of Congress, then nothing does!

A final way to portray the problem of deficit spending is that by the time it takes the average reader to read this book, the national debt will have increased by $162 million!

FIXING THE PROBLEM

How is it we can put men on the moon, but we can't find a way to get our representatives (public servants?) to work for us? Why can't we get them to tell the truth? Why can't politicians be honest to their bosses, the taxpayers? We deserve honest representation. Just look at what we are paying each year in taxes!

The fact is, Congress and the government are not like the weather. If we don't like it, we don't have to just talk about it – WE CAN CHANGE IT! Let's do something about it – now – before there's a $10 trillion debt, and we are paying twice as much in taxes. Don't believe for a second that there aren't workable solutions! Innovative individuals can find solutions to every problem, and we can find a realistic solution to this one.

One of the goals of this book is to help get America back on track, to lower the tax burden for everyone, and make the United States as great a country as it can be. Reducing the tax burden will be the result of less government spending and working our way toward a balanced budget. A realistic balanced budget has tremendous benefits to everyone in America. According to Federal Reserve Chairman Alan Greenspan, if we can balance the budget by the year 2002, we will have much lower interest rates, we will be more competitive in the world, enjoy higher productivity, a higher standard of living, lower trade deficits, and increased savings. There will be a boon to the economy that we haven't seen in recent memory. If that isn't incentive enough, I don't know what is! A brilliant report by the U.S. Chamber of Commerce from the *1995 Congressional Record* can be found in the appendix. This question and answer piece outlines in no uncertain terms why we must strive for a balanced budget – now.

CHAPTER 2

WHAT'S WRONG WITH OUR COUNTRY?

The United States of America is the greatest country to live in, according to popular world opinion. This is not taken from a biased poll. It is fact based upon the reality that millions of people migrate here from all parts of the world each year with the desire to make the United States a permanent residence.

Upon visiting other parts of the world, from highly industrialized nations to third world countries, it is common to hear that other countries are wonderful places to visit, but only for a short period of time. It is an extremely rare case where an American packs his bags and leaves the United States to call another nation home.

We are, however, not without fault. Due in large part to the diversity of the peoples of the U.S., there are many strong opinions regarding how the country should be run and where the money should be spent. As the world's most powerful nation, we maintain a strong armed force to cope with animosity throughout the world. As a nation of compassion, we spend billions to provide for the poor, the needy, and the aged.

It is my contention that you, the people who earn the money, should have the greatest say on where your money goes. The less you give to Washington, the more you will have to spend at your own discretion. After all, you earned the money. It's only fair that you should do with it as you wish.

However, somewhere during the history of this great

nation, we got into a position of spending more money than is taken in with taxes. This is quite a feat, since our tax intake has consistently risen (only twice in the last 35 years did the government not procure more revenue than the year before). Annual deficit spending has become routine, and until recently very little has been done to cope with the choking debt and mounting problem we now face.

Who is responsible for this mounting debt which has approached $5 trillion? The politicians who occupy the seats of the House of Representatives and the Senate are responsible. We will study the truth of why the Congress has not cleaned up its act, and why our elected officials have allowed this debt to swell to such proportion. By the end of this book, you will be hard pressed not to tell your politicians, "NO MORE!"

Let's put the problem of the national debt into perspective. It is presently growing at the rate of $388,000 per minute! That isn't federal spending – that's the amount the politicians are spending over and above what we are paying in taxes. Isn't that a frightening thought? Another way to look at it is that the debt is growing at the rate of over $760 for every person in the United States each year (at a current population of about 263,000,000). We are each going into debt almost a thousand dollars more each year, thanks to the devastatingly irresponsible spending of our "leaders."

As I said before, just about any problem can be corrected. But there are several basic steps that must take place in order for the correction to occur. First, we must admit that there is a problem. Most people would agree that over–budget spending of $388,000 per minute is a serious problem.

Next, we must agree on what the problem is. How did it come to be that we are in such debt? Since we are spending more than we are generating in tax revenue, either we are spending too much money or we aren't paying enough taxes. A simple solution, one that most politicians would cherish, although they wouldn't readily agree to publicly, is that taxes must be raised to handle this annual deficit. With a deficit of roughly $200 billion in 1995, the budget could be balanced by having each taxpayer pay an additional $1,100 per year in taxes, or roughly $4,400 for an average family of four. That sounds easy enough! The budget would be balanced for the first time in decades (only once in the last 35 years – in 1969), the politicians of each party could keep all of their pet spending programs, and the two parties would end the bickering, at least until they go over budget next year.

You say you already pay enough in taxes? Maybe you should be telling that to your "representative." So then, the problem isn't that we're not paying enough taxes, it's that the government is spending too much? Well, if that's the case, then we just have to find some ways to tighten our belts.

But how is this possible? After all, we've been told by any number of high-level politicians that any cutting in spending will result in great pain and devastation to the people who can least afford it – the elderly, the poor children, the disabled, the underprivileged, the impoverished, the destitute, and the indigent. Cutting any spending at all will cause great pain to these people, and we would be heartless and callous to even consider such a drastic notion!

It is my contention that the greatest pain that will be suffered by cutting spending will be felt by corrupt politicians and their pals, whose pockets they have lined for decades.

However, what if we could save some money? Maybe we could, not by cutting deeply into social welfare programs (although not leaving them out), but by finding savings elsewhere as well. The TRUTH is, there are hundreds of places to save billions of dollars from the fat of the bloated, pompous, bureaucratic political feeding frenzy called government. The TRUTH is, notwithstanding the greatness of the United States, this government is immensely inefficient! The opportunity for cost-effective reform is so mind-boggling that it staggers even the most lively imagination.

Why haven't our politicians solved the problem of the inflated government? Some of the many reasons are:

• Congress is too corrupt to do the job it was hired to do.

• We have allowed our officials to handle the most important negotiations behind closed doors where no scrutiny on our part is possible.

• The welfare program is a trillion dollar disappointment that has outgrown its original intent, and worked to destroy a generation of people instead of help them.

• Congress depends on pork for its power, and we haven't compelled our elected officials to end the shameless spending at our expense.

• Our elected officials have no incentive to save our money. On the contrary, the more they spend, the more power they preserve.

• Congress, through the tax laws it has conceived and its control over other monetary factors (interest rates, inflation), has covered up many of its mistakes and deceptions.

• The more inefficient, immense, and confusing government is, the more difficult it is for the public to understand it, scrutinize it, and object to it.

• Our elected "civil servants" have become arrogant, power–hungry elitists who, by their actions if not their words, show little regard for the future of our country and its people.

• A politician's most popular solutions to any budget, spending, or deficit crisis are to raise taxes (generally on the middle class and the wealthy), or to go further into debt.

Make no mistake. Politicians are good at two things – finding ways to seize our money, and finding ways to spend it (or worse yet, spending it before they get it, leaving us holding the debt).

By the way, we will illustrate that the same problems occur, and the same solutions apply for local government, as well as Congress.

As a further example of the lack of fiscal responsibility of the federal government, following is a reprint of an article by K. Alan Snyder for *The American Conservative Union, 1994,* also responsible for *The Grace Report:*

> What if you were asked to become a partner in a business, and upon investigating the health of that business you discovered the following: first, that the business could not find a large part of its records; second, that it was not sure how its money was being spent; third, that the employees took 35% more vacation time than in other businesses; fourth, that it was so far in debt that the only way to cover the debt would be to double the prices of its products?
>
> Then, to top it off, suppose you found that a management expert had come up with a solution to the whole mess without raising prices and that the company executives had tossed it in the trash? How eager would you be to tie your fortunes to the future of such a business? Amazingly enough, there is a business like this—it's called the Federal government. Even more amazing is the fact that someone has come up with a plan for bringing the system back from death, but nobody seems to care. No one is even trying to follow the plan. If the American people are tying their hopes to the future of the Federal government "business"; somebody needs to take the proposed solution seriously.
>
> The problem is well documented, so

well documented in fact that our familiarity with government mismanagement has rather numbed us to the dire consequences which await us if something does not change. Instead of being numbed, shouldn't we be shocked when we are told that Medicare payments are being sent to 8,500 dead people? Shouldn't we be a little bit outraged when a Minority Business Development Agency grant is used to rent townhouses and cars for its executives, who then in turn "forget" to pay over $300,000 in taxes? Or should the outrage be directed more at the government agency for not even noticing what was happening?

Private insurance companies can process a claim for $3 to $6; it only takes the Veterans Administration $100 to $140 to do the same. The private sector issues a payroll check at a cost of $1; the Army accomplishes the same task for a "mere" $4.20. Over at Health and Human Services, a letter needing the Secretary's signature whizzes through the bureaucracy in just 47 days. That should easily qualify for a new Olympic event–we could call it "The Big Government Shuffle"

Who pays for this? Who else but the taxpayer. That is why President Reagan set up a private sector commission, at no cost to taxpayers, to find ways to require some degree of efficiency in the Federal work force. This commission, under the guidance of corporate executive J. Peter Grace, found 2,478 ways to bring down the cost of government and streamline its inner workings – without tax increases or any cuts in defense or social welfare. This massive report is available to anyone who is interested in its conclusions. It

> can be purchased through a certain publishing company for $10; if ordered through the Government Printing Office, the cost is only $19. What else is new?
>
> Yet official Washington has sighed its usual weary sigh, clucked on about the "impossibility" of ever doing anything about the situation, and figuratively tossed the solution in the trash. Too many vested interests are at stake; too many pork barrels would have to be emptied. Yet the nation is at a crossroads—now is the time to act.
>
> The American public is not the Washington establishment – and vice versa. Common sense could still prevail. It is time for outrage and constructive action to overrule the petulant squeals from the Federal quarter. Wouldn't it be nice to save $424 billion in the next three years? If the Federal government were your business, what would you do? Come to think of it, it is your business—of the people, by the people, for the people, right? Are you going to allow it to perish from the face of the earth?

As you can see from Mr. Snyder's article, we the taxpayers have attempted solutions to our imposing and ever–expanding national debt. However, Washington and the Federal bureaucrats turn a deaf ear to solutions. I will show you why this occurs. Following is an example by another taxpayer advocate, the Citizens Against Government Waste (CAGW), and its President, Thomas A. Schatz, who spoke before the Joint Economic Committee on February 16, 1995. Portions of his presentation follow:

> Since 1986, the implementation of Grace Commission recommendations has

helped save taxpayers more than $250 billion. Other CAGW cost–cutting proposals enacted in 1993 and 1994 will save more than $100 billion over the next five years. CAGW has been working tirelessly to carry out the Grace Commission's mission to eliminate government waste.

But there is still more to do. A $4.7 trillion debt and chronically high budget deficits are clear indications that we have been living beyond our means. Unfortunately, spending must be drastically reduced, programs eliminated and priorities re–ordered to ensure a sound economic future. If taxpayers cannot get a real return on their investments from a program, then it should be eliminated. If a program is not significantly time-sensitive, it should be deferred until the budget is balanced.

Taxpayers are suffering from the costs of inefficient government. The national debt still grows by more than $388,000 each minute. We are calling on you to answer the call for reform and spending cuts that taxpayers made on Election Day.

Thomas Jefferson said almost 200 years ago: "The question whether one generation has the right to bind another by the deficit it imposes is a question of such consequence as to place it among the fundamental principles of government. We should consider ourselves unauthorized to saddle posterity with our debts, morally bound to pay them ourselves." Those words remain true today. That's why CAGW has supported a balanced budget amendment with a tax limitation.

For more than a quarter century, the federal budget has been unbalanced. Interest on the federal debt for FY 1995 is estimated at more than $310 billion, making it the second largest item in the budget next to Social Security. Even more frightening, the national debt will reach $6 trillion by 1998. The president's fiscal year 1996 budget does nothing to slow down the runaway debt freight train. Last year, the president projected a debt of $5.95 trillion in FY 1998 and $6.31 trillion in FY 1999. This year's budget projects a debt of $6.0 trillion in FY 1998 and $6.36 trillion in FY 1999. The president's budget not only punts on the deficit and debt, it punts backwards.

The current budget process has failed to prevent deficit spending or the enormous national debt that will destroy the standard of living for future generations. Past laws to restrain fiscal irresponsibility have been watered down or simply ignored. Only a constitutional amendment, followed by strong implementation legislation, will lead to a balanced budget.

CAGW supports current efforts in Congress to enact a balanced budget amendment. Senators Hatch, Craig, and Simon deserve recognition for introducing a balanced budget amendment to the Senate and providing solid, bipartisan leadership to ensure its passage. While we reiterate our support for a three-fifths tax-limitation provision to prevent increased taxes from being used to balance the budget, we recognize that the perfect must not interfere with the good.

Senator Gramm's Balanced Budget Implementation Act (BBIA) will help assure that Congress does in fact balance the budget. The Gramm proposal requires that the spending authority for all unearned entitlements and the most expensive one-third of discretionary programs expire before FY 1996. In order to continue funding for those programs, Congress must re-authorize them for that fiscal year. In FY 1997, authorization for all other discretionary spending programs expires. The plan exempts Social Security, veterans benefits, retirement programs, and Medicare from this process. The BBIA also creates a point of order in both houses against any bill or provision that appropriates money for programs without authorization, unless the point of order is waived by a three-fifths vote in both houses. Finally, the amendment requires that all discretionary spending and unearned entitlements be authorized every 10 years, beginning with the first session of Congress that follows the Census reapportionment. All unearned entitlements and the most expensive one-third of discretionary programs will expire in the first session; the rest in the second session.

Sunsetting requires programs to re-justify themselves, and eliminates the perpetual opportunity to appropriate funds for programs which have not been reviewed by the authorizing committees, sometimes for decades. In fact, CAGW would support a more frequent re-authorization process; perhaps every five years. CAGW suggested sunsetting entitlement programs in its July

1994 report on entitlement reform. If Congress would be forced to regularly consider entitlement programs, it is more likely that the programs would be reformed to reduce the fiscal risk to which the federal government is exposed.

The BBIA also maintains and extends the discretionary budget freeze, and caps growth in entitlement spending, except Social Security, for FY 1997–FY 2002. The growth rate is an aggregate cap equal to that of the Social Security growth rate over the same period. Individual entitlements may grow at faster rates, but aggregate growth is capped. If the aggregate growth exceeds the cap, then there is a point of order for an across-the-board sequester to eliminate excess growth, except Social Security. A three-fifths vote is required to exclude any other entitlement, which would remain excluded until Congress voted to bring the program back into the cap.

CAGW's July 1994 report on entitlement reform noted that sequestration would not specify the necessary reductions in individual programs that would be needed to avoid sequestration. The entitlement cap could allow members of Congress to hide behind the automatic sequester and avoid making the hard management decisions that would control entitlement spending. But the cover of an automatic sequester could be the answer to the political sensitivity of entitlement programs.

Sunsetting unearned entitlements subjects them to regular review. The earned entitlements, however, should also be subject to review, and not left simply to the sequestration process. Placing a limit on an entitlement program is no substitute for changing the policies controlling it.

Spending caps do not address the real problem of entitlement spending. Instead, they tackle the symptom — out-of-control spending — not the cause: entitlement programs are loosely governed by generous spending formulas and not the fiscal restraint which should determine federal spending decisions.

CAGW's preferred method of reducing entitlement programs is to go through each, one by one, searching for ways to cut benefits, limit eligibility, or force recipients to pay more in the way of premiums, fees, or other offsets. New program rules or tax laws could limit who qualifies for benefits, reduce the amount of benefits provided, or change the taxation of benefits. Essentially, the program-by-program approach is an attempt to put individual entitlement programs on a sound financial footing and eliminate wasteful spending.

The program-by-program approach is most difficult because of politicians' reluctance to take away congressional-mandated benefits and public resistance to giving up something many believe they have a right, or entitlement, to keep. Members of Congress can bury proposals in committee, use multiple committee referrals, and block reform measures. Special interests can use their influence to perpetuate many of the programs.

In 1984, the President's Private

Sector Survey on Cost Control, popularly known as the Grace Commission, observed that entitlement spending was a "driving" force in the uncontrolled growth of Federal spending"; The Grace Commission found that "adequate information does not exist to the degree to which the intended recipients of these subsidy programs are receiving sufficient benefits or, conversely, the degree to which benefits are being bestowed upon undeserving recipients to the detriment of all taxpayers. Indeed, there is no way to identify all the subsidies a particular person receives."

The Grace Commission observed that the information gap on administering subsidized programs or entitlements has caused a lack of control, resulting in significant mistargeting of benefits. To better target all federal benefits to those who deserve them, the Grace Commission recommended that each federal department or agency providing a subsidy to a specific beneficiary issue a form similar to a W–2 form, with a copy going to the Internal Revenue Service, that would total all payments to individuals and add the total to the beneficiary's earnings in order to arrive at total income. The commission recommended that a cut-off point be established below which subsidy payments would not be taxed — with everything above the cut-off point included in total income and taxable as any other income would be at the individual or corporation's given tax bracket.

The information provided as a result of the form would enable federal policy–

makers to determine the extent to which these targeted outlays are meeting stated objectives or, conversely, benefiting those who are not in need of subsidies. For beneficiaries above the cut-off point, the prospect of having to pay taxes would serve as a disincentive to receiving subsidized payments.

The Grace Commission also provided other principles for entitlement reform including reducing administrative costs, consolidating benefit programs to better target funds and reduce the number of uncoordinated programs that are attempting to serve the same objectives, improving federal agency accounting systems to provide accurate data on total administrative costs for subsidy programs, and redefining poverty statistics to include in-kind federal transfer payments.

The Grace Commission concluded that this kind of detailed data collected through the issuance and consolidation of subsidy forms (similar to the W–2 forms issued to wage-earners) is a critical first step in a process that will enable the federal government to manage means–tested programs more effectively — and in the process, save taxpayers billions of dollars. The Grace Commission approach would be highly effective combined with the program-by-program approach.

Senator Gramm's legislation establishes fixed deficit targets in order to balance the budget by the year 2002, by modifying and extending the existing maximum Gramm–Rudman (GR) deficit targets. It also extends the GR sequester mechanism to reach and maintain a balanced budget for FY 2002 and beyond. This provision again places a spending limitation by requiring a three-fifths vote to override the target deficit levels for each year and makes the point of order permanent to ensure the budget remains balanced.

The provisions of Senator Gramm's bill would help ensure that balancing the budget by FY 2002 becomes a reality. The "look back" provisions would assure that the targets are reached each year.

Spending limitations are an integral part of the balanced budget debate. Past measures to get the budget deficit under control failed in large part due to loopholes built into the legislation. Although the Gramm–Rudman Act was a serious means to balance the budget in 1985, it failed because Congress and the President chose to ignore the target reduction levels and further increase the debt. If the Gramm–Rudman Act had been applied as it was intended, the whole discussion about a balanced budget amendment would not be taking place today.

Senator Jon Kyl has proposed a Balanced Budget Spending Limitations Amendment (BBSLA) that would cap spending to 19 percent of the GNP. By making it an amendment, Congress would have no means to circumvent the procedure and increase spending as it has in the past. Rather, Congress would be forced to limit spending and encourage domestic growth. The higher the GNP, the more money Congress would have to spend, yet it would never be a larger portion of the economy.

Today, spending is roughly 23 percent of the GNP and only small cuts of .5 percent each year would be required to meet the 19 percent mark by 2002. James Buchanan of the Center for the Study of Public Choice at George Mason University claims that "reducing government as a share of GNP from its current level of 25% to, say, 20%, would generate roughly a 2% increase in the rate of the growth of GNP". Spending limitations have eluded Congress, thereby making a balanced budget impossible. Amending the Constitution with a balanced budget requirement coupled with spending and tax limits will make fiscal stability a reality. Senator Kyl's amendment is also pro-growth, because it is linked to private sector success or failure to generate money. Anti-growth regulations and mandates would be considered more carefully because of their impact on Congress's ability to spend. This amendment not only balances the budget, but limits spending in a way that benefits the economy.

Given the reality of the balanced budget amendment approved by the House and being considered in the Senate, Senator Kyl's bill, like the tax limitation, will be the subject of a future effort to strengthen the amendment. In either case, passing a balanced budget amendment is merely the first step.

Balancing the budget will still require Congress to make decisions on where and how to spend tax dollars. But George Will recently noted it's not necessarily a difficult endeavor:

Tending livestock in Nebraska in

February, that is hard work. Being a sod carrier in New Orleans in August is hard work. Teaching in an inner–city high school or giving critical care to the elderly is hard work. But in what sense is it hard work for legislators to decide to spend other people's money at a somewhat slower rate of acceleration than had been planned? That is what balancing the budget in seven years would involve.

The Congressional Budget Office estimates that Congress must eliminate $45 billion in spending each year to achieve a balanced budget by FY 2002.

Senator Mack has proposed a solution to make budget cuts by proposing to create a government spending reduction commission, which combines ideas from the Grace Commission, Gramm–Rudman, and the Base Closure and Realignment Commission to eliminate spending by the target deficit levels. The Grace Commission was not armed with the power to enact its proposals, but Senator Mack's commission has specific enforcement mechanisms just like those of the Base Closure Commission. The spending reduction commission will target deficit levels, and make binding budget decisions to balance the budget.

The Mack proposal sets specific guidelines to follow in the budget process and does not require action by the commission unless Congress fails to meet the deficit reduction level for that year. If necessary, the cuts the commission makes will be introduced as a non-amendable privileged motion to be voted on by September 30 or introduced for a roll call vote by the presiding officer. The spending reduction commission will prioritize spending, backed by economic analysis from the Office of Management and Budget to ensure that spending is reduced at the recommended $45 billion a year. Senator Mack's bill creates a Grace Commission with teeth to finally arrest runaway spending and deficits, and put America back on track to a stable and balanced budget.

CAGW believes sequestration is a necessary option, but one to be avoided. The spending reduction commission could provide the recommendations to meet the new Gramm–Rudman deficit targets should Congress fall short. Members of Congress would still have the opportunity to make the tough decisions before the sequestration ax would fall.

Mr. Chairman, Congress usually has good intentions when spending money, but the power to do good is also the power to do mischief with our tax dollars. Care must be taken when looking at individual programs and projects; the more open and honest you are, the more likely a project is to withstand the light of day.

Restoring fiscal sanity to our nation is the most important job for the 104th Congress. The country is awash in a sea of red ink, and every day slips perilously closer to bankruptcy. The national debt is expected to rise to nearly $6 trillion by the end of the century. This is not the legacy that we should leave to our children and grandchildren. Spending has not been cut to the bone.

> Money is being wasted daily and the clock is ticking. We're sitting on a fiscal time bomb that needs to be defused.

Despite the documented inefficiencies of our government, those in Washington want government to take over even more programs. Never mind that only 28 cents of every welfare dollar we give to Washington gets to those who need it. Is the problem that the taxpayers aren't compassionate, or that we should find ways to reform the bloated system? What if we were able to get 72 cents on the dollar to people who need the welfare help, and spend only 28 cents to get it to them? Wouldn't that be more compassionate than continuing to spend our hard-earned tax dollars on a solution that is only 28% efficient?

In 1823 Thomas Jefferson warned about government corruption.

Never shift the government offices from the states to Washington, he warned, where "further withdrawn from the eyes of the people, they may be more secretly bought and sold at market."

Mr. Jefferson was right, of course. He foresaw that we would not be able to keep a watchful eye on a government whose actions were hidden from us. Even though it's much easier to observe our local officials than those in Washington, plenty of corruption still exists at *local* levels.

There are many good reasons why the role of the federal government should be limited to functions that are inherently national in scope, such as defense. More importantly, functions that can be handled at the local level, should be. Local politicians are closer to, more in touch with, and therefore more accountable to the public. They know the "personality" of their constituency and can more readily customize policies to meet specific needs. It is impossible for the federal government, overseeing a vast nation of 263 million people, to provide a "cookie cutter" approach that will fit all areas and circumstances. For instance, local government in New York City would have significantly different programs and policies than local government in a small farming town in Wyoming.

The accountability issue comes in two forms. First of all, it is very easy for Washington politicians to ignore the needs of those citizens who are located over 2,000 miles away in obscure areas of the nation. Second, with Washington setting the agenda, the proposed bills are exceedingly lengthy and complicated, which makes scrutiny by the people that much more difficult.

Cost is another reason why the federal government should allow local governments to run local matters. When the federal government "oversees" local programs, it adds at least one extra layer of bureaucracy to the mix. We are paying for overlapping bureaucracies in hundreds of areas of government. By eliminating such overlap, we will be saving billions of dollars each year.

Money isn't our only problem. Although crime runs rampant in this country, and we haven't found ways to prevent the killing of Americans in America, we must send "peacekeeping" troops to Bosnia, Somalia, and Haiti. Why aren't peacekeeping troops being stationed in our largest cities, where the crime rate is, for the most part, the highest? Could it have anything to do with the fact that sending peacekeeping troops to points in America isn't as politically expedient as sending troops overseas, where we can overwhelm the aggressors and look good in the process? Would overwhelming aggressors in America seem too "drastic," or politically incorrect?

CHAPTER 3

A NATION OF INCONGRUITY

At no time in the history of the United States, including the Civil War, have we been more upside down in our priorities. The Bureaucrats of Washington (BOW) wonder why so many citizens are angry, weary, and frustrated with the government. They attempt to shift any blame from themselves by blaming talk radio, a unique occurrence, or misinformation. However, today, because of talk radio, the computer age, and other forms of communication, the public is more informed than ever before. This is why we are finally starting to take notice, and can see more readily what transgressions are occurring in Washington and beyond. For example:

- Instead of focusing on crucial issues, the first and foremost of which is the economy, politicians use the media to communicate their daily rhetoric on less consequential topics, in order to take the focus off of their own deficiency and negligence.
- People are punished every day for doing the right things – going to work, bringing up a family with proper values, consuming, paying taxes, obeying the laws, contributing to society, etc. How? These are the people who are told they aren't doing their fair share and need to pay more taxes. If they protest, they're told they are greedy and have no compassion for the needy. In most cases, the "needy" are the greedy politicians who seek a wider power base.
- People who do the wrong things are rewarded by the

liberal left with compassion and handouts. Never mind that, often, these are people who decided not to pursue an education. Never mind that, in many cases, these are people who consider work to be slave labor, and would rather have babies to increase their welfare benefits than try to improve themselves. These people are supported by society. Why should they try to support or improve themselves as long as there are champions for their cause in politics, fighting to keep them entrenched in a welfare state?

• Our elected officials, who pretend to work for us, are treated like royalty while we must support their every whim and desire. They brazenly lie to us, and we tolerate it, rationalize it, and just chalk it up to "politics as usual." They create debt for us that we will be paying for in years to come. On top of that, we reward them with handsome salaries and millionaire pensions. Where else could these people be treated so well? Why do we continue to follow them blindly, like sheep, and believe their stories? The truth is, they control our lives in a very negative way.

• How important is credibility at the White House? The President of the United States is the holder of the most powerful office in the world, and he has the nerve to play fast and loose with the truth, half truths, and mind games. The citizens of the United States, as well as world leaders, must be able to trust what comes out of the White House. Instead, we get nothing but rhetoric, arrogance, and politics as usual.

• Nowadays, a high percentage of students "graduate" from school, even though they can barely read, write, or exhibit basic math skills, all necessary for survival in the work world. In fact, according to "A Businessman's Guide to the Education Reform Debate" by Jeanne Allen and Michael J. McLaughlin, almost 94% of high school seniors were unable to solve multi-step math problems or use basic algebra. Yet, schools have the time and resources to teach children revisionist history and social issues that weren't taught just a generation ago.

• Our justice system is fraught with inequity. Swindlers can tie up innocent people in court for years, with the honorable party lucky to break even after paying attorneys' fees. Criminal lawyers have outsmarted prosecutors for years, and now criminals enjoy more protection than law-abiding citizens. Lawbreakers found guilty of crimes, no matter how heinous, are often pampered in prison, and may enjoy a more prosperous, safe, and healthy lifestyle in prison than they did outside of prison. And we taxpayers are paying for their room and board. Still, these prisoners have many allies who contend that they have it too rough, and who continue to fight for more rights and benefits for the lawbreakers.

• Illegal aliens flock into the country and, when they need health care, we foot the bill. When these illegal aliens have children, their children are automatically affirmed with the same rights as every U.S. citizen. Without paying a dime into the system, they may receive costly benefits such as health care, welfare, education, etc.

• Taxpayers have fewer rights than welfare recipients. Welfare recipients are given thousands of dollars each year for doing nothing. Taxpayers are taxed and scrutinized for working, trying to produce and contribute to society. However, any scrutiny aimed at welfare recipients is shunned and considered politically incorrect. How can others decide that we should support someone other than our own families with our hard-earned income?

• Higher wage-earners are targets, primarily of the left, but of the right as well. Why else would a person be penalized for making more money by having to pay a higher percentage of his income in taxes? Why, if a person works longer and harder for his money, isn't he allowed to enjoy the fruits of his labor? When did we decide that a person who works harder than his neighbor should pay a higher share of his income to support those who don't work at all, and who, in many cases, take much more from society than they contribute?

Instead of targeting the upper class wage-earners, why isn't there a non-partisan effort to target the politicians, their cronies, and accomplices who have profited from the billions of dollars of pork barrel projects thrown their way over the years? What is more fair: going after the wealthy who have made their money honestly as productive citizens in society, or targeting the politicians and their cronies, who have made billions of dollars at the expense of the rich, the middle class, and poor alike?

To paraphrase Rush Limbaugh, popular talk radio host with a weekly audience of over 20,000,000, who was talking about the current administration:

> Taxes are building at ever-increasing levels, both hidden and visible, to give money to those who say that they don't have as much, or to people who others say don't have as much and should have more. And what does the nation have to show for it? After 30 years of the Great Society, we still have poverty levels of the same percentage as the day that we began the Great Society. We have destroyed the American family with all of this compassion. We have illegitimacy rising to levels never before thought possible in the U.S. We have crime out of control. We have a value base that is slowly decaying. We have abortions happening to the tune of 1.5 million per year. We have lost the respect for human life that was once held in this country. We have deteriorating education. All because the federal government has attempted to equalize society by defining compassion as how much we give away to people who otherwise would be able to provide for themselves, were it not for the dependency that has been created by this so-

> called compassion that has been articulated by Mrs. Clinton.
>
> Quite simply, the middle class of this country has been bled dry by virtue of the fact that somebody ought to get something from someone else. This philosophy that somebody is entitled to something that someone else has just about bled the middle class dry. This [health care] is just another example of another government grab of the productivity of the private sector, and parcelling it out to those people who should get something from someone else. And Mrs. Clinton has the audacity to believe that it is mean for those who don't agree with her agenda.

Mrs. Clinton doesn't seem to understand that to give to people over and over again does not help them. People must learn to stand on their own, to grow, and not be forever dependent upon others.

CHAPTER 4

THE ECONOMICS AND CONSEQUENCES OF WASTEFUL GOVERNMENT

The focal point of government debate, during the past several years, has been the economy. Part of the credit for this debate should go to Ross Perot, who brought to the forefront of the 1992 elections much of the wastefulness and lack of credibility of the political process. Another venue focusing on this debate is talk radio. Many popular and vocal commentators, including Rush Limbaugh, have simplified the rhetoric and made politics interesting for millions of Americans. This has agitated and angered many politicians who, in the past, felt free to perform just as they pleased. After all, no one was looking. Now, more than ever, we are taking notice, we are seeing what's taking place, and we are ready to revolt.

But why revolt? After all, the United States is the most powerful nation in the world, and none of us are so fed up that we are ready to move to another country. Staunch patriots who blindly follow the lead of their elected officials will glumly proclaim, "If you don't like it here, then leave!" That's not the point. Those of us who condemn our elected officials do so because we love our country and want our government to work EVEN BETTER THAN IT DOES NOW! Don't criticize us for wanting to improve our country for our children and grandchildren. Instead, criticize those leaders who knowingly and willfully keep our country from being better to further their own selfish interests. You may understand this statement better when you read the following powerful quote from a former congressman:

> "I have never seen more senators express discontent with their jobs...I think the major cause is that deep down in our hearts we believe that we have been accomplices to doing something terrible and unforgivable to this wonderful country. Deep down in our hearts we know that we have bankrupted America and that we have given our children a legacy of bankruptcy...We have defrauded the country to get ourselves elected."
> Senator Jack Danforth (R–Missouri), 1992

The current budget debate is one of the most important issues ever argued regarding the present and future health of our country. It is the contention of this writer that, although there are a number of important differences between the parties, the ONLY reason we don't have a balanced budget and fiscal responsibility is the obsession for political power and partisan politics. Neither the Democrats nor Republicans want to give in to one another, which would be a recognition of the credibility of the other side. There have been a number of proposals made by nonpartisan patriots leading toward balancing the budget, but politicians on both sides ignore these suggestions. Both parties have too many partisan issues and constituencies to consider, and don't want to lose the support of a large voting block by giving into reasonable, commonsense solutions.

There is a tremendous amount of waste in government; yet the public is suffocated with so much propaganda from the compliant media that a frightening percentage of us are uninformed, misled, or suffer from apathy. But would you still be apathetic if you realized that what Washington is doing on a daily basis is taking money from your pocket and affecting how you live? Would you still be apathetic if you could see, firsthand, how your elected "representatives" are squandering your money on their own priorities, few of which you would support if you had the privilege of accepting or rejecting their actions in advance? Would you be apathetic if you could see how politicians have knowingly and willingly undermined your confidence, effectively robbing you of your (and your children's) future, and changing society as we used to know it? And finally, would you be apathetic if you could see some of the many deceptions and tricks politicians play on the taxpayers to hide programs they know would be unpopular to the vast majority of their constituents?

Although there have been thousands of examples of wasteful spending in government run programs, the CONSEQUENCES of these wasteful programs may not be clear. The following breaks this down into simple form:

Suppose that you, as a compassionate person, have no argument with the idea that the truly needy, helpless, and starving people of the United States need assistance. Although there is a fundamental argument between liberals and conservatives as to the definition of "needy," most people agree that there are a number of people who need sustenance (food and shelter) and cannot survive without help.

Let's further agree, for the purpose of this model, that it would cost approximately $5.00 per day to feed a starving, needy individual, and about $15.00 per day to house that same person. Thus, for $20.00 per day, the neediest person in the country could be fed and sheltered. As a compassionate society, most Americans would agree that $20.00 per day is not too much to spend to see that the truly needy, who cannot provide for themselves, get such help. Twenty dollars per day times 365 days per year means a cost of about $7,300.00 per year to feed and shelter a needy person.

Now let's illustrate how government waste affects the needy. Based upon the above model, for every $1 billion of taxes that are frivolously wasted each year, it may be said that we could feed and shelter 136,986 impoverished people for a whole year! This is a powerful reason why we should put the wasteful Washington bureaucrats out of business! The truth is they care more about advancing their own agendas than they do about the truly destitute in this country!

However, there are many conservative individuals who will say that, even though there are needy people out there who can't help themselves, it is difficult to provide for them when we are already in debt to the tune of $5,000,000,000,000.00 (5 trillion), and are incurring additional deficit spending of $200,000,000,000.00 (200 billion) per year. Thus, until we balance our books, we can't afford to be compassionate to others.

Would we still be arguing about helping the poor and needy if we didn't have the large deficit Washington has stuck us with?

TAXPAYER AGENDA VS. POLITICIAN AGENDA

Let's look at what the government is doing to us. The agendas of taxpayers and politicians are very different. Politicians believe that, because of the large number of taxpayers, spending or wasting a few billion dollars here or there is not significant for each taxpayer. After all, why would a taxpayer worry about paying an extra $10.00 per year, even if the money is wasted? It certainly isn't worth a person's effort to make a fuss over $10.00 per year. But look at it from the politician's side. That $10.00 per year from everyone in the U.S. represents over $2.6 billion! A politician can maintain plenty of power and favor by spending an extra billion in the right places. So it's an easy argument for the politician to rationalize. Even if $2.6 billion is wasted on a frivolous or wasteful project, it's only $10.00 per person. And who cares about $10 per year, right?

Now what does this mean to the taxpayer, assuming there is a limit that he can pay, and that there should be some fiscal responsibility? Every dollar that is wasted on frivolous government spending is taken away from a truly essential program, while wasteful programs are fed with increased budgets.

A politician constantly attempts to appeal to the emotion that someone else isn't paying their fair share. This is a wonderful strategy, because he is never targeting the group he is talking to. It's always the other guy. So there are two possibilities. Either someone pays more taxes to pay for a politician's spending bill, or we go deeper in debt, so everyone pays for it. Rarely, however, is the politician refused his largess.

The amount of wasteful spending that the bureaucrats have loaded upon us can be easily measured. The current national debt is now costing us over $330 billion per year for the interest alone! We haven't even begun to reduce the debt; we just continue to pay the interest on it. This annual interest payment represents a burden of over $1,250 for every American. Again, for a family of four, this is over $5,000 per year. And assuming that approximately 30% of the population pays no taxes, the burden on the taxpayer is increased by 30%. This results in an annual interest payment of $7,100 for a family of four. Remember, this is interest you are paying on a loan you didn't take out. You are repaying the loan so those in Congress can keep expanding their power.

In addition to interest costs, we are spending approximately $400 billion more than would be necessary if we were to rework the budget and cut out all the pork and wasteful spending. Our 8-step balanced budget plan outlined near the end of the book will detail what needs to be done. By following this proposed reform, the anticipated $400 billion savings would result in an additional savings of $1,520 for every American, $6,080 for a family of four, or $8,600 for the family of four when taking into account their increased burden based upon 30% of the population not paying any taxes.

In summary, when you total the aggregate interest payment and nonessential spending our elected officials, without conscience, saddle us with, the average family of four is paying over $15,700 more in taxes per year than it should be paying. This, my friends, is why we must focus on government spending. It has gotten out of control, and only we have the incentive to bring it in line; not the politicians.

What if we actually wanted to pay down the debt? Since there is still deficit spending, based upon the present tax and spending proposals, we won't end the deficit until it reaches $6 trillion. If, in fact, we ended deficit spending at $6 trillion and decided to pay down the debt once and for all, the calculations would look like this:

PAYING OFF THE DEBT

Six trillion dollars @ 6.5% over 40 years would be $421,528,903,300.00 per year. Thus, in 40 years, we could pay off the debt by paying just over $421 billion per year for 40 years, or $1,600.00 for every man, woman, and child in the United States for the next 40 years. The total amount paid over the 40 years, including principal and interest, would be $16.86 trillion, including almost $11 trillion in interest payments! This is the debt our high-priced politicians have saddled us with. Are you angry yet?

How many times have we heard from our politicians that balancing the budget is not necessary, that government spending is cut to the bone, and that the $5 trillion national debt is not a serious issue? Is it possible that these people simply don't know the numbers, or that they don't understand the consequences of their actions? No. They have access to the same facts and figures we have, yet they distort the truth to further their own selfish agendas. The nerve! I really wonder how some of these people can sleep at night.

There are thousands of examples of wasteful spending that have been brought up time and again, not only to the general public, but to the members of Congress as well. We know that it is the responsibility of Congress to appropriate spending. But whose responsibility is it to find savings? Unfortunately, we have little or no voice when it comes to saving our own money.

Even though many of you are aware of the waste in government, I thought that a small sampling might make your blood boil, as it does mine. Sometimes just being aware of the waste in government, which is nothing less than frivolously throwing away your money, is enough to make you decide to do something about it.

Pork Defined

It may be important to define exactly what "pork," or "pork-barrel," projects are. After all, a politician wants us to believe that any spending he is doing is necessary. It may be necessary, but perhaps only for his reelection.

It's easier to define pork by what it isn't. Any expenditure, in order to be defined as legitimate, must be authorized and must fall within budget limits. If it shows up suddenly during a House/Senate conference (usually behind closed doors and out of the public eye), it is considered pork. And, if the item is earmarked for a specific location, pet project, special interest, or organization, or is not competitively bid for, it is considered pork.

Pork may also be defined as the government's decision to spend money in a specific location, not because of efficiency or cost-effectiveness, but because of lobbying and pressure brought to bear by local politician(s) or special interests, at the expense of taxpayers.

EXAMPLES OF WASTE AND PORK-BARREL SPENDING

It's in the best interest of politicians to deflect the disgust of the public who must pay for their arrogance, deceit, and wastefulness. Here is just a small sampling of the litany of wasteful spending.

The Immigration and Naturalization Service, or INS, is the agency responsible for handling illegal immigration. In 1995, the INS decided it needed additional sites to train increasing numbers of border patrol agents and other immigration enforcement officers.

The best choices for the training sites included Eaker Air Force Base in Arkansas, Fort Bliss in Texas, and Fort McClellan in Alabama. It was concluded by the evaluation team that Eaker Air Force Base best met INS needs, since its accommodations (dorms) were only ten years old, and the grounds worked well for the training requirements.

On the other hand, a closed naval base in Charleston, South Carolina, was strongly recommended by Senator Ernest Hollings (D - S.C.). The problem with Charleston, however, was that the accommodations weren't suitable. Additional buildings and renovation of the existing facilities would be needed, at an additional cost to taxpayers of millions of dollars. Senator Hollings prematurely promised his constituents that Charleston would be chosen. After great debate, Hollings persuaded the INS to split the training among three different sites, including Charleston.

Because of Mr. Hollings' influence and hometown loyalty, the committee determined that we would pay an additional $10 million and delay the training of the extra border patrol agents for approximately 18 months. This is a typical example of pork-barrel politics. Thank you, Mr. Hollings.

Another example? The National Park Service (NPS) is a prime source for pork. In fact, President Clinton, of "the era of big government is over" declaration, had several interesting items hidden in his 1996 National Park Service budget, including: (1) $1.5 million for the Native Hawaiian Culture and Arts Program, (2) $500,000 of unspecified funding for the King Center in Atlanta, and (3) $1 million for replacement of the White House sidewalks. A General Accounting Office study reports that more than $27 million worth of National Park Service items are "lost, missing, or untraceable." Paul Pritchard, president of the National Parks and Conservation Association in Washington regularly criticizes any downsizing proposed by Congress, yet cannot comment on the mismanagement that is apparent in the NPS.

Non-partisan pork is the way of Congress. Once the latest $243 billion defense bill was approved by the House and Senate, it went to the conference committee to work out the "differences." One of the items the committee approved, that was not in the bill approved by the House or Senate, was a cyclone coastal patrol boat to be built at the Bollinger Shipyard in Lockport, LA, at a cost of $20 million. Remember, this wasn't requested by the Department of Defense, nor was it included in the bills that the House or Senate approved. Those who pushed for this pork were Senator Johnston (D - LA), House Appropriations Committee Chairman Bob Livingston (R - Metairie, LA), Rep. Billy Tauzin (R - Chackbay, LA), and Rep. William Jefferson (D - New Orleans, LA).

Why do we need a $243 billion defense budget? One reason is because of the money spent on weaponry that has no clearly defined mission, and that no one in the Pentagon requested. Take the B–2 bomber, for example. At a cost of $2.2 billion per plane, the B–2 not only hasn't performed as promised, but is overpriced, according to defense experts. Yet Congress wants to order 20 more planes, at a cost of over $44 billion. Instead of *reducing* the huge defense budget, or transferring the money to legitimate defense needs, Congress relies on each B–2 as a huge pork program to supply its needy supporters. Republicans, who are pushing hardest for a balanced budget, are the primary sponsors of this additional spending.

How poorly Congress protects our dollars is illustrated by the U.S. Helium Reserve. It is estimated by the Congressional Budget Office that realistic proposals to end the reserves could save taxpayers between $5–7 million per year over the next five years. Not only have we been storing up to 31 billion cubic feet of helium for over 66 years, but we still haven't been repaid the $250 million the Bureau of Mines borrowed to buy the helium in the first place. At present, the Treasury is owed approximately $1.4 billion and has no plans to receive payment soon.

The Peter J. **Grace Commission** was set up by President Reagan in the early 1980s to identify wasteful spending. Following are a few of their findings:

• Private insurance companies can process a claim for $3 – $6; it takes the Veterans Administration $100 – $140 to do a single claim.

• The private sector issues a payroll check at a cost of $1; the Army spends $4.20.

• Medicare payments are being sent to 8,500 dead people each year.

• HUD pork includes $1,000,000 to the Playhouse Square Foundation in Cleveland, Ohio, for redevelopment and restoration of the Allen Theater, and $450,000 for construction of the Center for Political Participation at the University of Maryland.

• Another maddening example of Washington's irresponsible culture of spending comes from HUD in August of 1995. A conference was held to train 194 public housing "tenant leaders" from across the country to be more effective tenant leaders. This four-day conference was held in Puerto Rico at one of its most expensive resorts, at a cost to taxpayers of $335,000, and was being promoted to the public housing tenants as an "unforgettable" vacation with "casinos, beaches, swimming, snorkeling, dancing, exotic shopping, and a beauty salon for complete pampering."

At a time when all government agencies are supposed to be downsizing and saving money, this event and its organizer, HUD official Edwin Moses, came under attack. Despite the criticism, Mr. Moses, who now works for the Chicago Housing Authority at a healthy salary of $120,000 per year, defended the vacation convention, as did his boss, CHA executive director Joseph Shuldiner. Shuldiner felt that these events were necessary, and supported other similar events that have taken place, as well as some other events at resorts that are scheduled, all paid for with taxpayer dollars.

The attitude that Messrs. Moses and Shuldiner have, that they can justify spending our tax dollars at will, is not only unacceptable but borders on a betrayal of the public trust. Government employees who do not understand fiscal responsibility should be let go immediately. They should be held personally responsible for this complete lack of financial restraint, and dealt with convincingly to demonstrate to all government employees that this behavior will no longer be tolerated.

• $93,000 was added in conference for the National Potato Trade and Tariff Association.

• $5,200,000 for construction of the Indiana Center for Interdisciplinary Research and Education at Indiana State University, the alma mater of House appropriator John Myers (R– IN).

• Over $80,000,000 for pork-barrel projects in the state of Senate Appropriations Committee Ranking Member Robert C. Byrd (D–WV), including $75,000,000 for highway Corridor H construction, $1,500,000 for southern West Virginia environmental restoration,

$805,000 for the Huntington waterfront park, $800,000 for West Virginia port development, $700,000 for the Tygart River, $400,000 for West Virginia trailhead facilities, $400,000 for Tug Valley greenway, $400,000 for the Cheat River Basin, $350,000 for a West Virginia comprehensive investigation, and $275,000 for the Charleston waterfront park. Senator Byrd voted against the balanced budget amendment.

The **Citizens Against Government Waste** (CAGW) is another think tank whose goal is to identify and make recommendations for the elimination of wasteful spending. To that end, they have identified hundreds of areas that should be targeted for savings:

• The National Council of Senior Citizens received $68.7 million, which is 97% of its entire budget, from the federal government. The NCSC then contributed $183,000 of it to political campaigns of more than 60 candidates for the 1994 elections.

• Although there are 19 military golf courses within close proximity to Washington, D.C., a third course is supposedly "needed" at Andrews Air Force Base for the exclusive use of active and retired military, members of Congress, their staffs, and the President, at a cost to the military of $5.1 million. An effort several years ago to open the military's 204 private golf courses to the cash–paying public, thereby saving an estimated $100 million per year, got lost in the rough.

• Scores of taxpayer-funded grants, totaling over $4.2 million, were given to the National Endowment for the Humanities (NEH) in half of 1995 alone. Some of the "essential" programs include:

$60,000 to NPR affiliate KPCC radio in California, which "will build on Los Angeles cār culture" by holding 13 two-hour "town meetings" during drive time.

$85,000 to the American Bar Association to hold

versations on "the covenant between society and ıals that forms the foundation of a law-based democratic society."

$85,000 for the National Council on Aging in Washington, D.C. to conduct six intergenerational conversations.

$125,000 to support a three-week summer program for ten K–12 teachers in Maine to "study the role of photography in forming an American identity."

$250,000 to the Association of American Colleges and Universities to hold a 10-day institute on curriculum reform and "new scholarship" for 180 academicians.

$19,275 for discussion groups and symposia on "The Role of the Press in the Public Life of America."

$220,000 for Brown University's Choices for the 21st Century Library Project.

$18,000 to the Vermont Center for the Book for a study project on the role of egalitarianism in democracy.

$40,000 to the Alaska Humanities Forum to support town hall meetings about "Anchorage as a unique pacific rim community" in the country's "last frontier."

$35,000 to Occidental College in Whittier, California, for conversations on the future of the college and two nearby communities. The program will attempt to spur dialogue with a bus tour, soccer match, and the showing of a documentary film.

$15,000 for a series of radio conversations on "Appalachian Pluralism and Identity."

• Even though the National Institute of Mental Health (NIMH) continues to request increased funding, they have enough money to spend:

$161,913 to study "Israeli Reactions to SCUD Attacks During the Gulf War."

$104,055 to study how people communicate through facial expressions.

$85,583 for design of a Leg Activity Monitor (
which could help scientists prevent insomnia-causing
odic limb movements (PLM)" and "restless legs (RL)" – neither of which has evidently been declared a syndrome.

$137,534 to study "The Development of Commitment in Heterosexual Relationships."

$105,163 to research the "Evolution of Monagamy in a Biparental Rodent."

$124,910 to find ways to reduce "school phobia" among children.

$1,708,696 to prevent "conduct disorder" in children.

$77,826 for "Coping with Change in Czechoslovakia."

$76,971 to study "Human Response to Repeated Floods."

$71,266 to study "Marital Violence in the Wake of the Great Flood of 1993."

$100,271 to determine if volunteering has health benefits for old people.

$311,868 to see if aerobic exercise will reduce depression in older people.

$319,580 to study the "Mental Health Consequences of Anti–Gay and Lesbian Violence."

. . . to name a few.

These must be considered serious studies by the NIMH; otherwise why would they receive such large sums while so many of the needy are hungry, shelterless, and without medical assistance?

Medicare Fraud

Despite all the rhetoric and scare-mongering ("Mediscare") aimed at frightening the elderly, and misleading them into thinking that a slowdown in the growth rate of Medicare funding will be its demise, the opposite is true. In fact, there are non-partisan studies that show that just eliminating the fraud and waste in Medicare will save the program, as well as lower its annual burden on taxpayers, without diminishing needed services. Medicare fraud is replete in many areas, including: organized crime and the drug trade, kickback scams, medical equipment scams, fraudulent billing, nursing home and home care fraud, prescription fraud, unnecessary or nonexistent laboratory tests, billing fraud, ambulance fraud, selling tainted medical supplies, and embezzlement of funds.

Fraud occurs partly because physicians, supply companies, and diagnostic labs have about three chances out of 1,000 of having Medicare audit their billing practices in any given year. This reality is a welcome mat for unscrupulous cheats.

Some startling facts and true stories include:

• June Gibbs Brown, Inspector General of the Department of Health and Human Services said, "fraud and abuse permeate all aspects of Medicare." She said up to $17 billion, 10 percent of Medicare's budget, will be wasted because of fraud.

This was taken from the *Congressional Quarterly, Congressional Monitor,* August 1, 1995, p. 7.

• The Government Accounting Office (GAO) reports that the Health Care Financing Administration (HCFA), responsible for administering Medicare, "is aware that flawed payment policies and abusive billing practices plague Medicare, but the exploitation of the program continues."

• Medicare has been charged rates as high as $600 per hour for speech and occupational therapy, though therapists' salaries range from under $20 to $32 per hour.

• A scam involving mobile physiology labs grew into a multi-million dollar fraud, initially involving Medicare before moving on to other public and private payers, by taking advantage of Medicare's weak control over billing numbers.

• Hospitals and other health providers owed Medicare millions of dollars because of incorrect payments. In the absence of HCFA guidance and monitoring, Uncle Sam failed to recover the losses due to the erroneous payments.

• A pharmaceutical salesman peddled $6 million in expired, mislabeled, unsterile, or secondhand pacemakers over an eight-year period, sometimes providing Hawaiian vacations or prostitutes as kickbacks to cardiologists who agreed to implant the adulterated devices in unsuspecting patients. On raiding his offices, authorities found "a number of bloody pacemakers, raising suspicions he was reselling devices surgically removed from other patients or even from corpses."

• A Georgia healthcare company has been accused of defrauding Medicare of more than $14 million. Unallowable costs charged to Medicare include $9.7 million in computer software, $84,341 for gourmet popcorn, $18,600 for lobbying, golf course memberships, vacations, and a new car for the CEO's son. One may ask if the people responsible for these atrocities have been prosecuted. Knowing the government's track record, it's doubtful.

• In Minnesota, a speech therapist pleaded guilty to six counts of mail fraud involving Medicare and Medicaid. Investigators say that on at least two occasions he billed for nearly 20 hours of speech therapy per day with nursing home patients. On another occasion he billed for working with flash cards with a blind patient.

• According to prosecutors, a company in New York lured Medicare beneficiaries into giving their Medicare identification numbers to the company in exchange for microwaves, air conditioners, or angora underwear. Investigators say the company then used those numbers to bill Medicare for expensive beds, using part of the money they received from Medicare to buy the items they had promised.

• In California, investigators believe a hospice company that cares for the terminally ill may have billed for patients who had already died.

• In Texas, ten home health agencies are being actively investigated. According to the inspector general for the Texas region, the suspected frauds average $2 million.

Clearly the problems with Medicare are critical. At stake is whether senior citizens will have a viable health-care system in the future, whether we can say we treated our parents as well as they treated us, and whether we can hand over a viable Medicare program to our children and grandchildren.

Taxpayers know that Medicare loses billions of dollars each year. In fact, the 10 percent going to waste equals the 10 percent increase in Medicare spending each year. We must act today to save, simplify, and strengthen Medicare. And the first step is to eliminate the fraud and abuse.

Based on the above information, it should be clear that politicians need to make an honest effort to deal with the fraud and abuse that dominate this overburdened program. Instead of politicians demanding more tax dollars, why not go after the abusers? Why make honest people pay for the billions of dollars being wasted each year?

As cited by Martin Gross, author of *Government Racket – Washington Waste From A To Z, A Call For Revolution,* and *The Tax Racket*, a small sampling of his findings include:

- In 1935, there were 20,000 employees working at the Department of Agriculture, overseeing 6.5 million farmers. Now, with only 2.1 million farmers, half of which are part-timers, the number of government farm employees, excluding Food Stamp and Forest Service personnel, has grown to 60,000. Based upon the number of farms and the increased technology, the personnel should be 7,000, not 60,000.
- In 1992, the General Service Administration (GSA), which handles our government buildings, held 15 million square feet of vacant space in thousands of federal buildings. Yet at the same time, they budgeted $5 billion for

new construction. Some of the projects included a new $22 million lab for the U.S. Geological Survey, a $38 million FBI field office, a $50 million Department of Transportation headquarters, a $25 million U.S. Courthouse in Louisiana, a $182 million Federal Building in Boston, a $21 million courthouse in Prince Georges County in the Washington suburb, a $69 million Federal Building and Courthouse annex in Minneapolis, a $33 million Courthouse annex in Oregon, an $81 million Federal Building in West Virginia, a $250 million Naval Command Center in Virginia, and so on.

• The GSA also spent over $100 million in building gifts to private institutions, ranging from the Forestry Science Complex at Northern Arizona University ($4.5 million), to a computer center at Iowa State University ($2.2 million), to a Primate Research Institute in Alamogordo, New Mexico ($4 million), among many others.

• In addition to the shameful waste of money associated with costs of government offices is the cost to decorate. Although no clear records are kept anywhere at the GSA, for apparent reasons, it is estimated by a top GSA spokesman that the annual spending on new furniture and decorating for 1992 alone was between $1.35 to $2 billion. Also, furniture that is replaced is offered to other agencies for free. If not taken within 30 days, it is offered to state and municipal agencies, then donated to charities.

• The federal payroll contained 237,000 middle managers and 116,000 "specialists" in the early 1990s, according to the Office of Personnel Management. The cost to taxpayers, including salaries, pension liabilities, overhead, and assistants was $50 billion per year. It is estimated that a 20% cut of the nonessentials from this group could be made without reducing productivity, and would save about $10 billion per year.

• Farm subsidies and other farm "welfare" programs are costing taxpayers approximately $30 billion per year.

• We paid $859,000 in 1993 for senators to move their offices to more desirable ones that were vacated by retired or defeated senators, plus the cost of moving telephone lines, computers, etc. for a total of more than $1 million.

• $23 million by the United States Post Office to find out how long it takes the mail to get delivered.

Here are a few samples of government waste as found in a recent *Readers Digest* article by William Ecenbarger:

• $1.2 billion was spent for a "service life extension program" for the gutting and rebuilding of the aircraft carrier *USS John F. Kennedy* at the Philadelphia Naval Shipyard, which was obsolete and ready to be shut down. Even though the Senate eventually voted 56 to 44 to defeat this spending bill, it was quietly restored the next evening in secret – a case of political deception at its worst.

Other bills sponsored by our representatives include:

• A $94,000 study of "apple quality" by Michigan State University, sponsored by Representative Bob Traxler (D - Mich.).

• $1 million to determine why people don't use bicycles or walking "as a means of transportation" more often, offered by Martin Olav Sabo (D - Minn.).

• $37,000 to develop "comprehensive management technologies" for the handling of animal manure, engineered by Representative David E. Bonior (D - Mich.).

• In the same defense bill that included the aforementioned *USS John F. Kennedy* restoration, $8 million was earmarked for a new building at Chicago's Loyola University, with the skillful persuasion of one of its alumni, Dan Rostenkowski (D - IL). When Loyola officials expressed guilt that they were taking dollars earmarked for defense, Rostenkowski cleverly had the Pentagon money transferred to the Education Department budget.

• Senator Robert C. Byrd (D - W.Va.), who is called the "prince of pork," is responsible for some of the following misuses of taxpayer money:

$150,000 for a "study" to determine if Bramwell, site of the third drugstore in the U.S. to sell the perfume Chanel No. 5, should be a historic site.

$325,000 to see if Wheeling, W.V. should be a "national heritage area."

$150,000 to see what the Hatfield/McCoy feud was about.

$310,000 for a local hiking trail group.

$4.5 million to transform a Huntington movie house into a multiscreen theater.

• Rep. John P. Murtha (D - Pa.) got $13 million to create a chain of "industrial heritage" parks at old manufacturing sites in Pennsylvania.

• $2 million was appropriated to help perpetuate "native Hawaiian culture and values," thanks to Sen. Daniel K. Akaka (D - Hawaii).

• $2.8 million went for a catfish farm, which is run by the Interior Department's Fish and Wildlife Service, thanks to Sen. Dale Bumpers (D - Ark.).

• Consider up to $140 million in mandated spending by then New York Governor Mario Cuomo, who pushed for requiring newly established limited liability companies to publish legal notices in two local New York papers for six weeks, costing up to $2,000 for each company. Many New York professionals contend that the rarely read notices are of little benefit, except to the newspapers and media-hungry Cuomo.

More Examples of Pork and Waste

Are we being misled by the politicians who promise smaller, more efficient government? Read this and find out. Despite cries for government reform from both sides of the aisle, an abundance of pork and waste is still being proposed in current bills, including:

• $40 million for major corporations such as General Electric, Westinghouse, and ASEA Brown Boveri to develop an advanced light-water reactor design, even though no new nuclear reactors have been built in the United States for over 20 years.

• $15 million being channeled through the Pentagon to support the 1996 Atlanta Olympics.

• $10.4 million to build a physical fitness center at the Puget Sound Naval Shipyard in Bremerton, Washington.

• $15 million for the High Frequency Active Auroral Research Project, which will attempt to draw energy from the Northern Lights, compliments of Senator Ted Stevens (R– Alaska).

• $36 billion to build 20 additional B–2 bombers, even though the need for the new bombers is questionable.

• $700 million this year for a third Seawolf submarine, which will cost a total of $2.4 billion over the next several years.

• $15 million to reduce the debt of the Port of Portland, Oregon, compliments of Sen. Mark Hatfield (R–Oregon).

• $1 million appropriation for "outreach for socially disadvantaged farmers," a program to teach beginning minority farmers how to farm.

• $110 million for the Agriculture Department's Market Promotion Program for 1996. These are tax dollars that go to major corporations, such as Ernest and Julio Gallo wines, to publicize their food products overseas. Gallo wines got over $2.5 million in 1994. In 1993, Pillsbury got $1.75 million, Jim Beam got $713,000, and Campbell soups got $1.1 million. In 1991, McDonald's got almost $500,000 to promote Chicken McNuggets overseas.

• In the GOP budget outlined at the end of 1995, a $265 billion defense appropriations bill was proposed. Many of these rich contracts include mandates that major contracts go, without competitive bidding, to the home states of Republican senators Trent Lott (Mississippi) and William S. Cohen (Maine), and Republican Representatives Curt Weldon (Pa.), Bob Livingston (La.), and Duncan Hunter (California). In more detail, these items include:

(1) The building of an amphibious landing ship, at a cost of almost $1 billion, even though the Navy didn't request one (Rep. Bob Livingston).

(2) A helicopter carrier ship, to be built in the hometown of Trent Lott, at a cost of $1.3 billion, even though not requested by the Army.

These indefensible examples of wasted tax dollars are just a handful of thousands of examples that prove our elected officials in Congress, as well as in the executive branch, do not deserve the power and spending authority we have given them for so long.

Is political pork anything more than uncontested handouts to the well connected? If people don't get excited by what they see in this book regarding frivolous government waste, they need to get their pulse rate checked, their T.Q. (Tolerance Quotient), or both.

The debate regarding how much and where we should pay taxes is clear. Do we determine that those individuals who work hard and earn their money should decide how it should be spent, or do we rely on the "wisdom" of those in Congress, who are responsible for the thousands of wasteful programs documented here and elsewhere, to decide what to do with our money?

What do the foregoing examples, as well as thousands of other documented examples of irresponsible spending, fraud, and abuse prove? The government has **too much** money to spend! Instead of taking more of our money, they should be taking less.

CHAPTER 5

REFORM – CONGRESS'S WAY

The Government Reform and Oversight Committee

Despite the evidence that Congress has robbed us of billions of dollars each year feeding their own pet projects, they have the audacity to attempt to "police" themselves with the Government Reform and Oversight Committee. The job description of this group of self-appointed overseers in the House of Representatives follows: "The Committee on Government Reform and Oversight shall review and study, on a continuing basis, the operation of government activities at all levels with a view to determining their economy and efficiency." The committee consists of 28 Republicans, 23 Democrats, and one Independent.

This committee was apparently contrived to take the place of the taxpayer's watchful eye on the Congress. We should feel comfortable that, since this committee has been formed, we no longer need to concern ourselves with the possibility of duplicity, trickery, or waste where Congress is concerned. The Committee on Government Reform and Oversight will make sure that Congress is working for the taxpayers and not on their own agendas. Right. The truth is we're in the debt we're in because we have let Congress oversee themselves for much too long.

Another wonderful example of reform and self-discipline in the House of Representatives is the *Ethics Manual For Members, Officers, and Employees of The U.S. House of Representatives*, developed by the Committee on

Standards of Official Conduct of the 102nd Congress. Among other things, the Code of Official Conduct states that a member, official, etc.:

"...must conduct himself at all times in a manner which shall reflect creditably on the House of Representatives."

"...shall receive no compensation nor shall he permit any compensation to accrue to his beneficial interest from any source, the receipt of which would occur by virtue of influence improperly exerted from his position in the Congress."

"...shall accept no honorarium for a speech, writing for publication, or other similar activity."

If books written by members of Congress count as "writing for publication," then a number of members of the House are in violation of this one.

The Ethics Manual Code of Ethics For Government Service, adopted in 1958, adds that all of Congress:

"...must put loyalty to the highest moral principles and to country above loyalty to government persons, party, or department."

What about pork-barrel spending and partisan politics?

"...seek to find and employ more efficient and economical ways of getting tasks accomplished."

Was the globetrotting of Energy Secretary Hazel O'Leary a good example of employing the most efficient and economical ways of getting tasks accomplished?

"...expose corruption wherever discovered."

There are only so many hours in the day.

Lacking in both Code of Ethics manuals are any punishment or discipline for those members who strayed from the letter of the ethics standards described therein. The full body of the manuals described above can be found in the appendix at the end of this book.

The Hidden Tax Burden

ANOTHER distortion, as it relates to taxes, is that no one really knows exactly how much their total tax bill is. For instance, in addition to the state, federal, and county income tax we pay each year, there are numerous taxes we pay without debate. To name a few, there are gasoline taxes, inheritance taxes, sin taxes, real estate taxes, sales taxes, social security taxes, utility taxes, personal property taxes, luxury taxes, self–employment taxes, environmental taxes, airline, hotel, and travel taxes, and so on, and so on. Thus, if you're in the 25% tax bracket, your real total tax bill could be approaching 50%! These taxes don't even include other costs of government, such as fees, mandates and regulations. As you can see, politicians have found neat, creative ways to take our money. Why can't they can't find any creative ways to save it?

The tax burden is on the producers. The fact is, the taxpayers whose incomes are in the top 5% of the country are already paying 44% of the taxes. In other words, these people are paying nine times their proportionate share, and these numbers include only income taxes. Add on the other taxes and the proportion goes even more out of whack. However, according to many bureaucrats, these people are still not paying their fair share.

Congress – Welfare's Best and Brightest

The ultimate question regarding government and taxes is this: who will spend money more efficiently and wisely - the people who have earned it by working, or the government who has the money handed to them? This is also one of the problems with welfare. Because the money is given to them, many welfare recipients don't know the value of a dollar and, in some cases, spend the money frivolously on items other than necessities. It could be said there is little difference between politicians and welfare recipients. Both subsist on other people's money.

CHAPTER 6

WHO'S TO BLAME?

The final blame for what happens in Washington lies with us, the voters. We haven't kept ourselves informed or paid attention to the things Washington is doing that affect our daily lives. But we shouldn't be too hard on ourselves. Most of us have been busy trying to earn a living, to survive, and have been working long hours just to pay our bills. We don't have the time, the energy, the patience, or the inclination to follow what is going on in Congress, or make sure the politicians are fulfilling their campaign promises.

Even so, we *do* have an obligation to become informed voters. There are several non-partisan organizations, the most prominent of which is Project Vote Smart, that track politicians' voting records. You can call this organization toll-free and request that they send you the voting record of any politician. It's just that easy to become an informed voter. You will feel more confident when you vote, and will be electing politicians based upon their actions instead of their rhetoric. See the appendix for more contact information on Project Vote Smart and other organizations.

Still, the odds are stacked against us. Not only do we not have time to keep an eye on our politicians, but they do their best to make sure we don't understand what's going on. They hire experts to tell them what we want to hear and teach them how to say it. They hire pollsters to find out what is important to us at any given moment (that's because they are so far removed from reality they can't figure it out for themselves). They enlist "spin doctors" to fix their public images when things go wrong. They engage advisors to counsel them about public opinion, and how to influence and control it. Politicians are playing hardball, and most of us are on the sidelines. We don't have a prayer of competing, unless we level the playing field.

The average American couldn't care less about politics. After all, for the most part, politics is boring. Also, with over 150 million people of voting age, we feel that a single vote can't make a difference, so why waste our time? I spent the first 35 years or so of my life not knowing the difference between a Republican and a Democrat. If you had asked me what party a president was a member of, I would only be guessing. Sports took up my leisure time. I found it much more interesting than politics.

However, several events stick in my mind that got me more interested in politics and what is going on in the country. In no particular order, I'd like to tell you what they were.

• In a televised address to the nation, President George Bush was proudly telling us that, with the demise of Russia as a superpower in the early 1990s, the cold war was over. This would result in a tremendous savings to us regarding military spending. Since we were now the only remaining superpower, and the threat of a major war was diminished, we could expect a savings of about $50 billion over the next 5 years. At first I thought, *Wow! This is great. $50 billion is a tremendous amount of money.* Then reality set in. *Wait a minute. $50 billion over 5 years is only $10 billion per year, which represents only about a 4% decrease in defense spending each year, and less than a 1% savings in the federal budget.* The way President Bush had been talking, I expected a gradual savings of $50 billion per year over time. This was my first sign that politicians aren't too excited about cutting budgets.

• I was watching TV one day in October 1991, and channel-surfed to the Clarence Thomas/Anita Hill "trial" which was being run by a number of congressmen. I was transfixed by the trial, and very disturbed and embarrassed by what I saw. Politicians from the left and the right took turns grilling Mr. Thomas and Ms. Hill. When one side finished, another took over and went over the same questioning and speeches. It struck me funny that all the Democrats clearly thought that Mr. Thomas was guilty of uncivil advances toward Ms. Hill, and all Republicans thought he was innocent. Until then, I hadn't fully understood the reality of partisan politics. After a while, this looked to me like a witch-hunt. Either Mr. Thomas was the most convincing actor and liar I had ever seen, or the Democrats were trying to destroy Mr. Thomas's life and reputation so he wouldn't be confirmed for a Supreme Court seat. This event showed me that politicians would do anything to forward their own agenda, regardless of the consequences, or of what individual or family may be destroyed in the process.

I also learned, while listening to the politicians, to consider the source. In other words, why does a politician say things? It turned out that Mr. Thomas, a brilliant individual who believes in personal responsibility and hard work to get ahead, was a threat to Democrats who would like everyone to believe that African-Americans don't have a chance to succeed without the welfare state, entitlement, or affirmative action. Thus, he was, and is, a threat to the liberal agenda.

• Ross Perot's joining the 1992 presidential campaign educated the public, and me, in ways no one understood until that point. Perot was to me the "nutty professor" who had an honest purpose in mind, and seemed more believable since he wasn't a politician. While most people get into politics for the power and the money, Perot already had both. His debate on the economy forced the voters (and politicians) to focus on the economy, the budget, and wasteful programs more than either political party wanted. That was clear to me. Many people felt that, in order to fix the tremendous budget problem that we face, we needed a strong leader with practical business knowledge and economic sense. Mr. Perot had the experience of building and running a huge billion-dollar business, while staying within budget. Politicians, despite their rhetoric, excuses, and rationalizations, have proven to us just the opposite. They have no practical business experience, they don't know how to fix a budget deficit, and they *don't deserve the responsibility*.

• President Clinton's February 15, 1993, address from the Oval Office, where, after less than a month in office, he said, "I had hoped to invest in [the middle class's] future... without asking more [taxes] of you. And I've worked harder than I've ever worked in my life to meet that goal. But I can't." This was on the heels of his introduction of a huge, $500 billion tax bill. It was amazing to me that he had the nerve, after three weeks in office, to tell us that he couldn't find any ways to save money in the government instead of raising taxes! The only alternative he saw was the largest tax bill in the history of the United States, which stuck it to the rich, middle class, and poor alike. Anyone with healthy cynicism should be surprised he waited three weeks to tell us he couldn't wait to tax us more. In fact, not only did it take him only three weeks to decide that he had no alternative but to raise our taxes, but during the three weeks, when he had worked harder than ever before, he also found time to craft his new tax bill.

To make up for the time he spent trying to find an alternative solution, he made the tax retroactive to the beginning of the year, before he even took office, so we would all have the "benefit" of the increased taxes sooner. This way, history could show that the tax bill he pushed down our throats was in effect before he took office, so he couldn't be responsible for it.

Politicians know that most people couldn't care less about what bill gets passed, especially if it doesn't affect that person directly. A $10 million wasteful pork project in Virginia has no interest for those outside of Virginia. The rest of the country doesn't even know about it. And those in Virginia consider their local representative a hero for bringing some pork, and therefore some jobs and prosperity, to their neighborhood. So, for the most part, the politician can't lose. The way politics is set up, as long as we get our perceived share of pork, we should be happy. But the biggest winners, far and away, are the politicians who solidify their employment and power base by the more pork they develop.

The Sport Fan's Methodology

Politicians have another thing going for them. There is a sport fan's methodology at work in the system. Sport fans invest much of their emotional well-being in the success of their favorite team. By the same token, we are generally "forced" to vote, or root, for one of two people, the Democrat or the Republican. The media, to a great extent, finds any other challenger without national party affiliation a non-entity. So when voting time comes, the media creates a tremendous name recognition advantage for the two major party candidates, and only multimillionaires (or billionaires, such as Ross Perot) can compete with such hype.

In most cases, once you have voted for your candidate of choice, you will stick with him and continue to support that candidate for as long as he decides to run (or until he ends up in jail). To do anything different would be to admit a mistake, and most of us shy away from admitting mistakes.

Why have politicians been able to control our lives and brainwash us into thinking that what they are doing is for our own good? They have been able to take advantage of our apathy and lack of education We are just too busy worrying about our own lives to continually scrutinize these people. Only a well-educated public will demand that we have a voice and are represented as promised by these politicians.

The Information Vacuum

Unfortunately, politicians realize that most voters are terribly uninformed. The most common sources of information for the average voter are television, radio, newspapers, and word of mouth. There are large numbers of voters whose vote is based strictly upon a candidate's party, appearance, charisma, charm, or the influence of a relative, friend, etc. There are just as many one-issue voters who vote only on a candidate's position on abortion, the death penalty, smoking, the speed limit, foreign affairs, the budget, etc. All issues are important, but some will have a more profound effect on your life, and the lives of your family, friends, and neighbors, than others.

The average person who attempts to learn about a candidate depends heavily upon the media for the information. In fact:

- Most voters who get their information from television or radio are either watching or listening to the news, which is often biased; to candidate's commercials, which are clearly biased; or to debates, which may show only which candidate is the most charismatic or most effective speaker.
- Most voters don't take the time to find out what a candidate really stands for and what he plans to do once he is elected. In the largest percentage of cases, a politician gets the winning number of votes by expressing through the media whatever he thinks the majority of voters want to hear. His true loyalty lies with his financial supporters, special interest groups able to provide large blocks of votes as well as financial support, and anyone else he can attract without offending his primary supporters.

In summary, the most popular place for the majority of the electorate to get information about candidates is the media, which has the least amount of credible, unbiased information. So how does the average person, without a lot of time, find out what he needs to know? Clearly, without reform of the present system, many voters will continue to be uninformed and choose candidates based upon erroneous beliefs.

What do I want in a candidate campaigning for an elected position? Before I hear him talk, I want to know what he has done in the past. The best orator in the world with flawed ideas can lead us to disaster. I want someone who speaks openly about his plans, does not withhold facts, gives me honest and open reports of governmental and fiscal activities, and shares practical, specific ideas, backed by factual data, for improving the United States. I want someone I can trust to make this a country for the *people*, not the elected officials.

I don't want to support a politician who has ever suggested or voted for a pork or wasteful bill, or has lied to his constituents or the public.

Simply, a politician who has lied and deceived us in the past will probably lie and deceive us in the future. It's a matter of character, and you can more confidently judge a person by his actions than by his rhetoric. I feel confident I am making the right choice when I vote for someone based upon his plans, goals, and past actions, rather than on what he is saying at the moment to get elected. If, when I listen to a politician, his words are inconsistent with his actions, I believe his *actions,* not his words.

CHAPTER 7

WHY BLAME POLITICIANS?

Try to answer the following multiple-choice question. People get into politics because:

(a) they sincerely want to serve their country, become public servants, and represent taxpayers.
(b) they are power-hungry.
(c) this is a way for people of insignificant accomplishment to impose their will and agenda on the public.
(d) of the money.
(e) they are otherwise unemployable.
(f) they figure it's the easiest way to get their whole family employed.
(g) they like playing "entrepreneur" with other people's money.
(h) they are opinionated blabbermouths who are full of hot air and just like to hear themselves talk.
(i) all of the above.
(j) none of the above.
(k) fill in the blank ____________________

Why not blame politicians? Who shall we blame? It is clear that the political process has stacked the deck against newcomers. This is evident in the reelection rates, despite the fact that, according to national polls, politicians are on the bottom of the totem pole when it comes to credibility, integrity, and honesty. Yet, to defend the political process you may say we have the opportunity to vote an elected official out of office if we don't like what he is doing. Unfortunately, it's not that simple!

THE POOR CHOICES GOVERNMENT MAKES ON OUR BEHALF

The workings of government are nothing less than a national disgrace. Our leaders, in order to support their own greed and self-interest, have come close to bankrupting this country. But for a remarkably resilient mass of people called Americans who, so far, have footed the bills for Congress, the United States would be bankrupt today.

Taxpayers are fighting an uphill battle because of the way the government "system" is set up. The government is set up to *spend* money, not *save* it.

For instance, although there have been countless studies that detail the waste of a bloated government and offer realistic solutions in many cases, the government continues to ignore savings. Why? For a number of reasons, including:

(1) Those who are in charge of spending, the politicians, are rewarded for their spending with loyalty and the financial support of their constituents and supporters. Lawmakers aren't quick to cut the waste. They want a share of pork to come to *their* constituents as well.

(2) Government agencies and programs receive money based upon what they spend, so by cutting spending they get less money. Therefore, the leaders of these agencies or programs have no incentive to cut spending. There are no incentives for them to find alternative solutions or procedures that may be more efficient. In the private sector, employees are frequently rewarded financially for submitting alternative, cost–cutting ideas to their superiors.

There are two government agencies whose job is, among other things, to identify government waste: the General Accounting Office (GAO), and the Inspector General's office (IG). Unfortunately, these two government agencies are regularly ignored by the agencies they review, as well as by Congress. In the past 18 years, the GAO has made thousands of recommendations to cut waste and make government more efficient. Over 2,000 recommendations, which would have saved taxpayers untold billions of dollars, have been ignored by these federal agencies. Perhaps that's because many of these suggestions would reduce Congress's spending, much of which has been promised to colleagues and supporters.

In many cases, these unheeded warnings led to major financial disasters. For instance, since 1972, the GAO has written over 100 reports about unneeded military surplus. Government auditors estimated the excess inventory at $30 billion, not including the storage costs of the excess items, which amount to millions of dollars each year. And all this does not take into account the fact that the items become old and obsolete the longer they are stored.

In 1985, the GAO warned that the S&L fund protecting savings and loans had significant problems, and four years later the fund collapsed. This S&L bailout directly cost taxpayers approximately $200 billion. It also cost the U.S. economy another $350 billion in lost real estate values, and caused a virtual standstill of construction and all related industries, resulting in the most personal bankruptcies in over 30 years from 1990–1994.

Inspectors of HUD have discovered billions of dollars of waste, fraud, and abuse in this agency for over 15 years. Not only has there been little or no attempt at positive reform, but the abuse continues to this day, as shown in other parts of this book.

These examples are just a small sample of the irresponsible decisions made by politicians every day. In the private sector, employees would be fired for making such harmful judgments. But in government, waste, fraud, and gross negligence is not only ignored, it is often rewarded with reelection and increased personal wealth.

Why is government reform necessary? The arrogance and misguided principles of so many in Congress are depicted in the following example. On the subject of government reform, Representative Mary Rose Oaker (D - Ohio) said, "I don't want some guidelines changed to inhibit my city's opportunity to use that money." This was in reference to her request for government funding to help build a $48 million rock 'n roll museum in Cleveland. Rep. Oaker just couldn't believe she wouldn't be able to spend money on pet projects as she saw fit.

THE STACKED DECK

Politicians stack the deck in their favor in many ways. For instance, politicians, our lawmakers, over the years have passed laws, rules, and bills that entrench themselves in office, making it more and more difficult for "outsiders" to break into their exclusive "club."

Unseating an incumbent has become almost impossible, due to:

Franking

Thanks to our tax dollars, Congress has access to free mailing. Mailings, when described as "official business," are sent out at taxpayer expense, at a cost of almost $100 million per year. This mail, with the politician's name all over it and propaganda to match, gives the incumbent additional name recognition with his constituents and a decided edge over any challenger. Often the contents are nothing more than "fact-filled" information describing the wonderful services the representative has provided for you, at your expense, of course.

Due to the franking privilege abuse by our elected officials, new rules are now being put in place to limit this perk. This is one example, which will be described in detail later, of why we need to scrutinize our politicians more closely. It is apparent that many politicians take advantage of every liberty available and still are not satisfied. And given the opportunity, they will do it regularly and habitually.

Candidates need sources of money. In 1992, for instance, the cost of political campaigns went over the $1 billion mark, according to the Federal Elections Commission.

Congress alone spent over $678 million for 535 representatives, or $1.27 million per representative, to get elected or reelected. Doesn't that reveal the TRUTH that there is more to politics than just a $133,000-a-year job?

The average House winner spent $550,000; the average Senate winner spent almost $4 million. The losers were outspent about 8 to 1 by the incumbents who won at a 93% rate. A question must be asked. Did the incumbents win by such a landslide because of the great job they were doing, or because of their prodigious spending capacity? Did they do such a great job representing the public, which is what they're elected for, or did they just do a great job getting reelected?

Matching Funds

Only Republicans and Democrats have received tax-supported matching funds of any significance. According to Federal Election Commission law, the government matches up to $27 million per candidate for those contributions of $250 or less. In 1992, we spent $42,742,815 matching what presidential candidates raised during the primary campaign. Note that these funds do not include money from any Political Action Committees (PACs), or other sources.

National Conventions

The Federal Election Commission also gave each party $11 million in 1992 for the national conventions. When those conventions ended, each party received an *additional* $55 million of taxpayer money.

Soft Money

Soft money is the term for those contribution amounts exceeding the contribution limits that a person can give a candidate which are sent to the candidate's political party for party expenses and general party advertising. In 1992, $63 million went toward federal campaigns, and much more for local battles. This little-known loophole circumvents the contribution limit law we thought applied to all politicians

PAC Money

The average House member received about $260,000 from PAC money. This is in addition to all other monies outlined earlier. PAC money not used is put in a bank account controlled by the party. Guess what happens if a politician loses favor with the party? He loses his excess share of the PAC dollars. This is just another form of influence, or "arm-twisting," the party has over our "representatives."

Indirect Campaign Committees

Despite all the talk about limits on campaign contributions and spending cuts, candidates have still another loophole. Any supporter can form a committee to directly assist a candidate to get elected, as long as there is no direct cooperation from that candidate. That law clearly shows that politicians are serious about campaign reform, doesn't it?

The truth is candidates don't need a lot of money to win an election. In fact, former Senator William Proxmire of Wisconsin spent $175 on stamps and stationery to return unsolicited donations in his 1976 campaign win. He won again in 1982. Campaign contributions, in the eyes of many, are nothing more than "buying" a politician's goodwill and patronage. Politicians regularly trade favors with individuals and corporations for financial contributions and other forms of support.

Political Favor

All it takes is money to procure political favor. We know that, in many cases, the money politicians receive from individuals and businesses is more than just an investment in principle. In fact, the money is buying loyalty, favors, and goodwill that can be translated into millions of dollars. Studies, including the recently published *The Buying of the President* by Charles Lewis and the Center for Public Integrity, have shown that politicians consistently show allegiance worth many times the original investment to their benefactors. Is this how government is supposed to be run? Of course not. But, *The Buying of the President* clearly shows that the loyalties of even the most high profile politicians can be, and often are, bought – at the expense of the taxpayers.

The Buying of the President gives example after example of political favor shown by current political candidates. However, presidential candidates are not the only ones who trade their political power for additional funding and support. Innumerable examples of favoritism by politicians past and present are documented in dozens of sources. Is it any wonder Congress represents its contributors more than it does its constituents?

Besides spending the money raised, and nearly $300 million of our tax dollars as well, politicians are harming us in other ways. Incumbents running for reelection spend much of the 18 months prior to election day campaigning at our expense. Not only are they about 30% efficient during that period because of campaign responsibilities, but much of our tax money is used to fly these candidates and their entourage all over the country for campaign visits.

Maybe we've accidentally hit upon something here. During any 18-month period before an election, politicians are in "campaign mode." Since representatives are elected for only two years, what does that mean? The TRUTH is that once a politician get into office, his main priority is to find ways to stay there. Therefore, he's *always* in campaign mode. Consequently, while a politician may be only 30% effective during the 18 months prior to a campaign, he is only 50% effective the other months he's in office. How can he legislate properly when he's so busy trying to find ways to win points with his voters?

In fact, former Senator Don Reigle even admitted that politicians spend from 50% to 80% of their time raising money during an election year. Is that what we hired them to do?

The easiest way to win points is not to lose any, which means: don't upset any large voting contingent. According to the polls, to vote safely, vote with the majority. And if public opinion isn't consistent with your agenda, it's up to you, with the assistance of a well-trained media, to sway public opinion to your side.

Another popular way to gain favor with your constituency, established by decades of selfish Washingtonites, is to present spending bills that bring some of the tax dollars to the voters. This pork-barrel spending is one of the fundamental assaults that has been leveled against taxpayers.

Pork-Barrel Spending

Over the years, politicians have developed a powerful, effective, yet destructive (to us) method to keep themselves in power. Wasteful spending bills and programs mentioned in this book, and dozens of others, are calculated tactics to keep the incumbent politician in power. When a district representative receives a $4 million government-financed pork project, he gets at least that same value in positive press to his local constituents, some of whom may profit from that project. He makes sure, before the next election, that all the government-financed community improvements are spelled out clearly in franked mailings to his constituents, showing how many jobs were created in the community as a result of his latest pork-barrel victory. When an incumbent can show voters he has been true to the community by bringing some of the tax dollars back home, how does a challenger have a chance?

As the game is played, with a nod and a wink among fellow politicians, there is a collusion that exists that would sicken the average taxpayer if he knew the truth. How often is wasteful spending pushed through by one politician giving another his vote in exchange for the promise that the favor will be returned when it's his turn to bring something back to his people? How many billions of dollars have been spent playing this game over the years? No one could make an exact guess, but based upon the amount of wasteful spending prevalent in Congress these days, the number would run into hundreds of billions of dollars, if not trillions. Is it any wonder that incumbents typically have such a high success rate of reelection?

People Are Intrinsically Afraid of Change

Many people feel comfortable with the demon they know, and don't want to take a chance on an unpredictable challenger. One of the incumbent's favorite arguments against any newcomer is the newcomer's lack of experience. However, is the experience an incumbent has gained over the years, as a Washington insider and dealmaker, the kind that should make the voting public feel more comfortable? Do we want an experienced politician who has given us this $5 trillion debt, or are we ready to take a chance on someone who isn't entrenched in the system and who may try to eliminate the waste?

Passion

The politicians' passion for power outweighs our passion to change things for the better. That's why we cheerfully ignore their wrongdoings that have cost us trillions of dollars, and go on with our lives. History has shown us that the more passion one side has, the better chance it has of winning. Sports history shows that the team that plays more passionately and works harder is going to win almost every time. Without passion for real change, we don't have a chance of reforming our ailing government. Unless we get angry enough at what has been done to our country by Congress, we will never be able to generate the passion needed to bring about change and improvement.

Gerrymandering

In order to stack the deck even more in their favor for future elections, politicians regularly change the map of their district, or "redistrict", to suit their purposes. Based upon specific demographic studies that they engage, at taxpayer expense, representatives may "gerrymander" a voting district to get a higher percentage of a specific voting group.

For example, after the 1990 Nevada census, two Republican incumbents moved Republican territory in south Las Vegas to the conservative 2nd District and moved predominantly black north Las Vegas to the 1st District, with the idea of keeping a stronghold for Republicans in the 2nd district.

Paid Staff

In addition to all the other advantages an incumbent gets credit for, he has a staff, provided by taxpayer money, whose activities include:

(1) Doing volunteer work for their boss.

(2) Preparing campaign propaganda, franked mail etc.

(3) Providing constituent services. These are services a congressman provides for the voters when they need help with a problem. A certain number of his staff are specifically designated to help the voters and retain their support.

We are evidently irrelevant in the eyes of many politicians, except when they need our votes, support, or contributions. They prove this on a daily basis by their actions. Why can't we see through their hypocrisy, and recognize that their rhetoric is a substitute for action?

We need protection from politicians who run on one agenda, set of promises, or platform, and then promote their own agenda without regard to promises made. Why shouldn't we have the right to force politicians to live up to the voters' high expectations? Why should we condone, or make excuses for, those people who make casual promises that they later break just as casually?

VOTING FOR BILLS - SIGHT UNSEEN

Lawmakers in both the Senate and the House of Representatives regularly vote for and sign bills they haven't read. Bills, for the most part, are voted on along party lines, and often their contents are a mystery to the lawmakers. Is this the prudent way to spend billions of taxpayer dollars – without even knowing what's in the package? Is there any defense for this blatant negligence?

An example of this abuse of power and authority is the Intermodal Surface Transportation Efficiency Act of 1991, which is otherwise known as the "Highway Bill." This bill, which cost taxpayers over $151 billion, was voted on before any of the legislators saw the final draft. How could the members of the House of Representatives vote overwhelmingly in favor (372–47) of a bill they hadn't read? Simply because each legislator who voted for the bill was promised that a valuable pork project he could proudly wave in front of his constituents would be included in the bill.

PARTISAN POLITICS

Politicians regularly change their stripes based upon partisan politics. For example, in 1994 Democrat Diane Feinstein, California Senator, supported a balanced budget amendment (BBA). However, when the GOP attempted to push through a BBA, she was against it. Why? Because Republicans were behind it now.

However, partisan politics is forced onto politicians with tremendous potency. If a politician doesn't vote along party lines, he or she may be black-listed, and unable to secure or retain a prestigious and powerful position as a committee chair.

THE ULTIMATE POWER OF CONGRESS AND GOVERNMENT

Congress commands tremendous power. Their power is enforced by the U.S. government. When they pass a bill or program, we as citizens must follow those rules. There is no decision-making on our part; it is not voluntary. We have no choice.

While charities must appeal to our compassion for our support, government doesn't have to appeal to anything. If we don't do what they want, we can be taken to court, thrown in jail, etc. There is no freedom from Congress's power.

We must strip away some of the foreboding power that government has assumed, but was not given. WE used to be the government, but we aren't anymore. The government can shut down your business, or deny your right to free speech. The tax code is another form of their power. Even though initially paying taxes was voluntary, it is anything but voluntary now. Congress has become arrogant with power, and there are no effective checks and balances to control it anymore.

THE REGULATION AND TAKING OF PRIVATE PROPERTY

Government regulates private property because some activists in power don't like what you're doing with it. If a property owner digs up a worm, or the home of an animal, there could be some agency telling the property owner to stop. If they don't stop they could be sued, and who can afford to fight these lawsuits? So, often these groups get their way. They place their own agenda, and in many cases animal rights, ahead of property owners' rights and human rights.

Who is the ultimate winner when the regulators come calling? The legal profession, of course. Why have regulations grown to such a stifling level over the past 30 years? Among other things, it keeps lawyers very busy. And most members of Congress were lawyers before they became elected civil servants.

POLITICIANS' PROPENSITY FOR PREVARICATION – OR – WHY THEY LIE

Politicians seldom try to be accurate if it doesn't serve their purpose. They don't mind if it means sidestepping the truth. We have learned that we can't take politicians at their word because, now more than ever before in memory, politicians have mastered the art of deception, fabrication, and half-truth. Never before have we seen those elected officials, who ostensibly work for us, attempt to fool us so blatantly and so often. This shows the utter lack of respect that politicians have for us.

An illustrative example of hateful, deceptive, and sophomoric speech occurred on October 5, 1995, when Richard Gephardt, Democratic leader, spoke to a group called Families USA in Washington, D.C. Following are some excerpts from his speech, which targeted the GOP Balanced Budget:

"...the Republican Congressional budget...is every bit as revolutionary..."

"The problem is, sometimes revolutions claim innocent lives."

"And sometimes, you make history through tragedy."

Mr. Gephardt scares his audience into believing that Republicans are heartless, and that their proposals will tragically claim innocent lives. Instead of backing up his statement with actual fact, he leaves the facts to the imagination of the audience.

"You see, this Republican budget represents something far more extreme, far more radical, far more destructive than most Americans realize."

Gephardt tells the audience that there are points in the Republican proposal that are extreme and destructive, even though he won't be specific as to what the extreme points are.

"...destroying our air, our water, and our forests in the process."

He tells the audience that rolling back some of the environmental regulations will destroy our air, water, and forests, even though he doesn't explain *how* that will happen.

"...slapping a tax increase on the families that are struggling to get into the middle class, and giving a massive tax cut to the wealthiest Americans, the very people who don't need it, and probably wouldn't want it at that price."

He misleads his audience by implying that the tax cut is going only to the wealthiest Americans,

even though it is aimed primarily at families with children. In fact, a $500 per child tax cut is much more beneficial to lower and middle class taxpayers that to the wealthy.

He contends that the wealthy (a term he does not define, but uses to intensify class warfare) don't "need" a tax cut, and "probably wouldn't want it." The nerve!

"...the Contract with America may have been an irrelevant, poll-driven distraction..."

The contract was a promise to the voters who demanded change and got it when the President didn't veto the reforms attempted. The reform of Congress, getting them to follow the laws they make, is not irrelevant. The balanced budget is not irrelevant. The line item veto is not irrelevant. Mr. Gephardt clearly suggests that the voters' wishes for change are irrelevant.

"America...has fallen to sixth in the world in standard of living..."

"It's a battle to save America's standard of living."

For whom? He's attempting only to save his job, and those of other Democrats, who like Mr. Gephardt, are prolonging class warfare, and the welfare state.

"...to save a middle class that may not survive this Republican budget bombshell."

This is another scare tactic aimed at the middle class. Mr. Gephardt once again uses paralyzing rhetoric instead of specifics.

"Many now wonder if their government can help them at all."

People help themselves. Government gets in the way of those who attempt to help themselves with onerous taxes, regulations, and mandates. No one has become prosperous by receiving a government welfare check.

"...the Reagan revolution...exploded the deficit by tenfold..."

Another exaggeration, or outright lie. According to the Budget of the United States Government, the deficit the year before Reagan took office (1980) was $73.835 billion. When Reagan left office in 1988, the deficit was $155.187 billion, which is more accurately a two-fold increase, not tenfold. Is Mr. Gephardt intentionally lying here to make a point, or is he just not familiar with the facts?

The Democrat-controlled Congress, which is responsible for spending and appropriations, increased spending during the Reagan years faster than Reagan's tax cuts increased tax revenue. According to the Budget of the United States Government, from the U.S. Government Printing Office (see Addendum Chart I), tax revenues increased from $599 billion in 1981 to $990 billion in 1989: a 65% increase. Spending increased from $678 billion in 1981 to $1,144 billion in 1989: a 69% increase.

"We came to power in 1992..."

As if the Democrats had nothing to do with the spending deficits prior to 1992. In fact, Democrats had control of the House and Senate for a full generation prior to 1992.

"It's [the Republican balanced budget] not what people want, it's not what they thought they were voting for last November..."

So says a nonpartisan observer? The more distortions that are made of the Republican budget, the more people will be turned off by it. That is Gephardt's strategy.

"...shutting them out of college educations..."

The GOP proposal does no such thing. It asks for payment of interest when the money is borrowed, rather than after graduation. In the real

world, payments on a loan begin as soon as the money is borrowed.

"And why do the wealthy get every perk, every privilege, every tax cut the Republicans ever dream of? Is that what a national crisis demands? Sacrifice from the many, for the exclusive benefit of the few?"

According to Mr. Gephardt, only the wealthy have families. That's who is receiving the bulk of the proposed tax cuts.

"..child would lose his school lunch, costing them about $53.00 per year."

First of all, the school lunch budget the Republicans proposed increased funding, despite the lies to the contrary.

Second, how many families can't find $53.00 *per year* to feed their own child and save him or her from starving? If this is Mr. Gephardt's idea of a good fight, he's lost already.

"..Republicans are slashing Medicaid, and making families fully liable for the cost of nursing home care, that could amount to a crushing $40,000 every year for a family."

Mr. Gephardt, you're from Missouri. SHOW US where it says that Republicans have taken away all options for families who are in need of nursing home care.

The Republican agenda "..is reckless, unconscionable, and fundamentally unfair."

Mr. Gephardt's hate speech, which is filled with misrepresentations and outright lies, is reckless, unconscionable, and fundamentally unfair. Preying on the emotions of the sick, the elderly, and the uninformed to further his own agenda is thoughtless and selfish.

"Let's face it: the party that opposed Social Security in 1935, and opposed Medicare in 1965, and opposed guaranteed health care in 1994, has outdone themselves this time."

Let's see: Social Security is scheduled to be

bankrupt within the next 5–7 years.

We paid in 1990 ten times what was projected for Medicare when it was conceived.

The Clinton socialized "guaranteed health care" was rejected by 75% of Americans in 1994.

Mr. Gephardt describes these programs as if they were all resounding successes.

"A plan...that would decimate a generation of life–saving doctors and researchers..."

What plan was that? The Clinton health care overhaul was rejected by the medical profession in resounding numbers.

"...huge tax increases for the poorest working families."

The poorest working families wouldn't be paying huge taxes, regardless of the budget proposal. The flat tax, for instance, exempts the first $36,000 of income, a level which no longer qualifies as "the poorest working families." Mr. Gephardt's own tax plan taxes everyone making less than $75,000, including the poorest working families, at a rate of 10%, which is 10% more than the flat tax takes.

"...rather than cutting...school lunches that nourish young minds."

This tugs at our emotions, but uses an outright lie in the process. Is Mr. Gephardt's philosophy to win at any cost?

Regarding fair trade policies: "..making them compete with rock–bottom wages, prison labor, and slave labor."

Didn't President Clinton push NAFTA?

"...and I'll be damned if I'm going to let a band of supply–side extremists destroy our middle class to pay for tax breaks for the wealthy."

"...trickle–down terrorists..."

Mr. Gephardt calls Republicans extreme, because they aren't willing to negotiate with the Democrats. And yet, would you negotiate with someone who must resort to name-calling?

"It is the Democrats, not the Republicans, who must stand for the families that have been ravaged by declining economic growth in these past twenty years."

And it is the Democrats, not the Republicans, who controlled Congress for those same twenty years.

"It is the Democrats, not the Republicans, who must explain how this Congress of secret plans and midnight massacres is threatening the very foundation of American family life."

And it was the Democrats, led by Hillary Clinton, who presided over secret plans and midnight massacres regarding the health care of our country.

"Because it is the Democrats, not the Republicans, who know better."

About what?

"...the false stereotype of Democrats as 'tax–and–spend' bureaucrats, tired servants of the status quo."

The crowning jewel of the Clinton administration, the Clinton Tax Bill of 1993, increased taxes *and* spending. So far Clinton has voted *for* the status quo by vetoing welfare reform and the Republican plan to save social security.

The speech above is an excellent example of why we must demand truth in government. Speeches like this are made daily throughout the country, and in political debates and political advertising. Such misrepresentations and blatant deceptions should be things of the past, but this can happen only with your support. You must let all politicians know that this unproductive and destructive behavior is not acceptable and will no longer be tolerated.

THE INFORMATION VACUUM

People seem smarter when they know more than the

next guy. Politicians have been withholding relevant information for decades, feeding us just enough select material necessary while still keeping us in the dark. The government, with all its laws, rules, bills, tax codes, etc., is so massive and foreboding that the average taxpayer finds it hard just to keep the government out of his way, let alone try to understand what's going on in Washington. It's tough enough to make a living and support a family.

SHUMER'S CONTRIBUTION TO PUBLIC POLICY

Why blame politicians? With all the important economic and social problems facing every American citizen, Representative Charles Shumer (D - Michigan) in 1995 decided to make a big issue of, and wage war against, cereal makers for charging too much! He actually wanted the Justice Department to look into this "momentous" issue. Is this not a flagrant waste of time and taxpayer money? Aren't there more important issues facing society at this time than the price of corn flakes? In fact, as a great fan of cereal, this author believes that cereal is one of the best food values around.

Mr. Shumer found a TV camera, and gravely proclaimed that cereal companies enjoy a monopoly, and therefore control the rising price of cereal. This contention is inane. First of all, there are a number of companies who have popular brands of cereal, so there can't be a monopoly. Next, we do have options besides cereal. If you decide you can't afford cereal, you may eat fruit, muffins, toast, eggs, bacon, etc. If you find some cereals too expensive, there are others that cost less. Surely a box of cereal that costs $4.50 and contains approximately ten large servings can be afforded by Mr. Shumer on his base salary of $136,600 per year.

Mr. Shumer, why focus only on cereals? Why shouldn't

the government decide what each commodity is worth, and what we should be paying for everything? Look at athletes' salaries. Perhaps cereals have to charge what they charge because athletes demand such large sums to endorse them.

Following the logic of Mr. Shumer, can you think of another operation that has a monopoly and charges too much? HOW ABOUT THE PRICE OF GOVERNMENT, MR. SHUMER, WHICH ***DOES*** HAVE A MONOPOLY ON ITS CITIZENS?! Shumer says that cereal costs too much. I say government and its "leaders" cost too much. Not only is there clearly a monopoly, but we certainly don't get our money's worth from them. Why don't we take a national poll, Mr. Shumer?

How many people feel we don't get our money's worth from . . .

. . . cereal?	_____%
. . . politicians?	_____%
. . . government?	_____%

I wonder why Mr. Shumer brought up the price of cereal. What else was going on at that time, that Mr. Shumer was attempting to take the focus away from?

Finally, Mr. Shumer, wouldn't your time be better spent focusing on the dire social and billion-dollar economic problems of the day instead of on pennies? Or did you decide to go after the cereal industry only because you received a large number of grave complaints from your electorate regarding the high price of cereal?

Why are we skeptical of politicians? When politicians present a so-called "reform" program, more often than not it is a watered-down version of a program we would really like to see. Politicians have become proficient at appeasing the public with rhetoric, and proposed bills that supposedly "solve" a problem but actually do little or nothing significant. Bills of any significance are typically ambiguous enough, or contain small print we are unaware of, to allow the politicians the opportunity to circumvent the original purpose of the reform. And how often has a bill that America wanted passed the vote in Congress, only to be overturned shortly thereafter with no scrutiny or publicity?

THE PRACTICE OF "POLITRICS"

Politicians have numerous ways of getting unpopular bills passed without taking any personal responsibility. Some of their techniques follow:

(1) When voting on a bill that is unpopular with the voters, Congress has been able to vote by voice. That way no one is on record with his vote.

(2) Conference committees, which are groups from the House and the Senate, are ostensibly put together once a bill passes the House and Senate, in order to "work out" the differences, if any, between the bills. What happens, in many instances, is that politically unpopular bills approved by both the House and Senate can be overturned in conference, giving the Congress members credit for their popular vote, and yet giving the Congress their way in the end. Or, they can revise a bill, removing proposals that were approved in both houses but are unpopular with the members of Congress.

Campaigners use shallow eloquence in debates in order to move away from main issues for which they have no genuine solution, such as the budget, welfare, health care, government waste, etc. They are masters when it come to manipulating the press and the masses with their pontificating.

There is abundant evidence of government waste, fraud, pork, illegal activity, and backroom dealings that have cost taxpayers literally trillions of dollars during this generation's lifetime. There are thousands of people in jail who have committed less serious and less costly crimes than those committed by our elected officials who have a fiduciary responsibility for our money. And yet, despite their scandalous activities, these politicians are still running our country.

Shouldn't we be suspicious of politicians who support spending $30 billion on a crime bill when the criminal justice system is broken? It is hard to argue with the idea that imposing more severe penalties on criminals who have been caught would be a strong deterrent to crime. At the very least, "truth in sentencing" would keep criminals off the streets for the full term of their sentence. There is example after example that shows the success of this practice. It stands to reason that fewer lawbreakers would take the chance of being caught, if they knew they would be dealt with harshly in prison. As the justice system presently stands, even when a lawbreaker is caught, the chance of his receiving harsh punishment is slim, the chance of his getting off is great, and if he is sent to jail, often he will enjoy better living conditions in jail than he did at home. Isn't the $30 billion crime bill just another example of spending good money on the same bad solutions?

The bureaucrats of Washington have antagonized Americans for so long that we have finally reached the point of revolt. We won't be pushed any further. We need to make changes right now. It's time to stop the bleeding, which consists of high taxes and regulations, that chokes the workers of this country, puts small and big concerns alike out of business, places more people on unemployment and welfare payrolls, and makes more people dependent upon government and the overburdened taxpayers. This is a viscious cycle that has to end. And the sooner it is stopped, the better chance we have of fixing our problem.

A STUDY IN MALPRACTICE

"A dereliction from professional duty or a failure to exercise an accepted degree of professional skill or learning by one rendering professional services which results in injury, loss, or damage."

"An injurious, negligent, or improper practice."

Do the above definitions describe what we know about the activities of politicians? If so, you should know that these definitions are found in *Webster's New Collegiate Dictionary*. The word Webster was defining is "malpractice." This is a strong word to use to describe the way our politicians transact business, but is it anything less than malpractice when someone takes advantage of his position to consistently conduct fraudulent and deceptive business practices?

The examples in this book, and hundreds of other examples that appear in newspapers across the country each month, clearly show that politicians are, quite often, negligent in their duties. Their improper practices and lack of discipline are chronicled daily.

Without question, the actions of politicians frequently result in injury, loss, or damage. I have discussed this so often it has become redundant. The politicians who, over the years have allowed wasting dollars to become the norm in Washington, have left an oppressive legacy of debt for future generations to pay. If an annual interest payment of $333 billion per year on our national debt ($1,266 for each United States citizen) isn't injurious and damaging to Americans, I don't know what is.

Have congress members misused their authority by making laws to increase their compensation, their pensions, their power, and their likelihood for reelection? It seems that ever since those in power realized they could spend tax dollars in the name of government, and not be responsible for paying the bills, the deficit and national debt have exploded.

Professionals of all types are subject to malpractice claims if they don't do the job they are hired to do if they betray the public trust, or if they behave dishonestly. Doctors, accountants, and even lawyers are fined, sued, fired, or put in jail for various levels of malpractice. Why are they treated differently when it comes to accountability and punishment?

In addition to malpractice, politicians are guilty of gross misrepresentation of facts in order to intentionally mislead the public. These distortions or misstatements of fact can result in billions of dollars of fraudulent spending that we must pay for. And yet, there is a louder outcry from the public when a sports team moves to another city or when a movie star gets married.

Malpractice is dealt with severely in every area except government and politics. Although I am the last to advocate every citizen suing the government whenever it makes a mistake, I believe it's time we take a stand against the waste, fraud, and abuse that our politicians have gotten away with for decades. Therefore, because of the fiduciary authority we give them, politicians and government employees should be answerable to the same set of standards and rules as every citizen.

A CLEAR CONFLICT OF INTEREST

Yes, folks, we have a problem. And the problem is a conflict of interest. Our lawmakers, the politicians, are the ones who make the rules and determine how large and intrusive government will become. And yet, the more efficient government is, the less money it spends, the more freedoms we Americans enjoy, the fewer taxes we need to pay, and the less power and dominance politicians possess. No, the politicians who control our pocketbooks don't have the incentive to find authentic solutions. Their idea of a solution is to throw more tax dollars at a problem, thereby expanding their influence. We have the incentives – our pocketbooks, our children's future, and survival as we know it – not the politicians who thrive on spending.

What is the extent of the problem caused by politicians? Politicians are working on destroying the formula which has given the American people a fighting chance for success. Working hard and playing by the rules no longer assures success, freedom, or prosperity. Because of the amount of taxes taken from us each year, a large portion of which is used to fund politicians' own preoccupations, it is more and more difficult for a family to live the American Dream.

FOR OUR OWN GOOD – A LITANY OF FAILED GOVERNMENT INVOLVEMENT

Despite any evidence to the contrary, our lawmakers in Congress continue to stretch the boundary of the authority accorded them in the Constitution of the United States. Somewhere along the way, they decided that they needed more to do. They weren't satisfied with plain old legislating; they had to find other ways to control our lives. The elected officials and their staffs, perhaps to justify a larger and more bloated organization, continue to find areas in our lives where they can "help" us. However, what we have found from experience is that the more we receive help from government, the worse we are for it. The more it costs, the less we get, and the more power the Congress acquires. It's a great deal for everyone except the citizens, the taxpayers. Want examples? I could fill a book, but I'll try to be brief.

Medicare was set up 30 years ago as a fine program to help the elderly afford health care. It was projected that its cost in 1990, adjusting for inflation, would be $12 billion. It actually cost $98 billion, which was eight times as much.

Oops! The 1995 budget for Medicare was $154 billion.

The Great Society was announced by Lyndon Johnson to provide a safety net for the poor. Instead of providing a safety net, however, it has become a way of life for millions of families who are given just enough money to remain poor. There was supposed to be approximately $9 billion per year spent on this program, and yet we are now spending TEN times that level on various entitlements. Instead of *reducing* the number of poor people, these programs have *encouraged* more to join the ranks, and have made it easy for many to scam the system. Not only are the poor continuing to suffer, but now so are the taxpayers. Only 28% of the money taxpayers pay towards these welfare programs actually reaches the needy. What happens to the other 72%? That goes into the layers of bureaucracy the government has devised.

Grazing Fees on Federal Land

The government charges $1.92 per month for each horse or cow grazing on its land, even though a rancher must pay anywhere from $8–15 for private land grazing.

Supercollider

In the early 1980s, a giant subatomic particle-smasher was conceived, with the purpose of discovering the origin of mass, in Waxahachie, Texas. In 1989, the estimated cost for this project was $5.9 billion. The GAO now admits that the cost has exceeded $11 billion, nearly twice the original estimate. This is a typical government scenario where an original estimate is lowballed by omitting or failing to investigate possible additional costs, just to get something approved. Bureaucrats have learned that once an undertaking is initially approved, it almost always survives, regardless of the cost to taxpayers.

Courthouses

Would you consider it mismanagement for Congress to

approve construction for new courthouses, costing hundreds of millions of dollars each, without holding hearings, getting firm budgets, or setting aside money for construction? That's what has happened for years with federal construction projects. Those spending the money have had no accountability as to the cost, viability, or necessity of a project.

Let me depict how recklessly those who spend our money treat that responsibility. Until 1987, the federal design guidelines for courthouses stated that they should be built "with a spirit of dignity and simplicity." No one can argue with this. In 1987, the guidelines were changed, so the courthouses were "monumental in design" and built "on a grand scale." Who pays for these monuments to the judges? We do. Who is responsible for the change in policy to allow more frivolous spending? Congress is. What has been done about this lack of fiscal sensitivity? Nothing!

The General Services Administration (GSA) has spent over $7 billion in recent years on new federal buildings, and did so without hearings. Senator John McCain (R - Arizona) has been a vocal dissident of this spending, and even he hasn't been able to determine who the ultimate culprits are.

One of the more notorious examples of waste is the Foley Square courthouse, a New York monument that cost us over $400 million. Among the atrocities demanded by "anonymous" officials were custom carpet at $114 per yard (adding $1.4 million to the cost of the carpet); custom doors and hardware at $9,000 per set (adding over $9 million to the door budget); custom windows (adding over $145,000); floor-to-ceiling paneling (adding an extra $5 million); marble flooring in the lobby (adding over $5 million); a bronze firehose cabinet (adding $5,500); drapes costing more than $1,100 per linear foot; and an underground tunnel leading to a correctional facility located across the street from the courthouse, at a cost of over $13 million. All told, the change orders requested by the judges totalled over $120 million. Actions like those listed above speak volumes about the arrogant judges and politicians who continue to heap more financial burdens on the taxpayers, in spite of their rhetoric to the contrary.

For the sake of comparison, following are general guidelines for first-class construction: carpet, $30 per yard; doors and hardware, $850 per set; and drapes, $150 per linear foot. The items purchased for the Foley Square courthouse weren't "monumental in design," they were designed for **royalty**.

Hazel O'Leary

The Energy Secretary of the United States, Hazel O'Leary, has found it necessary to take luxurious trips over the past few years at our expense. Here is a sampling of her unmatched globetrotting.

1993	1994	1995	1995 (continued)
Paris	Ivory Coast	India	Costa Rica
Vienna	India	Hong Kong	Moscow
Moscow	Brussels	Shanghai	South Africa
London	Pakistan	Beijing	Prague
Moscow	Moscow	Paris	Vienna
Stockholm	Azerbaijan	South Africa	Florence

It is clear that, had this scandal not been brought to public attention, Ms. O'Leary may have spent more time overseas than in the United States in 1996.

Her frequent travel isn't the only insult. She also invites an entourage, at huge expense to a nation already in debt. For instance, she spent $730,000 on her trip to India in 1994 and $663,000 on her trip to South Africa in 1995. Not only did she travel first class, but incurred numerous expenses (about $80,000 on her trip to India and about $175,000 on her trip to South Africa) that are unaccounted for. For one trip, she chartered a private jet owned by MGM, at a cost to taxpayers of $485,000.

Over the course of her various trips, Ms. O'Leary has accumulated over $1 million of unaccounted-for expenses, due at the very least to inferior bookkeeping. During this scandal, Ms. O'Leary has retained her position. And yet, when the Clintons found $10,000-$20,000 worth of financial mismanagement at the White House travel office, the employees were immediately dismissed, and the FBI was brought in. Ms. Clinton indicated that financial mismanagement of *any* kind would not be tolerated by this administration. Aside from partisan politics and hypocrisy, what is going on here?

With mismanagement like this, how can the government honestly say they should have more of our money to spend as THEY see fit?

CHAPTER 8

GOVERNMENT BY DECEPTION

EXAMPLES OF LIES, DECEPTION

We are so conditioned to politicians "stretching" the truth, it has reached the point where we are no longer upset when a politician lies to us. It has become standard operating procedure for a politician to say whatever he feels will advance his view, regardless of its accuracy. Although there are thousands of examples of this to choose from, here are a few:

• For years, Congress has reserved a large number of parking spaces at Washington's airports for its members, paid for by Congress (with taxpayer dollars). Shortly after this story was made public, the signs reserving the parking spaces that read, "RESERVED Supreme Court Justices – Members of Congress – Diplomats" were changed to "Restricted Parking – Authorized Users Only." This misleading sign change, also made at taxpayer expense, followed a bill that in 1994 would have eliminated that symbol of vanity and royalty, but was summarily rejected in the Senate. So, even though the Senate voted to hold on to that perk, they attempted to stem the criticism by changing the signs. This is their way of solving the problem.

• President Clinton blew his own horn for lowering the deficit shortly after he took office, although a large portion of the deficit reduction, better than $50 billion, was saved due to lower interest rates on the then $4 trillion national debt. The deficit was artificially lowered, not only by interest rates coming down, but also by his decision to change much of the borrowing from safer, long-term borrowing, to less expensive, short-term borrowing.

However, when interest rates rose in 1994, which pushed the deficit back up, he complained that he had no control over the higher interest rates, and therefore the increase in the deficit wasn't his fault. The TRUTH is, Mr. Clinton could have locked in low long-term interest rates in 1993, but threw the dice by going with the shorter term rates and short-term positive results. In effect, he gambled with our long-term prosperity by attempting to get some instant, short-term success, and we lost. President Clinton was fast to take the credit for the lower interest rates in 1993, but slow to take the responsibility for his risky decision to use short-term rates.

During his 1996 campaign trail, Mr. Clinton continues to insist that his budgets are the effective ones that save us money. After all, he says, the annual deficit in early 1996 is one-half what it was before he took office. What he fails to add, however, is that the deficit was cut not only by declining interest rates on the national debt, but by his tax increase of 1993, which included over $500 billion of tax increases from Americans. Cutting the deficit on the backs of hard-working Americans is not the solution we want or deserve.

Speaking of President Clinton's 1993 tax bill, is anyone fooled by the Administration's identification of that bill, the "Deficit Reduction Package of 1993"? Why not call it what it is, the "Tax Increase Bill of 1993"? Mr. Clinton wonders why he doesn't get credit for lowering the deficit. It is easy to lower the deficit by increasing our taxes. Had the deficit been lowered by spending cuts and eliminating government pork and waste, Mr. Clinton would have been due the credit he seeks from the American people. In fact, *taxes* and *spending* both rose during the period that he wants credit for lowering the deficit. The "Deficit Reduction Package of 1993" is an excellent example of a politician's rhetorical attempt to brainwash the public.

Baseline Budgeting, Current Services

Until recently, few outside of Washington understood the concept of baseline budgeting. Current services (baseline budgeting) is the automatic spending increase projected each year to maintain certain services. When politicians increase spending at a slower rate than projected in their baseline budget, they deceitfully call the difference a "cut" in spending, even though it was only a cut in the amount of increase. This misleading gimmick is another trick politicians use to fool the American public by having spending automatically increase with no vote required.

In effect, what politicians are saying is that they want to preserve the fraud, the waste, and the abuse. By using baseline budgeting, Congress doesn't have to vote on increases, since they occur automatically. It is one of many schemes politicians employ to circumvent politically unpopular activities. And as everyone knows, increasing spending and raising taxes are two politically unpopular activities.

An example of baseline budgeting is food stamps. Even though there was a dramatic drop in the number of food stamp participants over the past couple of years, the spending continues to rise. Anyone who attempts to reduce the amount of money in the program, even though not as much money is needed, is invariably attacked by a large segment of the population for being "heartless" and wanting to "starve the poor." Shouldn't a distinction be made between wanting to cut out the waste and fraud so we don't spend more than necessary, and being cruel?

The Interest on the National Debt Sham

Of the bits and pieces of information we are given regarding the United States budget, the interest on the $5 trillion national debt is one of the largest line items. We are led to believe that the interest on that debt is approximately $200 billion per year. How many of us realize, however, and how many politicians have told us, that the actual interest expense for 1995 is over $333 billion?! How are they able to deceive us?

Using creative accounting, which was borne out of necessity due to inefficient programs, the government subtracts from the interest we must pay certain interest proceeds from trust funds. Those funds include the civil service retirement and disability trust fund ($27 billion), the military retirement trust fund ($10 billion), the Medicare trust fund ($12 billion), interest received from "off-budget" trust funds ($33 billion), and other line items. This makes it appear that there is a lower interest amount on the debt. However, this is misrepresentation any way you look at it. The fact is the $333 billion on the national debt for 1995 has no bearing on or relationship with other interest surpluses or revenue generated from unrelated line items. Yet the politicians rationalize a "credit" from these other totally unrelated items. All this is just a way for politicians to mislead us into believing that the interest payment on the national debt is much lower than it really is.

Why would politicians want to do that? Because they know that they are the ones responsible for the national debt in the first place, so, by "softening the blow," they are attempting to soothe their guilty consciences. Also, if people realized the interest on the national debt is over $333 billion, they would know it is the largest single federal expenditure.

The average American finds it hard to comprehend that we paid $333 billion in 1995 (and will pay more each year) in interest payments on Congress's overspending. However, what if you were told that every American man, woman, and child must pay an average of $1,266 per year (and more each year)? That is an even more astounding figure because it really hits home! The amount for a family of four is $5,064! The average family of four cannot afford to pay an additional $5,064 per year, but Congress has the gall to continue to overspend each year and increase the burden on all of us. And what does Congress get for giving us this hardship? *They* receive salary increases at twice the rate of inflation, multi-million dollar pensions, and increased power for spending.

More of Congress' Creative Accounting

Members of Congress are encouraged to bring a large "entourage" on trips. The reported cost of a trip is "decreased" because, due to another creative accounting gimmick, a congressman is able to divide the cost of the trip by the number of staff he brings. The lower the cost he reports, the more frugal he looks, even though he has actually increased expenditures by inviting more staff.

Only Democrats are Allowed to Reduce Social Security

When the Balanced Budget Amendment was announced, the Democrats voted against it, saying they were afraid that Social Security would be touched and millions of senior citizens would be affected. However, in President Clinton's tax bill of 1993 (deceitfully called by his supporters a "Deficit Reduction Bill"), Clinton exposed more Social Security benefits going to the elderly as taxable income. He called it a "spending cut" instead of a "tax increase." In TRUTH, this act lowered by billions of dollars the net amount of Social Security benefits senior citizens would receive after paying taxes. Yet the Democrats proclaim in front of the TV cameras, while arguing against the Republican Balanced Budget Amendment, that they don't want to see senior citizens' Social Security "taken away from them."

Does anyone remember Mr. Clinton's campaign promise that he would not touch Social Security? Then, just months later, he proposed a net cut in Social Security in the form of lowering the income threshold where Social Security can be taxed, "saving" the government $24.5 billion. The TRUTH is he COST senior citizens $24.5 billion. Still his rhetoric continues to include a line about protecting the programs for children and senior citizens, avoiding the truth about his taking almost $25 billion from the pockets of senior citizens as a result of his Social Security tax grab.

What is learned here? We learn that senior citizens are easy targets, and that they are being manipulated by the rhetoric of these politicians and the media. It is clear that Social Security is not "untouchable" to the Democrats. When it serves their purpose, Democrats will use the "compassion" ploy to vote down any cuts that Republicans support.

Despite ongoing rhetoric that the Republicans are heartless and want to jettison senior citizens, the Republican Contract with America includes a provision, the Senior Citizens' Fairness Act, that would raise the Social Security earnings limit which currently forces many able seniors out of the workforce. It also repeals the 1993 Social Security benefit tax hike passed by Clinton.

The Word Game

The use of words has become an art form of deception. Instead of paying new taxes, we are asked to "sacrifice, contribute, invest, or spend." If the other party proposes new taxes, they are "destroying the middle class." Cutting programs is called "savings" or "reform." When the other party reduces spending, they are "slashing" or "cutting." When our party reduces spending, we are "saving."

Republicans are called "extreme" when they follow through on their campaign pledge, the Contract with America. Perhaps some politicians don't understand that the public *wants* their elected officials to keep their promises. We need each politician to outline in advance what his agenda is, so we know what to expect from him.

Hopefully, one day we will reach the point where we can expect the truth from campaigners, and where the concept of following through on a campaign pledge won't be considered extreme.

Both parties are guilty of manipulating the public. During balanced budget negotiations, Democrats scare the public into believing that the truly needy will be kicked out onto the streets, and use whatever ruse they can to "balance" the budget. Republicans "find" an extra $135 billion or so by manipulating the forecasted figures, in order to compromise and close in on negotiations with the Democrats. When will politicians realize that they will continue to lose their credibility as long as they play games with numbers and provide the public with watered-down reforms?

Solving the "Who's Telling the Truth" Dilemma –or – What's Behind Door #1?

High-level negotiations on the balanced budget, one of the most important issues to face our country in a generation, are held behind closed doors. And when the doors open, both sides have a totally different viewpoint of what occurred on the inside. Confusion is the order of the day. Why don't they negotiate in public, so we can determine who is dealing in good faith and who isn't? The highest level politicians are reduced to lying to save face. But the TRUTH is that many of us can see right through the sophomoric, transparent lies. Is it just our opinion that someone is lying? I don't think so, when both sides have totally opposite recollections of what occurred just moments earlier in those behind-the-door meetings.

The clear solution is that all budget summits should be held in public view so we can see what's going on with the negotiations. This is the only way we can be assured that the politicians are negotiating in good faith, on our behalf. We can also see who is not working for us. Back room negotiations and deal-making should be a thing of the past.

Politicians have resisted this open approach to the public, but so far I haven't heard a compelling reason for the closed-door meetings. We're just told that we won't understand what's going on and shouldn't stick our nose where it doesn't belong. Perhaps, if they talk very slowly, we will be able to follow their high-level negotiations.

From Mark Levin, Director of legal policy of the Landmark Legal Foundation:

> Tom Daschel, speaking to a group about the Republican Contract, proclaimed, "It's the struggle between the rich and the rest of us. Make no mistake. The Republican agenda is worse than indifferent to the needs of working families. It's downright hostile to them. It's trickle-down economics with a vengeance." (Is this not a perfect example of offensive and hateful rhetoric?)
>
> It is ironic (or is it hypocritical?) that Mr. Daschel should say this when, according to the National Taxpayers Union, he receives an annual taxpayer-financed salary of $148,000 per year, along with benefits and perks totaling $200,000. His wife, Linda Hall Daschel, was appointed deputy administrator of the FAA by the President and receives a yearly salary of $115,000, along with other benefits. Thus, the two make over $264,100 per year, plus benefits. They will receive about $1,000,000 in combined salaries during Clinton's term of office and, by Mr. Daschel's own standards, are among America's wealthiest citizens. And he has the nerve to try to inflame a crowd by talking about the "struggle between the rich and the rest of us"! Isn't this hypocrisy at its worst?

Mark Levin points out that Daschel and the other class warfare proponents have it all wrong. The struggle is not between the rich and the rest of us. The struggle is between the robber barons of big government and the people. It is Washington's ruling elite, powerful politicians like Mr. Daschel and the hordes of highly paid bureaucratic soldiers they enlist to their cause, who are taking food from the tables and clothes off the backs of working people, by forcing them to pay huge sums in taxes to the welfare state.

Isn't it unfortunate that a politician's longevity is based not upon telling the truth, but upon the big lie, and often continuous lies?

The media has been the politicians' pawn for decades. It is the media that repeats whatever politicians have to say. The fact is, if people hear a fabrication often enough over a long period of time, they will eventually believe it. Also, when someone sees something in the newspaper, he's inclined to believe it, unless the publication is not credible. Some examples of the willful spreading of falsehoods are:

• The continuation of the fallacy that the Republican budget is cutting the Medicare budget. In fact, the Republicans were attempting to slow the growth from 10% per year, which was bankrupting the program, to 7% per year, which was still twice the projected rate of inflation. By continuing to quote politicians who openly lied about the program, without disputing or verifying their information, the media was an accomplice to the lies.

• How much pain will a balanced budget produce? The Center on Budget and Policy Priorities states that Congress would need to cut spending by $1.4 trillion over the next seven years for us to achieve a balanced budget, and this would cause too much "pain." This is intentionally misleading and scares the public from supporting a balanced budget. Besides, their statement is mathematically incorrect. For instance, if Congress cut $200 billion out of next year's budget, and there were *no* tax increase, the budget would be balanced.

• The continuation of the fallacy that the Republican budget was cutting school lunches. Again, the Republican plan was attempting to slow the growth rate for school lunch money, while still providing more money each year, not less.

• President Clinton's first 1995 Balanced Budget (10-year) Plan contains these passages:

"Republicans...cutting Medicare ...deeply to fund a huge tax break for the wealthy...," and

"Republicans would simply cut over $430 billion from Medicare and Medicaid, enough to turn them into second-class health systems," while

"The President proposes to take a first, serious step towards health care reform, providing net savings of $124 billion in Medicare and $55 billion in Medicaid by 2002..."

Does anyone see something strange here? The President is proposing a "serious step" and a "net savings," while the Republicans are proposing a "cut," while "turning the program into a second-class health system."

Lest you believe that only federal politics is corrupt, there are hundreds of examples each year that illustrate the learning curve of local politicians and bureaucrats who follow the lead of their national counterparts.

Illinois Tollway

Officials of the Illinois State Tollway Authority (ISTA) have been actively defrauding taxpayers for years. Within the past two years, misconduct, deception, and waste have been discovered within the agency. Among other things, the executive director of the ISTA, Robert Hickman, has been found to:

(1) Use the ISTA helicopter for personal use.

(2) Direct a number of no–bid tollway contracts worth millions of dollars to a company his son worked for, without disclosing that information.

(3) Direct patronage jobs to family and friends, including a $64,000-a-year tollway job to his ex–wife, and a job to governor Jim Edgar's nephew.

When Mr. Hickman was forced to resign because of his part in the misconduct and fraud, he was given over $100,000 from the agency, comprised of unused vacation and sick time pay, and monies from a supplemental plan for top agency employees.

Waste, fraud, and abuse of the public trust isn't the only deception the ISTA is involved in. In order to "soften" the misconduct uncovered, and the resultant bad press, the ISTA delivered a "tough" Code of Ethics for all to see, and for ISTA employees to comply with. Taken from a page out of the *federal* lawmakers' play book, the code of ethics did little more than list the duties and responsibilities the tollway employees were *previously* supposed to adhere to. It is clear that the document conceived was nothing more than an attempt at some positive "PR" while the ISTA was being investigated for wrongdoings. Officials within the department indicated that this code of ethics was a good faith gesture to clean up and reform the agency. In fact, the code had many flaws.

(1) An employee signs the code, not because he has read it, but because he has received it.

(2) It states that a violation of the code *may* result in discipline. However, this is a vague response to a violation. What about punishment, loss of job, and reimbursement of damages? With strict and sure discipline in force, would the incidence of violation not diminish?

(3) The Code of Ethics does not include anything new

or different. In other words, there is nothing in the code that any employee of the ISTA isn't already familiar with.

The ISTA was involved in a questionable land sale in 1992, when former Chicago alderman and current State Representative, James S. Kotlarz, Jr., "brokered" 12 acres of tollway-owned land to WMX Technologies (formerly Waste Management, Inc.). Mr. Kotlarz received a brokerage fee of more than $100,000 from WMX for his role in the sale of the ISTA land. Seven months *prior* to the land sale, Mr. Kotlarz received $4,250 in donations from WMX and its officials.

The ISTA awarded over $100,000 of no-bid contracts for legal services to a former top lawyer at the ISTA, who had recently resigned. Additionally, upon his resignation, Malcolm Erickson collected $103,606 from a controversial double-pension plan that he had been instrumental in authorizing while he was with the Authority. Mr. Erickson was able to set himself up quite well. Not only did he provide a generous pension for himself upon retirement, but he received substantial earnings subsequent to his retirement with no-bid legal contracts.

Another example of local government corruption was discovered in 1994. This occurred with the Department of Central Management Services (DCMS), which is the state agency that leases office space for government use. The DCMS has had a long practice of leasing space and doing business without competitive bid (NO-BID CONTRACTS), to the benefit and profit of many political insiders.

To make a long story short, it was discovered that Charles Strock, a well-connected "entrepreneur," leased a building to the DCMS for $202,000 per year. In fact, Mr. Strock didn't even own the building, but was paying the owner $28,000 per year and *subleasing* to the state. This gave him a clear profit of $174,000 per year. To the best of my knowledge as of this writing, no one at the state has been reprimanded, accused, or fired for making such a poor deal for the taxpayers.

U.S. Post Office

Want more deception? How about the U.S. Post Office? I have no problem with the cost of a postage stamp, which has been raised numerous times up to its present $.32. For all the complaints and jokes regarding the post office, it is exceptionally efficient overall, considering the billions of pieces of mail it must sort, handle, and deliver each day. Its service is quite a bargain, to boot. However, I have dozens of stamps with LETTERS on them, not numbers, so I don't know what they're worth, and therefore don't use them. I still have some D, E, F and G stamps with no numbers on them. I even have a stamp that says, "This U.S. stamp along with 25 [cents] of additional U.S. postage is equivalent to the 'F' stamp rate." This certainly clarifies things!

I called four different post offices to ask about these stamps, and spoke to counter clerks and postmasters. The only explanation I got was that the stamps had to be printed prior to the final determination of the price of the stamp. I find that hard to believe because I recall that, in each case of a postage increase, the local post offices never had those new stamps in stock. Why weren't the new stamps printed when the value of the stamp was determined, and have the new price go into effect once the post offices had a sufficient supply? Not only are these unmarked stamps confusing, but once I've determined the amount of each stamp, I've had to use up to 10 stamps on an envelope in order to use them up. This slows down production at the post office, since they must verify correct postage. And the "lettered" stamps aren't commonly known to many of the post office counter personnel I spoke with.

Lottery

What about the lottery? Many states have a weekly lottery (and in some cases bi-weekly) that generates millions of dollars of revenue. In Illinois, the lottery was endorsed on the basis that all the net revenue after expenses would go to our schools. Although this was a noble promise, it has been difficult to determine how much of the hundreds of millions of dollars raised over the years has reached the school system. There has been much talk of abuse and fraud within the lottery system, which makes this program seem questionable, at the very least.

And finally...

Deficit Spending

Every year that we have deficit spending, our politicians are telling us that they can't do their job. Their job is no different from any other – run an ongoing operation, pay for essential services, and stay within budget.

However, politicians deceive us by increasing the debt, instead of increasing our taxes as they increase their spending. It is a gutless choice. They know that if they increased taxes enough to pay for all of their programs and special-interest-driven pet projects, there would be a taxpayer revolt!

The Republicans who propose a supermajority (2/3) vote of Congress to increase taxes are ignoring the *spending* problem, since they would still be able to increase spending and increase our deficit. This tax proposal without major *spending* reform is next to worthless.

Clearly politicians have lost touch with the American people. The American people have become cynical. We've been "turned off" by the constant lying and manipulation which has become more and more apparent as we have become more informed. Isn't it a shame that we no longer *expect* the truth from politicians, and therefore are not upset when we find they have lied to us? You have to wonder if their constant barrage of lies and misleading statements is part of their strategy. After a while, we will come to expect such deviant behavior, and we won't hold them up to the standards we once expected.

CHAPTER 9

THE TAX GRAB

Contrary to this author's discourse that politicians are incompetent, even I must admit that they are without peer when it comes to one thing – grabbing more tax dollars. Both sides of the aisle, regardless of their rhetoric and their intentions, have consistently produced higher revenues through various tax grabs throughout the history of the United States. In the last 35 years, there were only two years (1983, 1971) in which there was no increase in government tax revenue.

World War I

Note below that government expenditures increased significantly, for the first time, as a result of World War I; from $713 million in 1916, up to $6.358 billion in 1920. The increases during this period from the previous years are illustrative.

1916 – $713 million
1917 – $1.954 billion, a 174% increase.
1918 – $12.677 billion, a 548% increase.
1919 – $18.493 billion, a 45% increase.
1920 – $6.358 billion, a 65% decrease, (but an 800% increase from 1916!).

During the same period, taxes increased as follows:
1916 – $761 million
1917 – $1.101 billion, a 44% increase.
1918 – $3.645 billion, a 231% increase.
1919 – $5.130 billion, a 40% increase.

1920 – $6.649 billion, a 29% increase.
1921 – $5.571 billion, a 16% decrease.
1922 – $4.026 billion, a 28% decrease.

As the need for revenue decreased, so did the taxes. Our leaders at that time showed some fiscal constraint, although you will notice that taxes still rose from $761 million (pre-war) to $4.026 billion (post-war), an increase of 429%. At the same time, expenditures rose from $713 million (pre-war) to $3.289 billion, an increase of 361% in seven years. Thus, during the period from 1916–1922, taxes increased at a 1.19:1 ratio relative to expenditures, or at a 19% faster rate than reasonably necessary.

From that point on, although there were steady incremental increases in taxes, with consistent surpluses (what a concept!), there were no significant increases in taxes or expenditures, until the beginning of World War II...

World War II

Government expenditures were:
1940 – $9.468 billion.
1941 – $13.653 billion, a 44% increase.
1942 – $35.137 billion, a 157% increase.
1943 – $78.555 billion, a 123% increase.
1944 – $91.304 billion, a 16% increase.
1945 – $92.712 billion, a 1.5% increase.
1946 – $55.232 billion, a 41% decrease.
1947 – $34.496 billion, a 38% decrease.

During the same period, taxes increased as follows:
1940 – $6.548 billion.
1941 – $8.712 billion, a 33% increase.
1942 – $14.634 billion, a 68% increase.
1943 – $24.001 billion, a 64% increase.
1944 – $43.747 billion, an 82% increase.
1945 – $45.159 billion, a 3% increase.
1946 – $39.296 billion, a 13% decrease.

1947 – $38.514 billion, a 2% decrease.

Note once again that once World War II ended, a decrease in expenditures and taxes occurred. Overall, however, taxes and expenditures still increased significantly; taxes increased from $6.548 billion (pre-war) to $38.514 billion (post-war), an increase of 488%, while expenditures grew from $9.468 billion (pre-war) to $34.496 billion (post-war), a 264% increase.

You can see that from 1940–1947, taxes increased at a ratio of 1.84:1 as related to expenditures, or at an 84% faster rate.

Here is a common thread for you to consider. Although additional sums of money were necessary to fund major wars that clearly affected our freedom, the end of these wars saw tax revenues reach new heights and begin their ascension from that new level. It is apparent that politicians found ways to raise taxes at that time without the natural hue and cry from the public.

Other examples of TAX GRABS follow:

Capital Gains

There is an attempt, as of this writing, to reform the capital gains tax. This is one of the most unfair tax grabs the politicians have at their disposal. What are capital gains? These are gains that occur when someone sells a capital asset that he/she owns. The net profit, after all sales expenses are deducted, is the amount taxable at the "capital gains" rate.

For example, let's say you purchased a home in 1970 for $50,000. Now, you sell the home and have $200,000, after paying brokerage commission and closing costs. You have made a profit of $150,000 and must pay tax on that profit at the current capital gains rate of 28%, or $42,000. But, how fair is this? Has the property really increased in value by 300%, or is the gain expanded largely because of inflation? A dollar today is worth only about $.25 compared to 1970. So your $200,000 house is worth only $50,000 in real 1970 dollars. Yet you must pay taxes on a gain of $150,000, even though you've only broken even with the home value after accounting for inflation.

In order to simplify the preceding example, two available loopholes were omitted. First, the profit on the sale of a home isn't taxable if that money is used to purchase another home of equal or greater value within 18 months. Second, a person who sells his home once he reaches the age of 55 is eligible for a one-time tax exemption on the sale of a principal residence. These loopholes illustrate part of the complexity of the tax code. They also show how government can give ultimatums to its taxpayers: either buy another house, or suffer the consequences of paying a hefty tax bill.

Bracket Creep

The main idea of bracket creep is that a person may actually have less spending power as his income increases, due to a combination of inflation and higher tax brackets. In other words, when a person earns more money, the increased income may place him in a higher tax bracket, which in turn may increase his tax burden. The actual result of this may be less purchasing power even though he has earned more money.

For example, let's assume that you are a single taxpayer, with a taxable income of $23,000. Based upon the present (1996) tax rates, you would pay $3,450 in income taxes for net spendable income of $19,550 after taxes. Three years later, you receive cost of living adjustments in your salary. Now, based upon a 4% per year cost of living increase, you are making $25,872.

Your "raises" push you into the higher (28%) income tax bracket, so your tax is now $4,124, leaving you net spendable income of $21,748. However, when that $21,748 is adjusted for inflation, the net amount is $19,241. Thus, your spending ability has been *reduced* by $309, due to the fact that inflation pushed you into a higher income tax bracket. As your income grows, and you move into higher tax brackets, the effect of bracket creep is even more dramatic.

Real Estate Taxes

Real estate taxes also are not factored for inflation. A person who purchased a home in 1970 for $50,000 continues to receive increased real estate tax bills, even though no improvements have been made to increase the value of the home. Although his real estate taxes may have been only $275 in 1970, this person could be paying more than $850 today.

The TRUTH about real estate taxes is that a property is rarely assessed at its actual fair market value. That would make it too easy for informed property owners to protest the assessment and possibly reduce the tax rate. It would also be more difficult for local taxing authorities to maneuver the numbers in their favor. Cook County, Illinois (which includes Chicago and its outlying suburbs) has one of the most deceitful, misleading, and underhanded tax collection systems in the country.

Using an actual example of everyday bureaucratic deception, let us assume that you, a resident of Cook County, Illinois, are the proud owner of a small shopping center worth approximately $500,000. On your real estate tax bill, you see an "assessed valuation" of $86,300 and a "state equalization factor" of 2.1135 for an "equalized valuation" of $182,395. You then multiply that figure by a "tax rate" of 8.717% to give you an annual tax of $15,899.

Since you know your property is worth much more than $86,300 (the assessed valuation), or even the $182,395 (the equalized valuation), you are likely to keep quiet when your tax bill comes. You are deceived into believing that you are paying at a bargain rate. Because of the way the system is set up with all the multipliers, it is virtually impossible for you to protest the tax bill with any degree of certainty. You can't argue the assessed valuation while the state equalization factor and the tax rate are subject to change by the assessor's office, based upon the revenue need of the taxing district.

Double Taxation

Actually, this should be named "multiple taxation." Let's use a computer that sells for $1,000 as a common example of a manufactured product. This commodity begins with a lot of separate parts that are ordered from various suppliers.

The parts of the computer may have a total cost of approximately $90. The suppliers, assuming they are profitable, pay an income tax on the profit of the sale of the merchandise. Assuming a 20% gross profit margin for the suppliers, and a tax rate of 30%, the result would be a tax of $5.40. Now the parts are assembled in the warehouse, and the manufacturer ships the computer to a wholesaler, who purchases the computer for $300.00. The manufacturer's gross profit margin in this example is 20%, with a 30% tax rate, for a tax of $18.00. The wholesaler then sells the computer to a retailer at a price of $500.00, for a gross profit margin of 20% and a 30% tax rate. Thus, the wholesaler pays a tax of $30.00. Finally, the retailer sells the computer to a customer at a price of $1,000. After overhead and expenses, the retailer has a 25% profit margin, or $250.00. When taxed at 30%, the result is a tax of $75.00.

But we're not finished. During each of the steps mentioned above, part of the cost was attributed to labor. Assuming labor represented the largest percentage of the production costs, and less of the post-production costs, would mean employees were paid:

- at the suppliers' level, $50.40
- at the manufacturer's level, $168.00
- at the wholesaler's level, $60.00
- at the retailer's level, $100.00
- for a total taxable employee income of $378.40.

Using an average individual tax rate of 18% would result in an additional $68.11 in taxes. And let's not forget employee benefits, such as insurance, health, sick pay, maternity, etc. These would add, conservatively, 20% in expenses to the payroll for another $13.62 in taxes.

How can we forget real estate taxes? For the purposes of this example, we will assume these four businesses pay 2% of their gross revenue for real estate taxes, which adds another $37.80 to the cost of the computer.

Then there's sales tax which, depending on where you live, varies from 5% to over 8.5% of the price of the computer. For this example let's use 7%, for a sales tax of $70.00.

Now, when we add up all the taxes described in this example, it looks like the total amount of taxes paid to get this computer to the consumer is approximately $317.93, or 31.79% of the total price of the computer. We didn't even want to include other taxes such as import/export taxes, excise taxes, etc.

Are you ready for another "double taxation?" How about when you receive a salary (already taxed), put the money in the bank or some other investment, and must then pay taxes on the income derived from that investment? If you spend the money, you have to pay sales tax. The only way the government doesn't get more of your money in taxes is if you stash the money in your mattress or a shoebox.

Estate Taxes

The most offensive example of double taxation, however, may be the estate tax. You've earned money and accumulated assets, on which you've already paid taxes. Upon your death, however, the government now taxes its share of any amount in excess of $600,000, before it gets to your heirs. Depending upon the amount of money left upon your death, the tax rate will be anywhere from 37–55%. On what basis does the government feel that it deserves your assets more than your own family?

Since it is so difficult to recognize or review all the taxes we pay, it is no wonder that the flat tax is among one of the most popular reforms being considered at this time. Which brings us to. . .

REFORM OF THE TAX CODE

As shown in the previous example of the real estate taxes, if the government confuses the public enough, it can get away with more and more. And what's more confusing and ambiguous than the present tax code? Countless studies have shown that the tax code is so voluminous and muddled, more often than not even the experts can't agree on tax law. In fact, one study shows that a taxpayer with a moderately complicated tax question, calling the IRS 800# for assistance, will receive different answers to the same question. Also, we are expected to abide by thousands of pages of laws, rules, and regulations. Isn't there something wrong with a system that is so treacherous, you must spend money to hire a trained authority just to help you conform to the law? And in the likely event that you make an error due to the confusion of the tax law, you must pay penalties and other costs.

There are numerous reasons why the government must radically reform its method of taxation and collection. Following are some of the more compelling reasons.

(1) The federal government's 28% tax on capital gains isn't indexed for inflation. Thus, we are paying tax on "inflation profit," which is nothing more than an increase in value due to inflation.

(2) The present tax system stunts economic growth by double-taxing savings and investment. The result is a U.S. savings rate that has declined to about 1/3 of what it was forty years ago. The importance of the savings rate is that the more we are able to save during our most productive

years, the less financial assistance we will need when we become senior citizens. Just think how much money you senior citizens would have now, if you had saved three times as much as you have now, over the past 40 years. Wouldn't you be more comfortable with your own "nest egg," instead of the meager monthly checks that Social Security provides you?

(3) It has been estimated by political scientist James L. Payne that Americans (including businesses) spend over 5.4 billion hours figuring out their taxes and tax strategies. This loss of productivity is compelling justification enough for a "radical" solution.

(4) The present taxing system is aggressively intrusive to the citizens who support the country. The arrogance of government is illustrated when it demands law-abiding citizens to open their books at the whim of an auditing IRS. Aside from being an offensive invasion of privacy, it is very intimidating, costly, and a waste of the taxpayers' time.

In fact, the IRS may, at its whim, search and seize any property or financial documents it deems fit from a citizen, without a search warrant. For further information on the intrusiveness of the IRS, you can pick up a Cato Institute study entitled "Why You Can't Trust the IRS." See the appendix in the rear of this book for the address and phone number for the Cato Institute.

(5) The present Internal Revenue Service employs approximately 115,000 auditors and agents. Its cost to taxpayers exceeds $8 billion.

(6) Another indignity of the present system is that the current tax code contains hundreds of hidden taxes that are enacted at will, at the discretion of Congress. In a 17,000-page tax code, there are many taxes that are disguised or sufficiently ambiguous to mislead the unsuspecting public.

So what can be done? There are several options that are infinitely better than the present system. Two of the more practical ("radical" to some) changes that have been frequently discussed follow.

The Flat Tax

The flat tax certainly has plenty of appeal, but many politicians are afraid of it. Why? It's very simple. With a flat tax, it would be more difficult for legislators to raise our taxes covertly. With a flat tax in place, let's say 17%, it wouldn't be possible for lawmakers to add another tax to the tax code, as they've done in the past when more money was needed to help cover their spending. Previously, obscure taxes that would raise a few billion dollars would quietly appear in the tax code, usually hidden in a huge spending bill. Or a mandate that would force spending onto a specific industry or group would appear. And since the new tax affected just a small segment of the population, any public reaction was manageable by the politicians and their "spin doctors."

Another problem we have with politicians is that they provide favors to contributors by way of favorable legislation. A flat tax would eliminate the power legislators have to offer special favors which, in turn, may "dry up" a portion of contributions to politicians. And, as we all know, money is what keeps most politicians in power.

There are a number of arguments against the flat tax. But to intelligently debate the pros and cons of the flat tax, we must define which flat tax proposal we are debating. For the purposes of this discussion, we will assume that the flat tax under discussion is the Steve Forbes proposal, because of its simplicity. In essence, the Forbes Flat Tax proposal suggests that, for an average family of four, no taxes are paid on the first $36,000 of income earned, and a 17% tax on all earnings over that amount. There are no other deductions with his proposal. For corporate taxes, there would be a 17% tax on all net income after expenses and current deductions on capital expenditures, such as equipment. Following are some of the oppositions to the

Forbes flat tax:

(1) The flat tax is just a tax break for the wealthy.

If people are allowed to see the actual numbers, they can see that a flat tax is a tax break for almost everyone. The only people in the middle class who would be negatively affected by a flat tax would be those who are currently benefiting from an extraordinary amount of deductions.

In fact, the people who maintain this argument will be pleased to hear that the flat tax is actually a progressive tax, which means that the more money a person makes, the higher his tax rate, despite the "flat tax" label. How does this work? Look at the following table for a family of four:

INCOME	*LESS $36,000*	*EFFECTIVE TAXABLE INCOME*	*x 17%=TAX*	*INCOME TAX RATE*
$36,000	*($36,000)*	*$0*	*$ 0*	*0.00%*
$50,000	*($36,000)*	*$ 14,000*	*$ 2,380*	*4.76%*
$75,000	*($36,000)*	*$ 39,000*	*$6,630*	*8.84%*
$100,000	*($36,000)*	*$ 64,000*	*$10,880*	*10.88%*
$150,000	*($36,000)*	*$114,000*	*$19,380*	*12.92%*
$250,000	*($36,000)*	*$214,000*	*$36,380*	*14.55%*

As you can see, the more income there is, the less effect the $36,000 exclusion has on the tax rate. So, if you still prefer to see "the rich" pay a higher share of their income, this flat tax proposal is for you.

(2) The flat tax will cause a higher deficit because revenue collected will decrease.

It is true that revenue collected will initially decrease with the Forbes Flat Tax. However, this argument ignores some important facts.

(a) First of all, if individuals can keep more of what they earn by not giving it to the government, they will have more disposable income. The ensuing increased spending

will result in a more prosperous economy, which will fuel higher employment rates, higher incomes, and therefore higher tax revenues.

(b) History has shown that every time the government lowers taxes (the last time with President Reagan in the early 1980s) the economy booms, and more tax revenue is generated. The problem in the 1980s wasn't a lower tax rate, because tax revenue increased almost every year (see chart I in the appendix). The problem happened to be a Congress that kept increasing the rate of government spending at a rate even faster than the rate of increased tax revenue.

(3) By eliminating the home mortgage interest deduction, the value of homes will drop below the mortgage amounts, which will cause a disaster to the home market.

Even though there may be a temporary slide in home values, the fact is a home isn't necessarily purchased because of the tax benefits. Regardless of the after–tax savings, a person can only afford so much out–of–pocket spending, and the interest deduction is just an additional bonus at the end of the year.

The truth is that by eliminating the deduction for everyone at the same time, home prices will be static. The inherent value of the home isn't in the interest deduction, but in the features of the home, such as its location, size, quality, age, school district, amenities, etc. Using the argument that a home is only as valuable as the deduction doesn't make sense. Many people own their home free and clear, with no mortgage payments, and therefore no deductions. And those homes certainly haven't lost their value just because there aren't any mortgage and interest payments.

According to the Wall Street Journal, "only 25% of all filers take the mortgage interest deduction" and "fewer than half of all homeowners do." In fact, if these deductions are eliminated, the hardest hit segment of the population will be those making over $100,000 per year, since 78% of the fami-

lies in that group take a mortgage deduction, while only 18% of the families making less than $50,000 use that deduction while filing. Thus, if anything, the deduction is regressive, and eliminating it takes away a major tax rebate for the wealthy, not the heart of the middle class, as naysayers would like you to believe.

Flat tax analysts feel that a by-product of the flat tax will be lower interest rates, as much as 25% lower. The proposed flat tax would eliminate taxation on money lent on mortgages, lowering their costs and thus our costs. Therefore, with a flat tax in place, the savings in monthly interest payments by a family, outweighs the tax savings of a mortgage deduction. Also, interest savings are immediate. You realize a lower monthly interest payment each month. With a deduction, you must send the estimated withholding taxes to the government, and get a government credit on your taxes when you file the following year.

(4) By eliminating charitable donation deductions, charities will receive much less money, and those who need the charity the most will suffer.

Those who believe that a person gives to charities only because of the subsequent deduction are cynics who apparently don't understand what "charity" really is. Most people give to charities not because there are tax benefits, but because they feel good about helping others. And most people who can afford to give to charities do so, regardless of the bonus of a possible tax break.

Another side of the argument is that a person who has saved money on his income tax has more disposable income to spend on items of his own choosing, which may include charities. So, contributions to charities may actually increase, with charitable spending being based on acts of kindness and generosity, instead of some income tax strategy suggested by a CPA. During the last tax decrease of the 1980s, charitable contributions increased threefold.

(5) By eliminating taxes on capital gains, there will be less revenue coming into the government.

Again, it is true that a loss of revenue would occur if there were no taxes on capital gains. The logic that is misguided, however, is that if there is no tax on capital gains, two things will happen. First, the value of all capital items will automatically go up, since the net gain will be improved substantially. Then, instead of the money going to the government, the seller will get the money, and will spend or invest it much more wisely than Congress would.

Next, there will be a tremendous growth explosion due to the amount of real estate and other capital investments being sold. The transfer of monies will result in additional investments, leading to more jobs. The result of all this will be an economy that will grow at a rate greater than that of the 1980s, which was the longest period of growth without a recession in over a generation.

The resultant investment and job-creating growth will mean higher incomes, more production, and the purchase of more capital equipment and construction. This, in turn, will put more people to work, and generate more income tax than anticipated by the present tax system. At the same time, with the increased job creation, there will be additional government savings as people get off the welfare train.

(6) Elimination of income tax on interest income, stock dividends, inheritance, and other "rich people's" investment income is just another tax break for the wealthy.

People who dwell on this issue are either missing the point entirely of what the Forbes Flat Tax is, or are attempting to perpetuate the class envy card, which is even more sinister. What Mr. Forbes is trying to do here is to avoid the double taxation trap that the government has gotten away with for so long. Government should not be allowed to tax the same money twice, even though the politicians would surely find a way to spend the money if they could get their hands on it. You can understand the concept of double taxation using the following simple example.

Let's assume that you purchase 100 shares of

McDonald's stock. The company makes a profit for the quarter and, after paying taxes, sends you a dividend check of $100.00. Is it fair for you to pay taxes on the $100.00 dividend, considering that McDonald's has already paid taxes on its profit? What if McDonald's sent you a pre-tax dividend? Would you want to pay the taxes twice, if you are an advocate of double taxation? By suggesting that double taxation is OK, you are sending a dangerous message to a government that is finding all kinds of ways to get in your pocket.

(7) Steve Forbes is recommending the flat tax because of all the money he will save if it's passed.

The fact is it has been estimated by nonpartisan sources that Mr. Forbes would save about $200,000 per year if his proposed flat tax were adopted. However, according to the Federal Election Commission, Mr. Forbes has spent almost $30,000,000 on his presidential campaign. It would take him 150 years to recoup his campaigning costs based upon his projected savings from a flat tax. Obviously, Mr. Forbes' agenda is not his own savings.

What are some other benefits of the flat tax?

How about the savings, hundreds of billions of dollars a year, to individuals and corporations who no longer have to comply with onerous tax laws?

How about the current need for taxpayers to spend hundreds or thousands of dollars to have experts fill out tax forms or do preliminary tax planning, that would be eliminated with a simple flat tax?

How about the constant tax planning that would no longer be necessary with a simplified tax code? Isn't the peace of mind of knowing your daily life doesn't have to be consumed (and complicated) by the after-tax consequence of a business or personal decision worth something to you?

How about the savings the government would achieve with a simplified system? Not only would a flat tax eliminate the need for 95% of the technical help, but it would also eliminate the filing and review of forms, and thousands of other people at the IRS who are responsible for compliance, refunds, clerical duties, and logistics.

How about keeping the politicians and other bureaucrats out of the business of "fixing" the system for their contributors and friends by giving them tax breaks for their business or industry? The reduction in tax breaks to the well-connected could easily run into tens of billions of dollars a year.

How about getting the loopholes out of the system and bringing simplicity and honesty back in?

How about the number of trees saved with the reduction of paperwork? It is estimated that the net savings would be over 550,000 tons of paper each year. That's a lot of trees. The savings wouldn't be only for the forms themselves, but also for the countless booklets of regulations and rules that "explain" the details of the present system, and the tons of paperwork needed for the excessive numbers of forms for compliance.

So why can't the flat tax pass? Not because most people wouldn't welcome such a breath of fresh air. After all, wouldn't you actually like to know, once and for all, what you are paying in taxes? Wouldn't you like to eliminate all the games, deductions, codes, laws, mandates, etc., that the bureaucrats and the professionals profit from? Wouldn't you like to be able to understand how, why, and how much you're being taxed? Few people accurately understand the tax code. Yet, it is estimated that the nation, individuals and businesses alike, must spend hundreds of billions of dollars, and millions of man-hours, just to comply with the system each year.

By being so visible and understandable to the public, a flat tax would hold the politicians' feet to the fire. With politicians being unable to raise taxes whenever they see fit or create loopholes for their friends, and with people focusing for the first time on the deficit and national debt, government spending could be monitored and controlled much more closely. And politicians would have to be more accountable for their decisions when spending takes place.

But despite all the clear benefits there would be for most of us if a flat tax were enacted, politicians who are afraid of losing their power base will attempt to discredit it by using their most powerful weapon, their divisive and terrifying rhetoric, with the help of press. Instead of trying to find ways to make the flat tax work, and correct its shortfalls, many politicians who stay in power on the strength of large government and corporate sponsorship are panicking, and will come up with whatever misrepresentation it takes to scare those who are less familiar with the tax debate. These politicians have plenty of access to the valuable and effective media of television, radio, and the newspapers; and the more often a lie is told, the more people will accept it as fact. Richard Gephardt of Missouri is a master at forcing a lie into the media, and repeating it so often that after a while, you can see that he has started to believe it himself.

What is the biggest shortfall of the flat tax? The flat tax is an income tax, so the IRS will still have to exist in some form. With any form of *income* tax, the government will still be able to intrude into your personal financial records.

The National Retail Sales Tax

One thing that would scare politicians more than a flat tax is a national retail sales tax. If the objectives of tax reform are to make tax collection simpler and more fair, and to remove political fraud, deception, and favoritism, a national sales tax must be considered. What is the national retail sales tax? This is a tax paid on purchases of goods or services from retailers. The retailers will collect the national sales tax along with any state tax due.

The appeal of the national sales tax is that:

- It gives you more privacy. You no longer have to disclose your income to the government.

• It is easy to comply with. You don't have to file returns or pay professionals to assist you. Only retailers must file the tax returns, and most retailers (in 46 out of 50 states) are already used to collecting taxes and filling out the forms for the state sales tax.

• It is simpler. We can throw out the 17,000-page Internal Revenue Code. Because of its simplicity, the jobs of about 100,000 IRS agents could be eliminated over time, thus reducing tax collection costs by approximately $6 billion per year.

• You will never be audited or required to open up all aspects of your personal spending habits to IRS agents who are antagonistic, oppressive, and intimidating by nature.

• It takes away Congress's power to revise tax codes to favor special interests, or to raise taxes with hidden or obscure changes. It is therefore a very visible tax.

• It takes tax collection out of the hands of the federal government and puts it into the hands of the states, thereby eliminating a huge and powerful bureaucracy.

• The number of employees needed by the IRS would be reduced to a fraction of the present staff.

• It will encourage saving more than other tax reforms have done. Since savings and investment income would no longer be taxed, there would be more incentive for saving.

• It will end the double taxation that exists in the present system.

Although the most extreme, this reform may be the most fair and solve many problems the flat tax cannot. Studies done at the direction of the Cato Institute find the following positive consequences of a national retail sales tax:

(1) The national savings rate will more than double. This is important, as it will make people less dependent upon government, especially at retirement age.

(2) Interest rates will be reduced, since lenders would

not be subject to tax on their income. Also, with increased savings, there would be more money available to lend, and rates would decrease due to supply and demand.

(3) National output will be increased by nearly $400 billion. It is determined that, without an oppressive and regressive tax system, and with the savings that the public would gain by not having to comply with the burdensome taxes, the economy would swell.

Are there negative points to a national retail sales tax?

First of all, the national sales tax initially would be estimated at approximately 17.4%. It will take us a long time to get used to paying such a high sales tax, even though there will be more dollars coming in without income tax withholding. *It is also determined, according to this study, that over a period of less than ten years the sales tax rate would be reduced to 15.4%, then 13.9% due to its positive effect on the economy.*

Economist Dale Jorgenson, professor at Harvard University, estimates that it would take a 15% national sales tax rate to compensate for all the taxes now collected by federal, state, and local government.

Next, some believe that a national sales tax is harmful to those with lower incomes who otherwise would not pay income taxes. *The fact is, there are various ways to give credits or deductions in a national sales tax system. For instance, each family member could receive a credit for the first $5,000 dollars spent. Also, even though many people pay no income tax, they are already used to paying sales tax on many consumer items.*

Those who oppose a national sales tax say it will be difficult to catch "cheaters" in this type of system. *However, the IRS estimates that over $150 billion now goes uncollected each year (which means the amount may be closer to $300 billion). States have reported that it is easier to collect a sales tax than to collect personal income* *taxes. This may be due to the fact that they are dealing with businesses instead of individuals. Since there are fewer businesses than individuals, the number of collections is reduced, and is easier to monitor.*

Proponents of either a national retail sales tax or a flat tax should understand that politicians will fight them as aggressively as possible. Politicians will not willingly support any reform that takes away their freedom to legislate (spend or raise taxes) as they see fit. It is up to you and every other United States citizen to speak loudly for change. Without your voice, we will be stuck with politics as usual.

CHAPTER 10

GOVERNING AGAINST THE WILL OF THE PEOPLE

Although politicians are elected by us to run the country on our behalf, there are many examples of how they do just the opposite. In many cases, this is arrogantly done right in front of us, and at other times behind our backs, without our knowledge. Examples abound. For instance:

- President Clinton invested billions of dollars to prop up the Mexican government, which is known to be corrupt. Polls at that time indicated that over 80% of the United States citizens were against our risking billions of dollars in this manner. President Clinton ignored our will. Many feel that the reason Clinton did this was to save Mexico from defaulting on billions of dollars of loans made by some of America's largest banks and securities firms. This brings up the question as to whether we, the taxpayers, should be responsible for seeing that these financial institutions don't lose money on risky loans they made to Mexico. Note that one of Clinton's largest supporters has been Goldman Sachs, the investment banking firm, which has contributed over $100,000 to Clinton over his political career.
- The 1993 Crime Bill was a superb example of government at its worst. After the crime bill narrowly passed, President Clinton called it a great victory. But the politicians' and Clinton's victory is America's loss. Congress

voted, not against crime, but for another way to grab and spend more of our tax dollars. How did they garner support from the public for this bill? Simple. They played upon our senses, stating that it was time to be tough on crime, and that the bill would put 100,000 more policemen on the streets throughout the country.

Despite the continued rhetoric by the supporters of the crime bill, this was nothing but a huge deception. Even some of the newspapers got it right after a while. The TRUTH is that the bill provides for up to 100,000 policemen to be hired in communities throughout the country, but pays only a small portion of their salaries for a short period of time, and pays nothing for training, equipment, automobiles, etc. Therefore, many communities who were offered help with law enforcement, compliments of this bill, rejected the "help" on the basis that it wasn't affordable. Unfortunately, as in the case of many other deceptions of Congress, the media didn't catch the lies and expose them until after the bill was passed.

• Politicians are fully aware of the cause and effect of raising and lowering interest rates, tax rates, and mandates on business, etc. They use these controls to alter unemployment, inflation, and other economic fluctuations that affect our everyday lives. If the unemployment rate gets too low, they raise interest rates. They don't want to see 100% employment! To them the ideal unemployment range is 5-6%. Yet these are the politicians who say they are for the poor. By playing with the economy this way, they are effectively taking away the jobs of many, and putting people back into the welfare lines.

• What happens to excess campaign contributions? It's a little-known fact that there is an amendment in a 1979 law which states that members who took the oath of office before 1980 can keep any leftover campaign money for their personal use when they retire. Politicians get to keep those dollars, as long as they are reported as income! This is not common knowledge because politicians don't want us to focus on the various ways that they line their pockets at our expense. You may find that some of the money you think is being spent to fund a campaign can *legally* go right into a politician's bank account!

• For a number of reasons, the public has not focused on what Congress's overspending has meant to us. But despite the rhetoric coming out of Washington, we are forced to pay for the mistakes they make. Higher taxes, additional taxes, more regulations, and fewer freedoms are some of the ways through which Washington controls us.

THE BRAINWASHING OF SOCIETY

I was amazed to discover that the congressional record is tampered with by members of Congress. For instance, a speaker on the floor is able to revise or edit his speech prior to its inclusion in the congressional record, so we are "shielded" from what was actually discussed. If a congressman makes an impassioned speech he feels will not be popular with the public, he can edit it, even after he has had his say to influence his "comrades."

Campaign specialists spend tens of millions of dollars to sway public opinion, using whatever tactics they feel will work at a given time. In most cases, politicians aren't focusing on relevant issues. More often their campaigns consist of smears, innuendos, lies, and half-truths. Many thinking Americans can see through these messages. It is no wonder there are such low turnouts for elections nowadays. People are fed up with the immature and childish practices of these campaigners. Does anyone know how much money is spent on campaigns each year? Keep reading to find out.

Political strategy, which has been very effective over the years, is to divide the public into Republicans and Democrats, as if there are no other choices. Politics also divide us in other ways: liberals versus conservatives, rich versus poor, white versus black. Since politicians have been robbing us blind for decades, and for the most part gotten away with it, I suggest that all taxpayers should band together and, if there should be any division, let it be politician versus taxpayer.

Politicians retain their power by using taxpayers' money. Both parties are given millions of dollars to spend on advertising, promotion, and getting their word out to the nation. Democrats go even further. The basis of their party's survival is to feed and grow a dependency group, which they buy with taxpayer dollars spent on "social" programs. We have allowed them to retain a powerful constituency this way for all these years! We need to look more closely at not only what we are spending for social programs and entitlements, but at what the benefits of this spending are to the politicians who endorse these programs.

Most people in the United States have been conditioned over the years to believe there are only two viable parties. That's part of the psyche and "power base" that the two parties enjoy. Because of this, the media focuses primarily on the two main parties and gives very little credence to any outside challenger.

Politicians are very analytical in what they say and how they say it. They cleverly design their speeches to sway the public with innuendo, expression, and carefully chosen words.

Free Candy for Everyone

Politicians' campaigns are just a matter of packaging. They have little or nothing to do with substance, politicians' beliefs, or how they will represent the people once they are in office. This has been proven time and again throughout history. Politicians say what they believe their constituents want to hear, regardless of whether or not it is the truth.

For instance, President Clinton can make an impassioned speech about the responsibility and accountability of those who educate our children. He points out that there should be ways to score a teacher's performance, and to replace those teachers who aren't doing their job well. He also says that the bureaucracy in the Board of Education should be pared down to the bare minimum.

The Board of Education has been a huge supporter of Democrats and the Clintons over the years. If they thought President Clinton really intended to follow through on these bold statements, they'd be alarmed and would develop a huge campaign to counter his objectives. However, they realize that Clinton is only saying what the public wants to hear. They want Clinton reelected, so they just listen to the things he says, knowing full well that he doesn't believe them. They know he doesn't plan to take action against the Board of Education, or against *any* of his supporters.

When Republican Jim Edgar ran against Dawn Clark Netsch for the position of governor of the State of Illinois, he blasted her plan to lower property taxes and raise the income tax in order to effectively raise tax revenue by approximately $400 million. Eighteen months after he became governor, he proposed the same plan he had condemned Ms. Netsch for just a short time before. This unpopular decision distanced him from other Republican powerhouses in Illinois, and took him out of the running as a potential vice-presidential running mate for Bob Dole in the 1996 election. It also showed him to be a typical tax-and-spend politician, despite his campaign pledges to the contrary.

Politicians are masterful when it comes to making bold, wonderful-sounding promises during a campaign. Only those same promises are often ignored or forgotten when they get elected. Campaigning candidates should be required to disclose to the public the cost for those promises or programs, and offer long-term feasibility plans showing where the money will come from. This compelled fiscal responsibility could go a long way in keeping politicians from making promises they can't keep.

The Final Debate - Federal vs. Local Government Control

Despite the long-running debate among the most brilliant and credible political analysts, the answer to the question of whether or not we should return programs and spending to local government is clear. Consider the following.

The federal government, despite its penchant for saddling local government with hundreds of billions of dollars in unfunded mandates each year, has still accumulated a national debt of over $5 trillion, which is more than three times its annual budget.

State and local governments, despite being saddled with hundreds of billions of dollars of unfunded mandates each year by the federal government, are ordered to balance their budgets each year, which they regularly do. There is relatively small accumulated debt in local government, compared to that of federal government.

Why is this so? The main reason is that local politicians and leaders are more accountable to their citizens, because they are *among* them. Globetrotting congressmen are not as accessible, and don't have first-hand knowledge of the unique problems each community endures. Also, it is more difficult for smaller governments to hide their relatively smaller spending bills from their public.

Is local government perfect? Far from it! But if more spending and programs originated from local government, it would be easier for those paying the taxes to be involved and have influence over the local legislators who make the laws.

CIVIL SERVANTS, OR ROYALTY?

Our elected officials, those who make the rules, have provided very well for themselves over the years by passing bills, laws, and perks that benefit officeholders. Somehow the tables have turned. While we once were the owners of the country with politicians working for us, we now are catering to their every whim and desire. This is one reason why members of Congress are viewed by so many with such contempt. Consider the following:

Perks

After exhaustive research, I haven't found any corporate pension plan, regardless of corporate profitability, as generous as the one Congress has given itself.

According to an August 1992 *Money* magazine article, Congress costs us more than just salaries. Congress members receive many significant perks that make up large additional expense, such as:

Salary (1996)	$136,600
Pension plan (portion paid by taxpayers)	26,289
Thrift plan	6,475
Health insurance (portion paid by taxpayers)	3,106
Free parking on Capitol Hill	1,200
Tax deduction for living in Washington, D.C.	930
Subsidized gymnasiums	600
Taxpayer-paid portion of $128,000 in life insurance	302
Total value of perks*	38,902
Total salary and perks	$175,502

Some other perks that Congress has taken advantage of, at taxpayers' expense, are mentioned by *Money* magazine in its 1992 article. They include:

* Perks may have increased between 1992 and 1996

Video producer (about $44,000) – 89 producers and technicians

Chauffeur ($40,667)

Upholsterer ($35,640) – 4 house upholsterers to fix furniture in member's offices and meeting rooms, costing $138,000 annually

Senior hairstylist ($32,917)

Garage attendant – ($31,984) – 80 for Capitol's garages

Folding operator ($30,346) – 12 operate Senate folding machines for franked mail

OTHER PERKS for our civil servants:

• Congress spends upwards of $100 million of taxpayer dollars per year on mailings to constituents. This practice, called franking, gives politicians a decided edge over others attempting to unseat them at election time.

• The Office of the Attending Physicians Service, located at the Capitol, is a taxpayer-paid, private medical services perk for lawmakers only. It is strictly off limits to civilians who pay the taxes to support this institution.

• Free use of the House recording studio to produce radio and TV spots, and free satellite service for radio and TV transmissions.

• Discounted haircuts, manicures, shoeshines, and shoe repairs at the Senate and House barber and beauty shops located in the Senate and House office buildings.

• Subsidized meals at congressional restaurants. Until five years ago tabs were run, some exceeding $300,000 that took years to pay back.

• Free processing of passport applications.

• Special handling of "orange bag" franked mail that ensures one-day delivery.

• A special Capitol IRS office to help members with the preparation of their tax returns.

• And what about the House bank, which is open exclusively for the members of the House of Representatives? In 1991, it came to light that the bank was run in such a slip-shod manner that it allowed its "customers" to break all the rules. Who else but our representatives could believe that they deserve interest-free loans, and that they can freely bounce checks without concern of retribution? Could we, their employers, bounce checks and get away with it? Not for very long! Not only did they get free checking, they got free *bouncing*.

• Who determines the SALARIES of the members of Congress? They determine their own salaries! The Senate increased its pay 9.9% in 1990, and the House raised its pay 7.9%, to $98,360 per year. But that wasn't enough. They waited until after the election of 1990, and then both houses raised their pay an additional 25%, up to $129,500, plus an automatic annual cost of living increase of about 4% per year. This raised each salary to $133,600 in 1993. To justify this obscene raise they'd given themselves, they banned the acceptance of outside honoraria. However, small gifts from parties with no conflict of interest are not banned. So many politicians still enjoy gifts, trips, and vacations that are masked as business meetings or other events.

The members of Congress didn't just *vote* themselves a salary increase. They did it in a way that was meant to fool and deceive the taxpayers. The raise was hidden in a 1992 appropriations bill that read:

> "The rate of pay for the offices referred to under section 703 (a) (2) (B) of the Ethics Reform act of 1989 (5 U.S.C. 5318 note) shall be the rate of pay that would be payable for each such office if the provisions of section 703 (a) (2) (B) and 1101 (a) (1) (A) of such act (5 U.S.C. 5318 note and 5305) had not been enacted."

Whoever came up with this language of deception should be fired on the spot!

Congress justifies these salary increases by saying that they are only attempting to maintain parity with the average private sector, middle class management employee. However, the TRUTH, according to the General Accounting Office, is that these salaries are in the upper 5% of the nation's wage earners. If congressional perks were included in these figures the discrepancy would be more dramatic. If workers in private industry exhibited the same unsuccessful business record as those in Congress, they would have been fired long ago.

In fact, a 1994 study by the Carnegie Foundation, shows the following figures. Compare the salaries now being paid to congressmen (over $135,000), to a House staffer ($119,000), and to a Senate staffer ($124,900), with the following average incomes:

- full professors at universities – $68,700
- average pay for so–called professionals (doctors, lawyers, dentists) – $59,450
- median income for all adults who have earned doctorates – $49,437

We all understand that people should get paid what they're worth. However, Congress forgets that they are working for us. When was the last time an employee not only gave himself a raise, but with all his accumulated raises, was eventually paid much more than the employer?

Retirement Plans

Congress makes sure it has provided for its members' retirement quite generously. We and our children, however, will be saddled with the results of Congress's mismanagement, fraud, abuse, and lack of discretion for generations to come, in the form of higher taxes needed to pay the principal and interest on the national debt. In fact, Congress's retirement plan is 2–4 times more generous, at our expense, than that of public sector programs.

Since 1987, members of Congress could invest up to 10% of their base pay in a qualified 401(k) pension plan, even though taxpayers could invest only 7% in a qualified plan. An in-depth study of congressional pension programs discovered that over half the members of Congress will receive in excess of $1 million when they retire, with a few receiving over $4 million, and some receiving well over $100,000 per year. In addition, these pensions are fully protected by annual cost of living adjustments. No one can explain why these people who work for us are enjoying a pension that is 2-4 times more generous than the pension of the average wage earner.

Is this the clearest example yet of the arrogance of our politicians? Not only have they spent our country into bankruptcy, but they have the audacity to make themselves rich in the process. So much for Outcome Based Government!

Expense Accounts

Each House member may hire up to 21 staff members, for a cost totaling $441,120 per year, plus an intern at taxpayer expense. Each member receives a base "official duty" expense allowance of $67,000 per year, a minimum of $6,200 for travel, $6,000 for long-distance phone charges, and rent for a standard 2,500 s.f. office space. The total of these expenses ranges from $100,000 to over $300,000 per year, plus the cost of office furnishings and equipment.

Meanwhile, the average member of the Senate receives: an administrative and clerical assistance allowance based upon the population of his state, from $814,000 to $1.7 million (for California); a legislative assistance allowance (to hire employees representing them on their committees) of $269,000 per senator; and a senatorial official office expense allowance, ranging from $33,000 to $156,000.

What does all of this mean? It means that we are

spending over $2.5 billion per year on the expenses of the legislative branch, or more than $3.5 million per lawmaker. With all of this financial support, you would think a congressman could do the job he was sent there to do. His job is not to pad his own pockets and increase his power base, but to run our government efficiently and cost effectively. Maybe the problem is that he still doesn't know what his job is.

All these sources of money for politicians, including PAC tax dollars, contributions, franking, and other perks, and soft dollars, apparently aren't enough. We have recently seen that politicians are allowed to collect money in other ways. As a result of a number of scandals they are involved in, the President and Mrs. Clinton have incurred over a million dollars in legal bills. In June of 1994, they set up a legal defense fund so supporters can give them money to defray some of their legal bills. As of February, 1996, the fund had collected over $970,000.

In January, 1996, the media revealed that, because of the legal fees, the Clintons were close to bankruptcy. In fact, President Clinton stated to the media, "If I remain healthy, I'll be able to pay my debts, and we'll be OK" This tug at the hearts of Americans was short-lived when, less than two weeks later, it was discovered that insurance companies had already reimbursed him almost $900,000 for legal fees incurred.

The contributors to the Clinton legal fund include a number of corporate sponsors, such as Oscar Wyatt, chairman of natural-gas producer Coastal Corporation, Hollywood producer Merv Adelson, and Sara Lee chairman John Bryan. Does the public believe that government can be run equitably, impartially, and without bias when major corporations hand money to the people who have the power to change laws?

CONGRESSIONAL ACCOUNTABILITY AND SELF-DISCIPLINE

One of the most momentous problems facing our government is how to discipline our elected officials. Over the years, there have been numerous examples of elected officials taking advantage of their posts for their own gain. Congress is supposed to discipline itself, but there is a growing skepticism among the public that ethics committees are no more than a sham. Many believe that once the public show is over, most congressmen get off with little more than a slap on the wrist.

Just think about how difficult it is for Congress to honestly discipline itself. If a wrongdoer is caught, he is investigated by his peers. These are the same people, whether in his own party or not, who must work with him to get their respective bills and agendas passed. So it is very difficult for someone on an ethics committee to play hardball with a fellow congressman. This committee person may need a favor or a vote one day and, if he's too tough on his peers, may lose some of the IOU's he's accumulated over the years.

Congress passed many important laws that they felt they did not have to obey. This was changed in 1995, thanks to one of the promises made in the Republican Contract with America, a promise that is very unpopular with Democrats. In fact, H. Lon Henry, in his book entitled *Congress: America's Privileged Class,* writes, "Only a privileged class insists on exempting itself from many of the important laws it has imposed on its own electorate. Only a privileged class would consider many of its own statutes too onerous and intrusive to be endured by themselves. Only a privileged class considers its status to be so apart, so superior, to its constituency. The Congress of the United States is this type of privileged class."

We applaud Congress for finally deciding to obey the laws that it passes on to the rest of us. But it is a great example of the arrogance those same lawmakers had, to have considered that they were above those laws in the first place!

Until now, Congress felt they should be exempt from a number of laws. I'll name a few:

The Americans With Disabilities Act
The Privacy Act
The Social Security Act of 1933
The National Labor Relations Act of 1935
The Minimum Wage Act of 1963
The Civil Service Reform Act of 1978
The Equal Pay Act of 1963
The Civil Rights Act of 1964
The Freedom of Information Act of 1966
The Age Discrimination Act of 1967
The Occupational Safety and Health Act of 1970
The Equal Employment Opportunity Act of 1970
The Ethics in Government Act of 1978
The Conflict of Interest Laws
. . . and so on.

To illustrate the arrogance of the present Congress compared to that of our founding fathers, I quote this statement made by James Madison over 200 years ago. It proclaimed, "We [Congress] can make no law which will not have its full operation on ourselves and our friends, as well as on this great mass of society."

Must politicians wonder why so much of the public is thoroughly disgusted by their lack of sensitivity towards their constituents?

It would be simplistic for naysayers to discount the problems we have with our politicians by saying we can vote them out in the next election.

TAKING RESPONSIBILITY FOR THEIR ACTIONS

Politicians and government employees who work in the public sector should take personal responsibility for their actions, get the credit for their contributions, and accept the blame and punishment for their negative productivity and useless ideas.

For instance, President Clinton signed a deadbeat dad law, which states that deadbeat dads may have their drivers licenses taken away if they don't pay child support as decreed. But, if they can't get to work, how can they pay money for support? Is President Clinton trying to lose them their jobs so they end up on welfare and other government programs? Isn't there a more intelligent solution to this important problem? What about having the employer garnish the wages? There must be a more practical, effective answer.

And shouldn't politicians be held personally responsible for their pork-barrel bills that waste untold billions of dollars each year? Shouldn't they be held personally responsible for any and all lies, deceptions, and fraud that they perpetrate on the American public? Shouldn't they be held responsible when their intentional distortion of the facts causes the public to make uninformed decisions that cost us billions of dollars? And finally, shouldn't they be held personally responsible when they sneakily slip spending programs and other bills into law without our knowledge and consent?

CHAPTER 11

SOLUTIONS, SOLUTIONS, SOLUTIONS

AN OUTLINE FOR REFORM

Now that we have presented the problem in basic terms, what is the solution? After all, we are talking about a trillion-dollar problem, so the solution must be pretty complex, right? No. This solution is no more difficult to understand or implement than any other. But it will require the will of the people to follow through. Nothing will be done voluntarily by the politicians. After all, they have demonstrated for decades that they can't resist the temptations of all the money involved with being in office, and so cannot be *trusted* with power. It's going to take a lot of pressure from a lot people to make sure the politicians lead our country in the right direction.

In many cases, the solutions for problems are so simple that they almost insult the intelligence of every politician. For instance, we must tell them to not take bribes, to avoid conflicts of interest, to not lie or mislead those they work for, to give honest numbers and facts when imparting information to the public, to not waste taxpayers' money, and to treat the public with the respect and dignity it deserves. Perhaps we could send everyone in Congress the book, *All I Really Needed To Know, I Learned In Kindergarten,* by Robert Fulghum.

Yes, these solutions are an affront to the egos and

senses of most politicians, and yet we see reforms (even from members of Congress) that embody the above ideas all the time. Why is that? Because politicians have proven they cannot resist temptation and must be kept in line. So, even though many of the following may be nothing more than simple, common-sense ideas, here they are.

In short, the outline for reform includes:

A Well-Educated Public

The public must be fully aware of how Congress operates. It must have enough respect for itself and the money it is sending to Congress to demand the truth about the actions of our politicians. The public must demand reform *now*. It must insist that Congress is working for the United States citizens, and not the other way around, as has been the case for decades. Only with a well-informed public will we be able to see through the rhetoric and confusion politicians have relied on for so long, and find the candidates who will truly serve us in the way we deserve.

Getting the Facts Through the Media

The media, including newspapers, magazines, TV, and radio, must, for the benefit of the public and the future of the country, provide truth and facts on a consistent basis. This can come in a number of ways. There should be a mandate for the national media, as well as all publications with a minimum specified readership, to document information and include summaries of Congress's latest votes and actions. Only then will the public be given enough facts to see whether or not their representatives are truly working for them.

The media must make it a point to present the relevant facts in each campaign. This is one of the most important public services that the media may perform. There must be a decree to the media that they will, on a consistent basis, inform and educate the public on each candidate, and make known the following:

(1) the candidate's position on the issues, taken from a position paper that each candidate will be required to fill out before the official campaign period begins

(2) the experience, history, and track record of each candidate, including his voting record on the important and relevant issues of the day

(3) the "truth grade" a candidate earns during the campaign, as he speaks, debates, promotes, and advertises his candidacy

(4) the specific background and qualifications of each candidate, including information on how and why he/she will perform well in the position sought

How can the media be pushed to give us the truth?

The media needs to realize how important its job is. It has an enormous capacity to inform or misinform. It's time the media started taking the responsibility of presenting accurate information to the public. The future of the United States depends on a trustworthy, informative, and credible media to survive.

The media becomes more valuable to society when it is credible and educational. A well-informed reporting and writing staff is critical. Just as important, however, is the ability of the interviewer to **question** a politician when the politician makes a misleading or erroneous statement. Those in the media act irresponsibly when they allow erroneous messages to get by without comment or question.

The media will reap definite benefits by treating the political process more responsibly, and getting the truth to the public. The most important benefit will be improved credibility. This has been questioned over the years because of the frequent bias media has shown for certain candidates, positions, or parties. By giving the public relevant material, and helping to inform the citizens, the media will be serving a more useful purpose, and achieve a higher value in the eyes of its customers. It will also be doing the country a service by educating the nation.

Public Debates with Truth & Honesty Detection.

All public debates should be monitored by a non–partisan committee, with facts at their fingertips, who will be able to judge the factual nature of the debaters' statements. A truth detection quotient should be published the next day by the national media to let the viewing public know which politicians were the most factual, and which politicians attempted to deceive the public with inaccurate or misleading information.

Honest Campaigns with Truth & Honesty Detection

Again, truth detection should be provided with every ad and all publicity for a politician. Once more, the public deserves to know who is telling the truth and who isn't.

An Overhauled Tax System

Make it simple enough for us to understand what our real taxes are and when we are being overtaxed. A form of the flat tax or a national retail sales tax, that the majority of the public can agree on, should be implemented in order to eliminate the corruption, loopholes, and favoritism that have taken place over the years with the current confusing tax code. A simple flat tax or sales tax we can all understand will take a huge bite out of the corruption that has existed for decades.

Reform of the Political Process

Over the years, politicians have made laws and rules for their own benefit that have entrenched them in the system, making it almost impossible for challengers to have a fair chance at running against them. That is why 90% of incumbent politicians running for reelection are reelected. And this is so, despite the fact that the majority of Americans don't trust politicians or feel they're doing the job they were elected to do.

(1) Campaign reform.

As you have learned from the information previously discussed, challengers for government office have little or no chance of beating the entrenched incumbent. Meaningful campaign reform will come only from pressure outside of Congress. Don't depend on Congress to regulate itself.

The beginning of a campaign for any contender, new or existing, should begin with a "resume" or position paper, which outlines at least the following information about the candidate:

- his position on the major issues of the day (those issues to be determined by citizen committee prior to the beginning of the campaign)
- his experience, background, and qualifications, including any information that would make the candidate uniquely qualified for the position he is seeking
- if the candidate has had any previous experience in government, his historical voting record on major, relevant issues (standard "relevant issue list" to be determined by committee prior to the beginning of any campaign)
- age, or any relevant health problems that could affect his term in office

(2) Honesty quotient – truth detection.

A grade for honesty must be established for each activity of a candidate's campaign, including speeches, advertising, and debates. This will help eliminate the kind of campaigns that have offended so many voters and made them cynical about the political process. An honest, issue-oriented campaign will result in higher voter turnout, and will bring back some of the credibility that has been lost. It may even bring back to the American people some pride and respect for the government and the political process.

(3) Finances.

The amount of money spent on campaigns for all office seekers, both incumbents and challengers, should be restricted. This is necessary, because otherwise it is impossible for challengers, other than multi-millionaires, to effectively compete with the incumbents. Now, as in the past, most of the money spent on campaigns is spent on biased, slanted, or negative advertising. This biased advertising is very effective. Because of the amount of money spent, the public is deluged with it and may begin to believe those slanted ads, whether they're true or not.

Campaign financing should also be reduced, in order to give qualified challengers equal footing in an election, whether it be for the House, the Senate, Presidential, or local elections.

Our recommendation is that, instead of spending millions for each of these elections (see our discussion, "The Stacked Deck," which discusses the economics of elections), the campaign amount spent by an office-seeker for the House should be limited to $250,000; for the Senate, $500,000; and for the White House, $10,000,000. All local elections should be limited to $250,000, and statewide elections (governor) to $500,000. There should be no tax dollars used in the election process at all. Tax dollars should not be given to any office-seekers, their supporters, or their parties to spend on advertising, salaries, promotion, marketing, travel, or for any other campaign purpose. In addition to eliminating the monopoly of entrenched politicians, cleaning up the campaigns and reducing campaign costs will free incumbent politicians to spend more of their time doing their job more efficiently.

How do you enforce the limits on campaign dollars? For every dollar an office-seeker spends *over* the allotted amount, two dollars must be given to each of his opponents. That way, no one will have an edge if one candidate overspends. Another effective penalty would be to disqualify a candidate for discounted TV, radio, and newspaper spots for those campaigns that exceed the stated limits.

Less money will be needed if campaign time is shortened from 18 months to 8 months. A shorter campaign will require less money for marketing, promotion, travel, the organization, etc. After all, our elected official's first job is to be our representative, not to campaign. The less time they spend on the campaign trail, the more time they will spend working for us.

Less money will be needed because all major media will make advertising available to all candidates at lower rates than in the past. Less advertising could also result in more positive messages from the candidates. With a responsible media presenting accurate and extensive information about the candidates, any biased, negative advertising will be less effective.

(4) Signing and enforcing the Contract with Americans.

Each candidate must be willing to sign the Contract with Americans. A refusal to do so would be a red flag to each voter, indicating that the candidate has no intention of representing the citizens of the United States as he so eagerly promises.

(5) Accountability of everyone in public office, from the top down.

One very important issue is the accountability and responsibility agreement. When people work for the government in any capacity, there must be a chain of responsibility, and the responsible parties must be dealt with according to their actions. Any spending, regardless of the amount, must begin with someone requesting it. All spending requests must be in writing, with at least two signatures, including a supervisor. Both parties will then be responsible for any overspending or fraud that takes place as to the appropriation of those funds. Also, approval and funding may not occur without the funding body also approving the request, and the individual who gives that approval shall be responsible as well.

What are we talking about? Wasted programs costing billions of dollars begin with an idea. The person whose idea it is cannot get the funding without it first being approved, and then being sent to the funding (appropriations) body. Instead of blaming the waste, fraud, overspending, and abuse on "the government," the actual *responsible parties* should be dealt with severely.

For instance, a scandal has been reported over the years regarding the building of exorbitantly costly courthouses across the country, wasting hundreds of millions of taxpayer dollars. Despite Congressional hearings on the matter, no one has been able to point a finger to the responsible party. However, *someone* must have requested, and others approved, the top-of-the-line construction materials and majestic design that, in some cases, doubled and tripled the cost of these buildings. Some individual requested, and someone else approved, custom doors on one building that added millions of dollars to the cost of construction. But at the hearings, no one could specify who authorized what. Cover-ups like this should be a thing of the past.

The corruption of government construction is far-reaching. As we learned from the racket of the court construction, most of the cheating occurred after the bid was won by a contractor, and the work begun. During the construction process, there were a number of changes requested (change orders) that were tacked onto the cost of the job. For the most part, because of time constraints, these types of changes usually are made without bid, so the contractor doing the job is able to charge whatever he wants, within reason. Thus, profit margins are usually much higher for contractors on change orders. In fact, there is the possibility that a contractor can win the bid by giving a low (below-cost) estimate on the job, with the understanding that he will make up his profit through extensive change orders.

There must be more checks and balances, with the actual individuals signing off on all requests prior to an approval. A request for funding must include the purpose of the request, the cost, the benefit, where the money is to come from, and specifically where the money is going.

Anyone who spends our money, or approves the payment of our money without proper approvals, should be dealt with convincingly and surely. If a government check is sent out without proper paperwork, then whoever sent the check out should be dealt with severely. This is the only way cost overruns can be cut to a fraction of what they have been in the past.

(6) Real term limits.

What are term limits and why are they so important? Term limits are proposed to limit the time a politician can remain in office, in order to effectively end careerism in Washington. The term limits under most discussion have been: two terms for the Senate, for a total of 12 years; and six terms for the House, for a total of 12 years. There are a number of reasons why term limits are important for the government to be run as it should. For instance:

- As previously discussed, incumbents are entrenched in the system, based upon their unfair "stacking of the deck" when it comes to elections. Mandated term limits are the only way to get a reasonable turnover of lawmakers.
- Politicians who feel they have an advantage during the electoral process will not be as responsive and accountable to the citizens. This is illustrated by the regular deficit spending, the arrogant overstepping of power and authority, and the political scandals and fraud that have become commonplace in daily news.
- Although most Americans favor Congressional term limits, Congress, because of its obvious self-interest, has done little to move the cause forward.

• The founding fathers expected a "citizen legislature": a government run by its citizens, not by career politicians.

• The average length of office for committee chairmen, the Speaker, majority leader, and House Whip is 27 years.

• The longer a politician remains in office, the more he is able to play the political game, and the farther he gets away from reality. Those individuals in Congress who are responsible for making the rules that run our lives forget what life is like on the outside because of all the power and authority that is handed to them. Making a living, keeping a job, and paying the bills become foreign to politicians the longer they are in office, where their staffs take care of everything for them.

• The longer a politician is in office, the more contacts and "friends" he makes, the more special interests he gets involved with, the more "favors" he can do for supporters, and the less accountable he needs to be to the citizens he is ostensibly working for. Additionally, he becomes more "familiar" and friendly with other members of Congress, and feels more comfortable making deals that benefit the insiders.

With term limits *in place*, a politician knows that, within a short period of time, he will be back home in the private sector, and will have to live under the laws and conditions he has legislated. Thus, he will try harder to make the laws and conditions reasonable, not only for his constituents, but for himself and his family as well.

Hopefully, with a limited time as legislators, members would spend their time working on the more substantive issues instead of their own pet projects.

State of Arkansas (Term Limit) Amendment 73 said, in part, "elected officials who remain in office too long become preoccupied with reelection and ignore their duties as representatives of the people."

Too many politicians see Congress as a permanent career and, instead of conducting the business at hand, focus their efforts on their reelection. They're often rewarded by being reelected, while others who are doing the job that they were hired to do are penalized for not spending enough time preparing for their own reelection.

Unfortunately, politicians care more about the next election than about the next generation.

Why do most special interests oppose term limits? Because, as a representative of the American Enterprise Institute admits, "They [special interests] have invested a lot in learning how to take advantage of the current system, and any change would involve heavy transition costs." Getting the special interests out of the business of setting the agenda for our country is a great argument for term limits.

By remaining in Washington so long, politicians are out of touch with the public and their day-to-day lifestyles. This is proven more than ever, since politicians rely on *polls* to form their agenda when they aren't legislating favors for their supporters and lobbyists.

Non-professional politicians would be more likely to consider themselves citizens of the United States, and less likely to fall in step with the bureaucrats and political insiders when it comes to making deals.

Finally, term limits would limit the extravagant pensions that members of Congress can accumulate. As discussed previously, we have been rewarding career politicians by paying them higher pensions, until now there are dozens of Congressional veterans who will retire with multi-million-dollar pensions. And look what they left us with — a $5 trillion debt, and no light at the end of the tunnel. Studies show that, with term limits, politicians would retire with pensions of approximately $30,000, instead of over $100,000 per year, which is the present average for those who have accumulated million-dollar pensions.

The entrenched politicians who are fighting term limits are doing so based upon the following arguments:

• Voters have the power to limit the terms of members of Congress by their vote. *We have seen by the statistics, however, that these are the same politicians who have incrementally changed the rules to entrench themselves, and who have used their positions of power to buy their own reelections, making it nearly impossible for challengers to compete.*

• It takes a long time for a newcomer to learn the procedures and the issues of importance. *But it is the established, experienced Congress, without term limits, that has given us this $5 trillion debt that is rising daily by more than half a billion dollars. Maybe we need less experience, and more expertise and honesty.*

• Politicians who are limited in their service will only be thinking about the short term ("hit-and-run" legislation) since they won't be around very long to answer for the mess they created. *Who allowed us to run up the more than $5 trillion in debt that our children and grandchildren will be paying off for several generations? Who is proposing "balanced" budgets where most of the difficult cuts are in the last two years, after those politicians are out of office?*

• 1994 showed that when a public wants change, they are able to do it at the ballot box. *This is an intentionally misleading statement. The fact is, 24 of 26 Senate incumbents were reelected (well over 90%), and over 90% of the House members who sought reelection won. The change, and much of the turnover, apparently occurred through voluntarily vacated seats.*

Congressional Gift Reform (Bill S. 101)

Why should elected officials accept any gifts at all? The opportunity for conflict of interest is too great. High-stakes decisions involving our tax dollars should not be left to the discretion of those in Congress being tempted by all those gift dollars. Receipt of any gift worth over $25.00 should be banned.

Instead of depending on Congress to resist temptation, why not remove the temptation in the first place? That alone will restore some of Washington's credibility. Only when full disclosure and honest representation are implemented will Congress receive the respect and dignity it deserves.

All Significant Dealings and Negotiations to Occur in the Public Eye

The only way the public will be honestly informed and educated is for them to be privy to negotiations about spending and other legislation. Clearly, national security interests should be discreet, but there is no logical reason why we should be kept in the dark about high-stakes bargaining regarding our national budget, health care reform, or any other major issues of national significance and scope. With all the cable channels available these days, and with the media's cooperation, it should be possible to keep the public informed about what is happening in all of these critical discussions.

There were lessons to be learned as we were treated to the coverage of the O.J. Simpson trial. In spite of the disadvantages of having cameras in the court, with some participants "playing to the cameras," there were a number of advantages as well. For instance:

(1) Those who watched the trial were able to get all the untarnished information first-hand, instead of relying on media who may intentionally or unintentionally alter or omit important facts.

(2) By observing the players, we were able to see their reactions to different conditions and situations.

(3) The nation learned a great deal about how a court is run, saw how the legal system works, and became famil-

iar with legal jargon that was previously unknown to millions of people.

(4) With all the information received, we were able to make a more educated, well-informed decision as to whether or not we thought O.J. was innocent.

(5) Because of the cameras in the courtroom, the media hype was greater, the public was more aware and more interested, and the learning experience was greater overall.

The same thing can happen, given the right setting, with Congress at work. Granted, we have C–SPAN, which brings plenty of action to us day and night. However, viewing of actual committee debates over the important issues, such as the budget, may cause a great deal of interest (especially now since O.J.'s latest trial isn't being televised, and millions of people with "O.J. shock" are looking for other places to occupy their minds).

Cost/Benefit Analysis for all Government Spending

Any new spending bills or proposed programs should include a cost-benefit analysis, and specify where the money is coming from. The bill's sponsor should no longer have the option of saying that the money will come from borrowing.

Any time the government plans to spend money, a detailed, long-range feasibility plan should be prepared, and the sponsors' names and signatures should be prominent on the request. Details, as discussed previously, should be included in the proposal, and THERE SHOULD BE NO MORE NO-BID CONTRACTS. All projects over a specific dollar value (to be determined), should be bid on by no fewer than three qualified vendors or contractors. All bid information should be reasonably available for public inspection upon request.

All new or increased spending bills should require a 2/3 majority vote in both houses to pass and, in the case of a Presidential veto or line item veto, an override should require at least a 70% majority vote in both houses to pass. This will go a long way in determining whether the additional spending is necessary prior to its being put into law.

No-Bid Contracts a Thing of the Past

One of the most flagrant use of a bureaucrat's power is that of giving favorable treatment to supporters, special interests, or friends, in the form of no-bid contracts. This is the worst example of the abuse of one's office, and this way of doing business has cost us billions of dollars in unfavorable contracts each year.

Despite the arguments and rationale politicians may come up with, there are few valid reasons why no–bid contracts should be awarded. Anyone who requests funding for a job, and who requests a no-bid contract, should show specific reasons why it isn't feasible to get competitive bids for the work being done.

No-bid contracts and the deficit spending that government has sustained for decades are two of the best examples of political hypocrisy. The same politicians who support those two behaviors would not do so if it were their own money being spent. This shows the utter disregard they have for our hard-earned tax dollars.

The "It's Not My Fault" Defense

A politician may not vote for a bill that he hasn't read and is not familiar with.

A politician who votes for a bill is alleging that he has read it and is familiar with all of its provisions. Although he can't be responsible for the success or failure of each bill, he should be responsible for any or all pork-barrel or other government waste proposed in the bill. Perhaps this is a radical idea, but I wouldn't mind seeing an occasional "pop quiz" given to the members of the Congress who voted for a bill, just to make sure they knew what they voted for. It could be like periodic, surprise drug testing for athletes.

Line Item Veto

A line item veto will give the President the power, authority, and RESPONSIBILITY to line out any wasteful spending proposed in a bill. Although this provision gives the President an excessive amount of power over Congress (subject to Congress's overturning the President with a 2/3 majority vote in both houses), it also places the responsibility for any wasteful spending directly on his shoulders.

No Campaign Travel Expenses Should Be Paid From Taxes

It's bad enough that politicians spend a major part of their 18-month campaign period raising money and trying to get reelected, instead of doing their job. Just as insulting is the fact that many incumbents freely spend our tax dollars on trips that are disguised as official government business, but are nothing more than campaigning on their own behalf, or supporting a colleague. The amount of dollars being spent on this partisan travel runs in the tens of millions for each campaign. Tighter checks and balances are needed to put this activity to rest.

Sponsor–Relationship Disclosure

A politician, upon proposal of a bill, must disclose whether any affected parties of the bill have contributed to his personal campaign or party.

The sponsor of the bill must fill out a standard request form containing a section which discloses any possible conflict of interest, or benefit a contributor or supporter may receive if the bill becomes law. At the very least, there should be an attached contributor or supporter list that shows the top 50 entities that support that candidate, and includes names, addresses, phone numbers, and the amount spent on this campaign, as well as on previous campaigns going back at least ten years. This disclosure will help educate the public and keep our officials in line.

For instance, if Bob Dole sponsors or attempts to push through a bill that affects Archer Daniels Midland, a huge agricultural corporation, he must disclose on the form that he has received over $200,000 in financial support from them over the years.

Or, if Bill Clinton lobbies for a bill to suppress legal reform, he must disclose his relationships with the law firms that have contributed to him over the years, during his political career in Arkansas and Washington.

End All Devious Voting Schemes

All votes must be made public record. No *voice votes* or other tactics shall be used to avoid the responsibility of a vote.

Over the years, politicians have found numerous ways to avoid being recognized for an unpopular vote. One way is by a voice vote that is not placed on official record. In that way, no politician takes the credit or the blame for voting for a wasteful bill.

Another way for Congress to hide a vote is to have the bureaucrats in committee vote bill into law, and to have staff write the law the bureaucrats are voting for. Since the Congressmen don't have their hands on the bill, or the vote, they can distance themselves from it and appear not to be responsible for it. Yet, when we are damaged by the contents of an ill-founded bill, we must go to our representative for help or for a favor. When they help us out of our jam, we are often so grateful that we vote for them the next time around. So, the strategy is to bury people with laws that get them into trouble, so they need the "help" of the politician. This is a sad, but effective way of maintaining power over a grateful constituency.

Conference Committee

Conference committee is another way Congress avoids voting for unpopular programs. Conference committees, which usually operate behind closed doors, are groups of congressmen who are responsible for working out the differences between the House and Senate versions of a bill. Even though the House and Senate may approve a bill in public, the conference committee can negotiate away items they couldn't vote against in public. As was discussed before, a vote in Congress to reject $700 million in spending on an outdated Navy ship was overturned in conference later that night. So, even though those in Congress got credit for the right vote by rejecting a pork-barrel spending bill, the bill was approved anyway, costing us taxpayers an extra $700 million.

Another example of a conference "override" took place in 1989, when the Senate voted 83-8 to cut almost $100 million from Congress's franking, with the savings going to drug treatment for pregnant women (the "Wilson Amendment"). The House voted 245-137 for the amendment, but conferees overturned the vote just a few hours later in private. Thus, although the politicians were on record with a popular vote, they continued to receive their franking by sleight of hand.

One more way for Congress to avoid voting on unpopular bills is to use *automatic votes*. For instance, Rule XLIX automatically raises the debt ceiling when Congress continues to overspend. Since overspending and the required raising of the debt ceiling are unpopular, the House need not vote on its raising, and is therefore not accountable for the overspending. Instead of just eliminating Rule XLIX, we should find out *which* politician initiated it, and make it known publicly who was responsible for the trickery and deceit that Rule XLIX was designed for.

The "It's Not Perfect" Pretense

Another reason the public cannot trust and believe politicians is that politicians are unlikely to reform themselves unless they are forced to do so, or until the public gets involved. There have been any number of bills sponsored that would help reform some of the questionable practices and deception in Congress. Those bills are rarely passed, however, because other members who want to maintain politics as usual will come up with numerous arguments to defeat the bill. The most insincere argument is, "There is no way I can vote for this bill, because there are still too many loopholes." In other words, politicians reject reform using the pretense that, until the bill is perfect and complete, they won't vote for it.

Following are some examples of Congressional reform bills that have been sponsored by members of Congress, and where they are today.

Truth in Voting

The minimum in reform needed is what is called the "Truth in Voting" legislation, outlined by Representative Mike Crapo (R-ID). This bill, originally named H.R. 3633 when first introduced November 22, 1993, and then renamed H.R. 215 when introduced again January 4, 1995, attempts to cut out a significant amount of the trickery and deception politicians have used to fool us. Some of the provisions include:

(1) No proxy or absentee voting for any measure whatsoever.

(2) Open committee meetings, except for matters of national security.

This would override a clause that said, "The closed committee meeting is a privilege made available by the House..." *Why members of the House deserve a "privilege" to transact our business behind our back in the first place cannot be explained.*

(3) The Freedom of Information Act should apply to Congress, to the same extent that Executive agencies are subject to it.

(4) The repeal of the aforementioned Rule XLIX.

(5) Conference committees. "Their report shall not

fund any program, project, or activity at a level higher than that contained in the bill or resolution as passed the House or as passed the Senate, and committed to the conference committee, or fund any program, project, or activity not contained in that bill or resolution as passed the House or as passed the Senate." *This takes away some of the deception that conference committees and the Congress have used on taxpayers for years.*

(6) Economic and Employment Impact Statements

(a) Preparation. The Comptroller General of the United States shall prepare an economic and employment impact statement, as described in subsection (b), to accompany each bill, resolution, or conference report reported by any committee of the House of Representatives or the Senate or considered on the floor of either house.

(b) Contents. The economic and employment impact statement required by subsection (a) shall...

(1) state the extent to which enactment of the bill, resolution, or conference report would result in increased costs to the private sector, individuals, or state and local governments; and

(2) include, at a minimum, a detailed assessment of the annual impact of the bill, resolution, or conference report (projected annually over a 5-year period from its effective date, and, to the extent feasible, expressed in each case in monetary terms) on. . .

(A) costs to United States consumers;

(B) costs to United States business;

(C) national employment;

(D) the ability of United States industries to compete internationally;

(E) affected state and local governments, fiscal and otherwise;

(F) outlays and revenues by the federal government as compared to outlays and revenues for the same activity in the current fiscal year (as reported by the Congressional Budget Office); and

(G) impact on gross domestic product.

(c) Exception. The above isn't necessary if preliminary analysis indicates that the aggregate effect of the bill, resolution, or conference report as measured by the criteria set forth...is less than $100,000 or 1,000 jobs in national employment.

The threshold should be reduced to 10% of the proposed numbers. It's too convenient for a politician to circumvent the design of this provision by spending almost $100,000, or affecting almost 1,000 jobs; both of which are significant numbers.

(d) Statement With All Legislation. The economic and employment impact statement required by this section shall accompany each bill, resolution, or conference report before such bill, resolution, or conference report may be reported or otherwise considered on the floor of either house.

What has happened to this bill, which attempts to reform Congress in ways that few members have attempted in the past? Apparently there is legislation more urgent than self-reform in Congress. The bill, as of the first quarter of 1996, is lost in space, in three separate committees: the Budget Committee; the Rules Committee (reassigned to the subcommittee on rules and organization of the House); and the Government Reform and Oversight Committee (reassigned to the subcommittee on government management). There have been no votes or affirmative action on this bill for over a year, even though it would go a long way towards bringing some credibility back to our elected officials.

Citizen Congress Act

Another attempt at congressional reform, first introduced November 8, 1995, was made by Senator Frist. This bill, entitled the "Citizen Congress Act," aspires to enhance disclosure rules, and change those things done in

Washington that give Congress many unfair benefits. Following are some provisions in the bill:

> (1) Makes members of Congress (Members) ineligible to participate in the Civil Service Retirement System (CSRS) or the Federal Employees' Retirement System (FERS) except as otherwise provided under this Act.
>
> (2) Allows Members to participate in the Thrift Savings Plan at any time during the 12-year period beginning on the date the Member begins his or her first term. Permits refunds to be made in accordance with otherwise applicable law on account of an individual becoming ineligible to participate in CSRS or FERS as a result of this Act's enactment (provides that, for purposes of any such refund, a Member who becomes ineligible to participate in either of the retirement systems shall be treated as if separated from service).
>
> (3) Amends the Legislative Branch Appropriations Act of 1965 to provide for the disclosure of information necessary to enable the public to accurately compute the federal retirement benefits of each Member based on various assumptions of years of service and age of separation from service by reason of retirement.
>
> (4) Eliminates for Members automatic: (1) annuity cost-of-living adjustments; and (2) pay adjustments under the Legislative Reorganization Act of 1946.
>
> (5) Requires a roll call vote for any matter relating to congressional pay.

(6) Permits any travel award that accrues by reason of official travel of a house member, officer, or employee to be used only for official travel.

(7) Expresses the intent of the Congress that a Member or Member-elect may not mail any mass mailing as franked mail.

(8) Prohibits a Member from receiving transportation in an aircraft of the Military Air Command unless: (a) the transportation is provided on a space-available basis as part of the aircraft's scheduled operations; (b) the use of the aircraft is necessary because the Member's destination or an airfield located within reasonable distance thereof is inaccessible by regularly scheduled flights of commercial aircraft; or (c) such use is the least expensive method for the Member to reach the destination by aircraft.

(9) Bars a Member from receiving medical or dental care in a facility of any uniformed service unless: (a) such Member is eligible or entitled to such care as a member or former member of a uniformed service or as a covered beneficiary; or (b) such care is provided on an emergency basis unrelated to the person's status as a Member.

(10) Prohibits the Metropolitan Washington Airports Authority from providing reserved parking areas free of charge to Members, other government officials, or diplomats at Washington National Airport or Washington Dulles International Airport. Directs such Authority to estab-

> lish a parking policy for such airports that provides equal access to the public and does not provide preferential parking privileges to such individuals.

Where is this bill now? As of the first quarter of 1996, there was no action on the bill. It has been pushed aside for ostensibly more important legislative activity, such as spending our money, and reelection activities.

Limit Franking Privileges

The franking privilege, now costing us about $100 million a year, has been abused by Congress for years. It's another one of those special privileges lawmakers gave themselves to hold one more unfair advantage over potential challengers, and to solidify their stay in office for as long as possible.

As the original intent of franking was stated, politicians were to use free mailings for essential government business. This meant it was to be used to respond to their constituents' individual requests for information, to solve problems, or to disseminate informational material when needed. In fact, only 8% of the franked mail sent out is in response to such constituent requests. Franking was not intended to be an incumbent perk, nor to be used for mass mailings during election years. However, over time, politicians have found ways to distribute information not specifically asked for to their whole constituency, adding their own propaganda to help solidify their approval rating with the voters.

If politicians can't be trusted to limit franked mail to specific requests by individual constituents as originally intended, then the privilege should be taken from them. In fact, based upon the above analysis of its abuse, that's not such a bad idea. If franked mailing *was* taken away, these offices would spend only $8.00 for every $100.00 that they once spent of our money previously. That's a pretty good return on our investment, isn't it?

No Lifetime Appointees

The president has the power to choose Supreme Court judges, who hold some of the most powerful positions in the country. These people are given their positions for life, which means that once they're appointed, they can't be fired. The arguments for lifetime appointees are tenuous at best. These appointments give a president influence over lawmaking long after he has left office. It has also been argued that Supreme Court judges have on occasion revised the interpretation of the Constitution. This lifetime appointment allows a Supreme Court judge to wield power and authority that few contemplated when our founding fathers designed the Constitution.

Why a president would command this authority is beyond me. These judges should be voted in like other government officials. After all, we the people want some control over who is writing and rewriting our laws. No one person, not even the president, should have such domination over us.

GUIDELINES FOR CHOOSING A CANDIDATE

The solution starts with a well-educated public; one that is able to elect responsible, honest representatives, and that can see through the tricks and lies of disreputable candidates. The challenge is knowing *who* to elect.

Choosing politicians to represent you and your country is no different from the analogy given in the first chapter, where the business owner is choosing someone to run *his* business. You, as a citizen of the United States, are the owner of this country, and must make careful decisions regarding *who* will make the laws and *how* your representatives will spend your money.

As you consider the various applicants, you should find a person who:

(1) Has had actual experience in running a business or organization profitably, with the responsibility of staying within certain well-defined budgets.

(2) Has a demonstrated track record of fiscal responsibility, instead of a history of frivolous spending.

(3) States *specific* ideas about improving the country, instead of speaking vaguely in magnificent sound bites.

(4) Has a history of honesty, integrity, and truthfulness, and answers questions directly and honestly. A person whose history is one of documented lying has no respect for you, and won't represent your interests, regardless of promises made.

(5) Doesn't avoid answering specific questions that are important to you. If a candidate hasn't given satisfactory answers to relevant questions, you won't be able to make informed decisions.

(6) Honestly and completely answers all relevant questions posed to him, rather than depending on his appearance, charisma, or eloquence.

(7) Doesn't expect you to "trust him" when he says something, but encourages you to check out his answers by giving you easy access to references and documentation.

Following the above model will take you a long way towards choosing a candidate who will truly represent you, and will eliminate many "con men" who want to hold office for reasons other than serious, honest representation.

A CONTRACT WITH AMERICANS

Each elected official, and every government employee, should sign a Contract with Americans as follows on the next page. Many of the items in *this* contract are similar to the Code of Ethics that have been in place for years (see appendix).

CONTRACT WITH AMERICANS

I,____________________ (fill in your name here), do solemnly swear to uphold the laws of the United States of America, and of the Constitution of the United States of America. I understand that I am acting as a fiduciary of the citizens of the United States and, as such, I have authority and responsibility that I will never abuse or take for granted. Therefore, I promise:

(1) To honestly represent the people of the United States.

(2) To never lie to the people of the United States.

(3) To never to sponsor, promote, or vote for a law, bill, or amendment which will knowingly waste taxpayers' money.

(4) To never to put my personal interests, or those of my relatives, friends, financial backers, contributors, supporters, or special interests ahead of the broader interests of the citizens of the United States of America.

(5) To never to handle any dealings affecting the nation or its people behind closed doors, unless such privacy is necessary for national security.

(6) To never to profit from my office, other than by earned salary and benefits, by receiving gifts of any size or manner prior to coming into office, while in office, or after leaving office; and to report in writing to the proper authorities, anyone who offers me such illegal gifts.

(7) To return to the government any and all unused campaign contributions and funding at the end of my term in office, which will be used towards paying down the national debt.

(8) To fill out a quarterly report that details the work I have done and the votes I have made on specified bills, so the voters can see that I am diligently following through on the promises that I made to them.

(9) To never distribute any false or misleading infor-

mation to the public, either during a political campaign or while in public office.

(10) To take personal responsibility for the breach of any promises I make to the citizens of the United States; and to strive towards seeking, speaking, and demanding the truth in governing the country, and in politics.

(11) To never to take advantage of loopholes to circumvent promises made to the American public.

(12) To do my best to find ways to run the country as efficiently and economically as possible.

Should I break any of the promises described herein, I understand that I will be severely punished for such actions, and agree:

(1) To forfeit my office as soon as possible, and with it all perks, salary, and accumulated pension earned.

(2) To never become eligible for another public office which is paid for by tax dollars.

(3) To be prohibited from any lobbying activities, or any other compensated activities, that result in government or political influence.

(4) To be subject to any other penalty or punishment according to the laws of the United States.

Sworn and signed this _____ day of ___________, 19__.

By: ________________________________

Will the current pedigree of politicians balk at signing the above Contract with Americans? You bet. They will become indignant, and look upon this as an insult to their integrity.

But Congress has attempted "self-reform" for years, and things haven't changed. They've had their chance. Now it is our turn to reform Congress and politics as we know it. Just as we need laws to punish criminals and combat crime, we need laws, rules, and punishments to enforce discipline in government.

Politicians may scoff at the idea of being forced to sign a contract such as the one suggested here. However, if a politician intends to honestly perform his duties as outlined in the contract, why would he hesitate to put that promise in writing? Just because politicians have enjoyed a free ride all these years doesn't mean that we don't have an inherent right, as their bosses, to expect them to sign a "letter of employment."

And for those of you who feel that making a pledge to the citizens of the United States like the one above is beneath you, hear this. If you don't feel that a civil servant should put his promises in writing, or if you aren't satisfied with a more reasonable compensation package than the one you now receive, I propose that you find a career that treats you more equitably. In a nation of 263 million talented people, we could find able replacements for everyone in government.

SPECIFIC SOLUTIONS FOR SPECIFIC PROBLEMS

Following are a number of specific problems with excessive government spending that have realistic solutions. Further solutions to government spending can be found in suggested reading by Martin Gross, and the Congressional Record. See the appendix for further details.

For pork-barrel spending and similar abuse:

"Pass a house rule that no member of a committee, especially an appropriation committee, can use a bill to authorize any additional monies for his district, or for the district of any member of the same committee." (Gross)

Violators of the letter of this rule, along with that of any rule passed to regulate Congress, should be fined, dismissed, and have their pension eradicated.

For lying to the press, or going after whistle blowers (those who expose government abuses):

"The Inspector General should recommend their firing, and publicly expose lies and liars for what they are." (Gross)

Hidden spending

All spending must be appropriated, in full view and scrutiny of the public, and the individual responsible for signing on the spending must be responsible for same.

Consultants, costing \$3 - \$5 billion per year:

"...should easily be reduced to no more than \$1 billion per year." (Gross)

"Travel spending of \$7 billion per year" (Gross)

Using commercial flights instead of private government jets, being fiscally responsible, and showing a supervisor, in advance of the trip, why the trip is necessary and why government should pay for it, could most likely save \$5 billion in travel costs.

"Outdated and useless federal agencies" (Gross)

Immediately get rid of all obsolete agencies, as well as those that duplicate the work of other agencies, or those that serve no significant useful purpose other than keeping bureaucrats at work.

"Close down the Economic Development Administration" (Gross)

Formed in 1966 to help those poor areas in the country with the highest unemployment, it now is a tremendous source of pork. Most communities now qualify, even those with lower unemployment, and its annual budget of \$230 million produces few jobs.

"Interstate Commerce Commission" (Gross)

The ICC once regulated railroads, trucks, barges, buses, etc. But now these forms of transportation are completely deregulated, so we can save the $53 million that is spent annually on this agency.

"Legislative Service Organizations "LSO's" (Gross)

28 various legislative groups get together for meetings, luncheons, and parties, and spend $5 million each year of our tax dollars. This must be halted immediately.

"Community Development Block Grant" (Gross)

This was to be used by cities to help the poor. But misuse and fraud is prevalent. Most of the money isn't going to help the poor who need it, so the $4 billion would more effectively be used to reduce the deficit.

"Helium Reserve" (Gross)

Here is a project that serves no useful purpose and costs taxpayers $100 million per year. There is no shortage of helium, and the United States should not be in the helium business.

"Federal Advisory Commissions" (Gross)

There are as many as 700 different groups created by the White House and Congress to advise the government on any and all topics, from animals to public diplomacy. At $150 million per year, these organizations include such wasteful and frivolous groups as the U.S. Board of Tea Experts, one for a Dictionary of Occupational Titles, etc.

"Unfunded Mandates" (Gross)

The federal government sets laws that the states and local government must adhere to and enforce, without giving the states any financial assistance. Washington uses this sleazy method to avoid raising additional tax revenue, so the regrettable task is forced onto the states and local government. These unfunded mandates are costly, amounting to almost $600 billion in 1993 alone. This represents almost $5,000 per household. When this sum is added to the taxes we pay and Congress's deficit spending, we are paying a total tax rate of over 53%. Here are some examples of the inequity and deficiency of unfunded mandates taken from the 1995 Congressional Record:

> The city of Lubbock, with a population of 190,000, is located in an arid area. It receives less than 20 inches of rain a year. Here are two examples of the problems they are having:
>
> Subtitle D regulations, governing landfills, require landfills to have, among other things, clay liners to protect from ground water contamination. Because it is an arid area, there is little threat of groundwater contamination due to rains which might cause landfill leaching. Over the next 8 months, it is going to cost Lubbock $500,000 for a clay liner for one cell in the landfill. It is being paid for by an increase in garbage rates.
>
> The Clean Water Act requires municipalities with a population of 100,000 or more to obtain National Pollutant Discharge Elimination System (NPDES) permits. Due to staff limitations, and the real need to conduct other city business, to meet the deadline for submitting the permit application Lubbock had to spend $750,000 to contract an outside consultant to prepare the voluminous documentation required for a permit application. Once the permit is issued, they can expect additional compliance costs of between $500,000 and $900,000.
>
> In April 1990, and again in December 1991, the city of Brownwood experienced floods. Brownwood is in the area where it is only expected to flood once every 100 years. The EPA, under its effluent discharge regulations, requires storm

water treatment plants to make plans to upgrade when they reach 75 percent of capacity, and be under construction to upgrade when plants reach 95 percent of capacity. Because of the back-to-back floods, Brownwood exceeded 95 percent of plant capacity for three months in a row. That's how the EPA makes its determination that additional construction is necessary--exceeding 95 percent of capacity for three months in a row, regardless of natural disasters, such as floods.

Brownwood is being required to spend $8.1 million to accomplish this. This is on top of the $2.5 million spent in 1982 and the $3.6 million spent in 1986 to upgrade the plant. Brownwood is still paying debt service on the 1982 and 1986 construction. On subtitle D landfill regulations, Brownwood is required to be bonded for $300,000 per landfill cell for a 30-year period.

Over the next five years, the citizens of Brownwood will spend $7.2 million to comply with landfill regulations. To accomplish this, landfill use rates will increase 28 percent this year, an additional 28 percent in 1994, and another 10 percent in 1995. Sewer charges will increase 17 percent this year and another 17 percent next year. Brownwood city officials estimate that 37.5 percent of the budget for the water department, the sewer department, and the landfill is directly related to unfunded federal mandates. Brownwood has a population of 18,300.

Abilene is spending $1 million for a clay liner for their landfill. Abilene has clay soil and no problem with leaching.

College Station is being required to set aside $500,000 per year for 13 years to assure that the landfill will be covered when it is no longer in use.

In Odessa, 18 percent of the $65.7 million 1994 budget is allocated to pay for unfunded state-and federal-mandated projects. Perhaps one of the most costly items is the $1.2 million that the city must spend to install a clay liner and monitoring wells at the municipal landfill in order to comply with tough environmental regulations.

In order to meet its EPA-mandated water requirements, San Antonio tacked $1.99 per month onto every household water bill and hundreds per month onto every commercial water bill. To effect the increase, the city council of San Antonio had to pass a bill, which it appropriately titled, "The Federal Storm Water Fee." Of the ten most costly unfunded mandates, eight deal with environmental matters. This is what these mandates cost some selected Texas cities:

Town	**Cost**	**Population**
Amarillo	$27,092,500	157,615
Bryan	984,284	55,002
Plano	6,642,015	149,188
Nacogdoches	1,257,564	30,872
Waco	2,894,039	7,000
Lubbock	11,199,789	186,206
Brownsville	1,633,435	102,000
Corpus Christi	5,674,303	273,677
Grand Prairie	4,263,036	102,557
San Marcos	1,266,133	28,173

These towns are put in the position of paying for unfunded federal mandates while sacrificing the things they want and need most: local police and fire protection, schools, and the like.

States and municipalities must be given the flexibility to ensure good environmental quality through rational, logical, and affordable approaches. There must be a way to address legitimate environmental concerns without bankrupting our towns and cities. S.993 goes a long way toward doing that.

New York City isn't left out of the unfunded mandate boondoggle. A few of the recent mandates on the taxpayers of New York include:

(1) $400,000 a year to wash jail windows four times a year
(2) $175,000 a year for newspapers for inmates of city jails
(3) $300 million to make jail meals warmer

Finally, although not a mandate, it is estimated that New York has as many as 400,000 illegal aliens within its borders, thanks to the inability of the United States to effectively patrol and secure its borders.

Washington continues to inflict these unfunded mandates on us, despite the fact that it is unconstitutional, per the Tenth Amendment to the Constitution, the last item in the Bill of Rights, ratified on December 15, 1791. The Tenth Amendment states:

"The powers not delegated to the United States by the Constitution, nor prohibited by it to the states, are reserved to the states respectively, or to the people."

Our founding fathers didn't want the federal government to become too powerful and oppressive by giving them dictatorial lawmaking authority. However, the federal government has clearly ignored the Tenth Amendment. Washington thrives on power, and the more power we let Washington seize, the more it will take.

Regulations

As of 1993, the total number of federal employees assigned to issuing and enforcing federal regulations reached an all-time high of 128,615. The federal government spent over $14 billion in 1993, another all-time high, to carry out all the regulatory programs. This must be President Clinton's way of reducing the size of government. "The era of big government is over," he says.

"The Department of Education" (Gross)

One of our most embarrassing sources of waste, with its annual budget of $31 billion, is producing little or no benefit. Begun in 1979 by Jimmy Carter, the Department of Education was created with the stated purpose of improving the educational system in America. Records show that the quality of education of our young has deteriorated at an alarming rate since the introduction of the Department of Education.

For example, the D of E spends $130 million per year on research and statistics, which hasn't helped anyone's education, and spends another $60 million a year on outside consultants.

Eliminating the $31 billion per year being spent on the incompetent Department of Education would go a long way towards helping balance our budget.

The Department of Energy

As discussed previously, this department has so much money that Hazel O'Leary, its chief, can spend millions of dollars traveling with an entourage of dozens of people at taxpayer expense. There is so much excess money in the Department of Energy that, even faced with the facts of Ms. O'Leary's spending, Vice President Gore continued to sing her praises on national television. The Vice President points to the effectiveness of the travel, without acknowledging that it could have been handled more efficiently. Just more examples of partisanship, and a Washington spending culture.

Local Government

Local governments have many advantages over the

federal government. Local people, with more intimate knowledge of the people in their area, should be better able to run most programs as needed. Because of the vast size and differences between one community and another throughout the country, it is not reasonable for the federal government to use a cookie-cutter approach, and run each community the same as the other.

However, local government has observed the model of the federal government, and has selfishly decided to become bloated and dictatorial as well.

The cost of local government has gone up 350% in real dollars since 1960. Since 1980, the number of local government employees has increased by 3.5 million people, even though the actual population of the states hasn't increased much at all!

In many cases, local bureaucrats are just as power-hungry as their peers in Washington. Many communities attempt to control all aspects of capitalism in order to flaunt their imagined power. Developers attempting to build in a community typically must bribe the local community with additional green space, ponds, money for schools, expensive sewage revamping, acreage for parks, etc. They must adhere to the orders of various traffic and safety commissions, consisting of people with little or no experience related to traffic engineering or development.

Developers must adhere to the demands of appearance committees who dictate that a developer do it "their way or no way"; i.e., size of signs and type of letters to be used, exterior colors to be used on the buildings, etc. Developers must adhere to the rules of zoning committees, made up of local residents, which tell the developers what is best for the site, how much parking is necessary, and what type of tenants are best for the space once it is built.

All this government control is necessary, in spite of the fact that it is the *developer* who has the experience. It is the *developer* who is building a project that will add tax revenue and jobs to the community. It is the *developer* who is putting his reputation on the line to build a quality project. It is the *developer* who must risk his net worth, and in many cases his whole livelihood, on a project. And yet power-hungry people, with little or no expertise regarding development, can single-handedly put the developer out of business with their misguided "suggestions."

What happens when the developer complies with the local regulators, and builds according to the whims of those in charge? What happens if the project is no longer economically feasible, if the developer loses his shirt, and if he and his family must go bankrupt? What happens to the local bureaucrats who knew better? You can bet they will find some rationale to blame the failed project on the *developer*, and then go on to the next issue de jour.

"State spending has continued to rise at alarming rates." In 1960, state budgets took only 4% of the gross domestic product. In 1970, state budgets took 7% of the GDP.

Now, state budgets have risen to 9% of the GDP, or over half a trillion dollars. In fairness to the state spending, let's acknowledge that this includes a huge amount of unfunded mandates the federal government has compelled the states to fund.

As of 1993, there were over 86,000 local governments, consisting of over 3,000 counties, 19,000 municipalities, 16,000 townships, 33,000 special districts (from pool to day-care centers), and 16,000 school and related districts, many of which are duplicated.

It is suggested (by Martin Gross) that an entire layer of bureaucracy, counties, could be eliminated. In fact, there is evidence that counties are not necessary. Two states, Connecticut and Rhode Island, have no counties whatsoever, and therefore no county budget. The 3,043 county governments in the United States have over 2.3 million employees, with total budgets of $150 billion.

Based upon the examples of Connecticut and Rhode

Island, it is feasible that many counties, if not all, could be eliminated at a taxpayer savings of approximately $150 billion per year.

Mr. Gross's solution to reduce the cost of state and local government follows:

> (1) Pass the Condit Bill and make all unfunded federal mandates illegal.
> (2) In the case of shared mandates, like Medicaid, states should be given the right to not accept any part of the federal aid and still keep those parts they want.
> (3) All the states should eliminate all of their counties.
> (4) Eliminate 5 million of the 16 million state and local government employees through attrition. By rehiring 20% of those who leave, die, or retire, the reduction can become a reality in a six-year term.

How heartless and cruel is this? Remember, we're not suggesting that anyone gets fired, we're just talking about those positions that are vacated for reasons other than firing. And the feasibility of replacing those people with just one-fifth of the workforce is realistic. After all, how many "nonessential" government workers did we discover when Congress was fighting over the balanced budget in 1995 and 1996? When you and I go into debt, aren't *we* required to eliminate some nonessential spending?

To handle each major U.S. problem, we should get a volunteer task force of experts in that field, not politicians, not paid political consultants, patrons, etc. There are many talented people who will be glad to volunteer their time for the good of their country, once they see that the government is working for them once again.

CHAPTER 12

DEBT IS A FOUR-LETTER WORD

A BALANCED BUDGET THAT WILL REALLY WORK

Promises for a balanced budget, from both sides of the aisle, are disappointing at best. The representation that the parties have made cuts of over half a trillion dollars to reach a real balanced budget is disingenuous at best, and deceitful at worst. Anyone paying attention to the fight between the two parties, and the sketchy details received through the media, can see by the way negotiations are going that a *real* balanced budget is not in the works. Again, the smart money is on those who feel there will be no balanced budget in fiscal year 2002. Why are we skeptical?

What is being discussed are proposed cuts in spending in some areas. But much of the "balancing act" relies on a healthier economy for the next seven years, with increased government spending and a plan for increased tax revenue. Note that over the seven-year period, most of the discretionary spending, which represents over $300 billion a year, isn't projected for cuts, or savings, until the last two years of the budget. By pushing the pain as far away as possible, a reelected President Clinton would receiving credit for a so-called balanced budget signed today, and would be gone long before any of the supposed cuts occur.

What the President and most politicians don't realize is that we aren't excited about a balanced budget being "signed." We will be excited about a balanced budget when it takes place. There is a difference. Fewer and fewer people get excited when a politician makes promises. Too many promises have been broken over the years for us to be able to count on what a politician says. We now know the difference between a promise and the follow-up action needed for the event to occur.

Another Analogy - The Balanced Budget

There's a right way and wrong way to achieve a balanced budget.

Suppose you are the owner of a business which began losing money. For a seven-year budget plan, you receive three proposals: one from your controller, one from your vice president of operations, and one from your brother-in-law. All you know for sure is that unless you lower your expenses by at least 58% over the next seven years, you will be bankrupt.

The controller suggests that you begin to cut all variable expenses, including salaries and overhead, by 3% per year in order to reduce your losses and become profitable again. This, he says, will reduce expenses in real terms by 58%. The reasoning is that, in addition to an annual 3% cut, there would no longer be the budgeted inflation increase of 3% per year. Thus, the effective cut of 6% per year over the expenses normally budgeted would result in overall expense cuts of 58%. Assuming conservatively that there is no growth of revenues over that period, the goal is met.

The vice president proposes the same amount of cuts, or 58% over the next seven years. The difference in his plan is that he will raise expenses by only 1% per year for the first five years (a 2% per year savings over the previously budgeted inflation level of 3%), and will chop expenses by 22% in each of the last two years in order to achieve the same 58% reduction. He too, is conservatively assuming no revenue growth during the seven-year period.

Your brother-in-law feels a reduction in expenses isn't

necessary at all. In fact, because of inflation and the strength of the economy and your industry, you will be just fine if you maintain your spending at the planned inflation increases. According to his calculations and projections, there will be a decided increase in revenue that will increase profits and make a cut unnecessary. Instead of reducing expenses by 58%, he expects to take care of planned expense increases by the revenue generated over the next seven years.

As the owner of the business, you must decide which plan will realistically keep you in business. The easiest solution, your brother-in-law's plan, is to make no cuts and let projected economic growth take care of future income and expense problems. Unfortunately, who can look into the future and confidently determine that the next seven years will see guaranteed economic growth?

The next easiest solution would be to follow your vice president's plan for the first five years by increasing the budget by 1% per year, instead of the 3% per year projected. But there is no feasible or realistic way to slash 22% from expenses in any one year in order to achieve the stated goal.

Thus, you realize that the only realistic approach is to make steady cuts. This is more readily achievable than a deep cut in years six and seven, and is more of a "sure thing" than your brother-in-law's plan to let inflation and projected increased revenue take care of the problem. Since you can't take a chance on bankruptcy, you decide to go with the controller's steady, most realistic plan.

SO WHAT'S THE POINT TO THIS ANALOGY? The point is that a balanced budget will never occur as long as politicians are afraid to cut spending in enough programs to effectively balance the budget.

There are many people who insist that we can't afford any cuts, and that the resulting pain that will occur with the spending cuts isn't really necessary. They insist that the budget cuts, projected growth, and increased tax revenue generated by the growth will take care of some of the extra spending that is projected.

ONCE AGAIN, is this a prudent way to run the government or balance a checkbook? The idea that we will be able to count on growth to fund our spending projects is questionable, at best. The idea that we will be able to cut spending by over 20% in each of the last two years of the seven-year term, when we aren't able to make a miniscule 3% cut any year for the first five years, is not only a misrepresentation of the facts, but an insult to the intelligence of every rational, thoughtful person in the United States.

The politicians who are afraid of an unpopular cut now are perpetrating a fraud against the citizens of the United States. It makes no sense to be afraid of possible pain at this time, considering the following areas where savings can reasonably be accomplished.

•There are hundreds, maybe thousands, of documented examples that show where we can save hundreds of billions of dollars per year in waste, failed programs, fraud, abuse, and pork-barrel spending.

•There are just as many examples of areas where we can eliminate bloated staff, offices, outdated programs, etc.

•There is natural attrition in the government bureaucracy when people retire, move, pass away, or take a different position in the private sector. In fact, just by rehiring only 20% of those positions that are vacated, we can eliminate almost a third of the government workforce over a six-year period, without firing anyone or putting anyone on welfare. And those government workers who remain will not only have greater responsibility, but will be more valuable, thus increasing their job security.

Finally, what happens if the government becomes more efficient, and we cut government spending to the point that there is actually a tax surplus? Two things will happen. First of all, we can use part of that surplus to reduce the national debt, which would help improve life for our children and grandchildren. Second, we can reduce taxes and put more money into the hands of the real producers, the citizens of the United States.

Most important, however, is to recognize the ongoing pain that is a result of the lack of guts of those politicians who are obviously too afraid of losing votes to make tough decisions. How much longer can they expect to spend at these deficit levels without taxpayers finally reaching a breaking point? The consequences of this deficit spending are enormous, as can be seen in the question and answer chapter regarding the balanced budget, near the end of the book. The annual interest on the debt, now over $330 billion, is a large price to pay for a politicians' reelection concerns. As we discussed earlier, even if the budget is balanced within the next seven years, it will still cost us over $16 TRILLION to repay the debt, including interest, over the next 40 years. Thank you, Washington!

The TRUTH is those individuals who rationalize or defend the deficit and the national debt are not leaders, and don't deserve anyone's support. They are gutless individuals who don't give a damn about the future of our children, our grandchildren, or our country. Those people are not worthy to be our leaders, and certainly should not be telling other people how to live. In fact, those politicians are just the people who need someone with a realistic vision of the future to tell *them* what to do!

Soooo... how do politicians seriously work on cutting government and balancing the budget? Here is an 8-step program:

8 STEPS TO A BALANCED BUDGET

(1) Immediate cut of fat, pork, unnecessary and outdated programs.

Identify the top 535 wasteful spending programs in

government, and give each congressman (both House and Senate) the responsibility of studying one program, examining its viability, and finding ways to eliminate or cut it to its most efficient level. Each congressman has a vast staff, some of whom could be kept busy working to cut or reduce said program, instead of on their congressman's reelection activities. After all, since we taxpayers are ultimately paying the salaries and other expenses of these bloated staffs, they should be working for us. We shouldn't be paying them to work on having their incumbent reelected.

Once the congressman completes the study and makes his recommendations to Congress, there should be swift and immediate follow-through on those suggestions. All hearings and recommendations should, of course, be held in public. If the congressman is unwilling or unable to make the necessary cuts, action should be taken to find out why, and the public should be informed that the politician has been ineffective when it comes to cutting a spending program with fat in it.

After the congressman completes the necessary study and cutting of the program assigned, he should be given another program to work on.

If this program isn't the most useful way a congressman can spend his time, I don't know what is.

(2) Re-evaluation of existing programs, including all entitlements.

Using the same model as above, have a known critic in Congress become responsible for cutting or eliminating a specific entitlement program, until each congressman has a program to work on. There are dozens of bloated entitlements, and a number of creative ways to slow down or eliminate the waste and fraud in these programs that cost billions of dollars each year. For instance, research has been done on the waste and fraud in Medicare. Without cutting Medicare benefits for those legitimately entitled to the program, billions of dollars can be saved just by following the lead of those non-partisan think tanks and groups who have studied the inefficiencies of Medicare. We don't need closed-door committees; we need dependable people who are sincerely interested in solving the problem.

(3) No increase in spending without a 2/3 vote of both houses of Congress.

There should be an immediate amendment stating that no less than a 2/3 vote in both houses is required in order to increase spending beyond the current budget. The 50% level makes it too easy for the party in power to control spending, and to continue or begin pet projects that the public would not approve. In most instances, a 2/3 vote would require some approval of both parties, thus taking away some of the partisanship of the spending. This would make overspending much more difficult, and would force discipline on a Congress which has shown little self-control over the past 30 to 40 years.

In short, the advantage of the 2/3 vote is that we will no longer be held hostage to partisan politics, since a spending program will have to be agreeable to both parties in order for it to be approved.

(4) A real plan to repay the $5 - $6 trillion national debt (over 40 years?).

If we are fortunate enough to return honest representation to our government, and cut out Washington infringement and overspending, we will be able to effect a real plan. Not only will we be able to eliminate the deficit, but we can start paying down the national debt, which now stands at about $5 trillion and is expected to reach $6 trillion before we achieve a balanced budget. Until now, we've been paying only the interest on the debt, which is not unlike an expensive credit card debt that never goes away. The more interest we advance without attempting to pay down the principal, the more expensive the original borrowing becomes, since we are going a longer time with the debt in place.

Proponents of deficits and debt apparently aren't concerned about the additional billions of dollars of extra tax dollars hard-working American families must pay to support this negligent spending by the select few in Congress. Using debt numbers projected for the turn of the century, the cost to pay down the debt will be about $16.8, including over $10.8 trillion in interest, which is $16.8 trillion of additional tax dollars we must fund over the next 40 years. How much higher do they want to go?

Another possible way to repay the national debt is for the government to begin an aggressive campaign to sell off the assets of the United States that generate no revenue. For instance, it owns millions of acres of land; thousands of buildings; oil, mineral, and water rights; and thousands of vehicles, aircraft, and other equipment worth billions of dollars.

In addition to all the unused buildings the United States now owns, just think about how many more could be sold if the government downsized as discussed herein. If one-third of all government staff were cut over the next six years, thousands of additional buildings would become available.

It is estimated that these assets are worth over $10 trillion! An aggressive strategy to sell these assets over time could result in net revenue of approximately $500 billion per year. This money should be allocated solely for the purpose of paying down the national debt, and not for any spending programs or current deficit reduction. If this occurred, the national debt could be paid off in less than ten years, keeping intact the principal and interest plan discussed previously. The interest, projected to be over $10.8 trillion, would be reduced to $2.1 trillion, saving over *$8.7 trillion* in interest payments!

Why should we sell the assets of the United States? If you owed the bank money and couldn't afford the repayment, you would be forced to sell off some assets. Why should our children and grandchildren continue to pay over decades for the overspending and corruption of our present politicians, whom they never even elected? If you could save future generations over $421 billion in principal and interest payments each year, wouldn't you want to do so?

In fact, why should we or our elected officials have the right to saddle future generations with our irresponsible spending and poor choices? Our children didn't spend the money. They didn't vote for the politicians who spent the money. It shouldn't be their responsibility to pay the interest on our debt. Whoever suggests that we should leave our debt to our children is without conscience.

IT SHOULD BE ABSOLUTELY ILLEGAL FOR ONE GENERATION TO FORCE FUTURE GENERATIONS TO PAY THEIR BILLS

(5) Reform or eliminate lobbying activities.

There are many powerful lobbyists who exercise undue influence over the politicians who set the rules and laws of the land. If such power were just in the form of public debate, they should be protected by the First Amendment's freedom of speech provision. Unfortunately, most of the influence peddling and deal-making is not done in public. On the contrary, special interest group lobbyists have, in many cases, influenced the policy-makers with money for campaigns, PACs, and other forms of enticement. It's a difficult stretch of our imagination to believe that money doesn't influence the decision-making of politicians. And if it does, as is expected, it is a sad realization that those with the money to spend can bribe our officials in order to influence the laws.

Why is this issue so important? If a lobbyist who represents a defense contractor, for instance, contributes $100,000 to the campaign of the head of appropriations (or anyone in power, for that matter), he may be able to influence the decision-makers to order more arms from his client. This causes a double problem for the taxpayer: whether or not the arms in question are necessary, and whether or not we are overpaying for them.

Or what about the tobacco industry, which spend millions of dollars during each campaign, working hard to help elect those candidates who are most sympathetic to the "plight" of the tobacco industry? When the candidates are elected, they are expected to do favors for the lobbyists employed by those companies in return for their support during the election. The favors may include a bill supporting tobacco subsidies to farmers, lighter restrictions on the sale of cigarettes, lower sin taxes on the sale of tobacco, less restriction on advertising, etc.

The elimination of lobbyists is not practicable, since the First Amendment protects this activity. The only other solution is to find ways to reform lobbying to keep its practice as honest and ethical as possible. The most popular and practical reform available has to do with disclosure. Only with appropriate disclosure rules and regulations can the average citizen of the United States be assured that the activities and techniques of lobbyists for special interests are properly executed.

Over the years, disclosure propositions have come up for discussion, and have been just as quickly discarded by members of Congress. Now is the time for total disclosure. Until that takes place, Congress, lobbyists, special interests, and contributors will have their way when it comes to behind-the-scenes control of legislation. Any politician who votes against stringent and complete lobbying disclosure shows that he is not serious about reform, and is clearly trying to protect politics as usual.

Whatever lobbying reform is passed in Congress will not be as vigorous as it should be. Why? Because the more disclosure that is enforced, the fewer temptations will be sent their way. Reform of Congress really is not difficult.

However, it is made difficult by Congress. They must be seen as sincerely striving for reform by passing a bill, but they really want to draft the reform in such a way that it leaves them enough loopholes to be able to conduct business as usual. Again, this problem isn't limited to lobby reform, but it applies to every piece of legislation Congress must consider, whose ultimate effect is to limit power, authority, and perks to its rank and file.

(6) Campaign finance reform.

Only through meaningful and complete finance reform will the public actually get representative government. We must eliminate all schemes that politicians have established over the years to entrench themselves in office. Only when people can run on an even playing field will we truly attract folks who will make Congress accountable to the *public* interest and reject the powerful influence of *special* interests.

(7) Slash or eliminate the use of outside consultants.

The government spends billions of dollars a year on the use of outside consultants and professionals, with most of the spoils going to law firms. It's time to take advantage of the talented staff and employees of the government on all levels, and to reduce spending dramatically in this area. This is another one of those areas where, in too many instances, the well-connected firms or campaign contributors are handed the government largess. Maybe some pro bono (volunteer) work done by all the firms who have made millions off of the government over the past 20 years would be in order.

(8) Reform all government activities.

As the world's largest business, with a budget of over $2.6 trillion, the government is a target for a myriad of corrupt behaviors involving our leadership, other government employees, contractors, and vendors. Even though each government employee has a vested interest in the financial well-being of the government, many people erroneously believe that the government can afford their plundering, since it can just print more money or raise taxes to compensate for the unethical behavior.

Due in large part to the magnitude of our government, and the power and authority that it wields, our leaders are constantly tempted by special interests, lobbyists, and other unscrupulous parties to get their share of the pie. The only way to end this abuse that we all pay for is to reevaluate our checks and balances to make sure that the chosen few are no longer given that capability in the future.

(a) All spending must be signed off by an authorized signatory. That authorized signatory will be responsible and accountable as to the legality and ethical nature of any monies disbursed by his authority.

Any new proposed bills, laws, or regulations must include its benefits, costs, where the money to fund the program is coming from, and what the consequences of the proposal will be to any influenced parties.

Although a bill, regulation, or law may have co-sponsors, this tactic is sometimes used to deflect the accountability away from an individual. Any idea must begin with an individual, and that individual should be identified as the original sponsor of the bill, while others can be identified as co-sponsors. If someone doesn't want to be named the original sponsor of a bill, the bill should not be seriously considered.

(b) Cut congressional staffs.

The money saved in salaries and other costs of staffs would be relatively minimal in the scheme of the national budget. However, the significant effects of smaller staffs would go well beyond the immediate, obvious savings. For instance, if congressmen didn't have as many people to run errands for their supporters, constituents, and special interests, they wouldn't command as much power and partisan favoritism.

If the staffs were smaller, Congress would have less time to spend on the minutia, and more time to focus on major issues, like the budget, that need attention.

During the election process, staff handles reelection priorities. A smaller staff makes that advantage for the incumbent less meaningful.

A smaller staff would require less complicated regulations. As it is, many bills proposed are so extensive and sweeping that few legislators have the time or the inclination to read them entirely. How many lawmakers read the whole crime bill before voting on it? The smart money is on less than 5%.

How do congressional staffs get cut? Don't expect Congress to volunteer to do it. Even the Republicans, who consistently run on the plank of smaller government, make proposals that sound good, but barely scratch the surface. A couple of years ago, they proposed to cut 50% of the House committee staff. Even though this sounds like a large cut, the committee staff represents less than 10% of all congressional employees, making the overall cut less than 5%.

(c) Force lawmakers to stick to their job of legislating according to their "job description."

This means that Congress should focus on the issues of immediate import, such as education, government waste, and national security, instead of various "feel-good" programs that affect only specific interests. Congress has grabbed the power to oversee every aspect of our lives, and the sooner it is taken away from them, the better.

(d) Congressmen should not spend twelve months a year in Washington.

In fact, they should spend at least four months at home, living with their constituents. This is one way for them to stay in touch with the concerns of the public. Since Congress typically meets only three days a week, it should be easy them to switch to a five-day week and shorten their legislative year. The less time they spend together finding ways to spend our money, the more we will save.

As discussed previously, a major complaint about long-term politicians is that they lose touch with reality; therefore some of their legislation, although it may look good on paper, may not be feasible in real life. An example?

Take the Americans With Disabilities Act (ADA) of 1991. This was a noble idea to be sure. Congress wanted to ensure that individuals with disabilities had equal access to all public buildings. So, property owners of all public buildings were mandated to "renovate" their property, sometimes at backbreaking costs, in order to comply with the regulations. Renovations included building wheelchair ramps, widening doorways, enlarging and retrofitting bathrooms, moving switches (including elevator buttons) that were out of reach of people in wheelchairs, etc.

Those property owners who didn't comply, or who couldn't afford to obey the regulations, were fined or put out of business. Putting large companies out of business not only feeds the "falling of the giant" (class envy), but also puts the employees of those companies out of work. Many other businesses and landlords made the regulated changes, sometimes at tremendous costs they could barely afford. So, this bill that originated out of compassion wasn't so compassionate after all.

Not only did the ADA force property owners to spend whatever it took to comply, but its timing couldn't have been worse. This mandate occurred right in the middle of one of the worst real estate depressions of this generation. With escalating tenant bankruptcies, the Gulf War debacle, the failure of hundreds of savings and loans, the Resolution Trust Corporation takeover (where hundreds of billions of dollars of real estate were sold at rock-bottom prices), and some of the highest vacancy rates and foreclosures recorded in the modern era, the ADA couldn't have come at a worse time.

Another example of a damaging bill is the 1986 Tax Reform Bill. With the stroke of the pen, this bill cost business and individuals untold billions of dollars in losses: lost value in real estate partnerships; lost value in commercial and residential real estate; losses to the housing and commercial building construction industry, which put thousands of contractors and vendors out of business; the highest number of bankruptcies ever recorded; the savings and loan debacle, which cost the government (the taxpayers) tens of billions of dollars in losses on loans, both real estate and business; and the dissolution of hundreds of savings and loans.

As devastating as the flat tax's elimination of mortgage interest deductions supposedly would be to the home market, the 1986 Tax Reform Bill was even more lethal to the commercial real estate market. The reason is that the commercial market is based on real estate *investment*, which is much more sensitive to after-tax returns. While taxes are a consideration in the home market, a tax adjustment would not be as devastating to the value of a home used principally as a residence.

Would the legislators have voted for these regulations if they had been more cognizant of their consequences in the real world? Hopefully not. As Eric Felten, author of *The Ruling Class - Inside The Imperial Congress,* states, "A definite end to sessions will also communicate to congressmen that they are representatives rather than managers of the permanent bureaucracy."

(e) Government regulation and control at all levels is to be assessed and reduced where deemed arbitrary or stifling to the citizens' civil rights, which shall always take precedent. A person who invests in a property should have the right to do with it what he wants, within reason. Local government should have to prove that an owner's operation of his land will negatively affect his neighbors. Government shouldn't force property owners to conduct studies unless there is a justification for such study.

(f) Daily governmental activities, including detailed proposed bill information and voting records, are to be outlined in national dailies, and in all cities of at least 1,000,000 population (or circulation of at least 200,000).

(g) Hire a Big Six accounting firm to audit Congress's books each year. This would be another step toward making Congress accountable to us, its bosses. It may eliminate some of the waste and mismanagement that has occurred, due in part to Congress's free reign over its activities and its shoddy bookkeeping.

EPILOGUE

The more one learns about the government, the more he can see that it doesn't work because it is loaded with conflicts of interest. Politicians depend on donations from their supporters who, in turn, often expect special treatment in the form of tax subsidies or other goodies. Lobbying requires disclosure, but the more disclosure there is, the less effective lobbying becomes. Congress's power depends on spending bills, yet we depend on Congress to cut costs and save our tax dollars. The House and Senate fight over decentralizing power from Washington, but that is like asking someone to voluntarily give up a position of authority. Congress promises to eliminate pork-barrel spending, but pork is one of their reelection tools. Congress attempts to reform its voting rules to eliminate deceit, but *they* are the ones who put those rules there in the first place. The Government Reform and Oversight Committee consists of 52 Congressmen, picked to oversee their own ethics and standards. Congress stacks the deck against outsiders running for political office, and limits the amount of money outsiders can receive for their campaign. The problems created by the necessity for two-income families increase the caseloads for a large segment of law enforcement officials, including lawyers, judges, etc. Congress is expected to vote to limit its own terms of office, reform its outrageous pension benefits, adopt a balanced budget amendment to limit its own spending, limit the gifts it receives from "supporters," and voluntarily increase disclosure in areas they once considered sacred.

Fat chance.

APPENDICES

Balanced Budget, Question and Answer

The following question-and-answer segment is taken from the Congressional Record, 1995. It answers questions regarding the government and a Balanced Budget Amendment:

The Economic Effects of the Balanced Budget Amendment. The U.S. Chamber of Commerce, the nation's largest business federation, has endorsed S.J. Res. 41, the Balanced Budget Amendment to the U.S. Constitution. The Chamber believes that this measure, sponsored by Sens. Simon (D-IL), Hatch (R-UT), and Craig (R-ID), will help move the federal government toward fiscal responsibility. This paper discusses the most significant economic questions raised by this landmark legislation, along with some of the conclusions reached by the U.S. Chamber.

Question. Why should we balance the federal budget?

Answer. There are several reasons why the federal budget should be balanced. Most fundamentally, the Balanced Budget Amendment would improve accountability in federal spending decisions. Government officials are generally inclined to increase government spending to improve services to their constituents. This, of course, is countered by their reluctance to raise taxes. But since borrowing can substitute for raising taxes, legislators find they can offer a high level of services without the pain of raising the current level of taxes. Consequently, when it's time to make tough spending decisions, Congress finds it can dodge the question by just borrowing the difference. The proper counterweight to higher government spending--raising taxes--is circumvented by the seemingly painless act of federal borrowing. This leaves us with more government than taxpayers are willing to pay for. Over time, such borrowing leaves us with a bloated government sector and the problem of paying off the debt.

The Balanced Budget Amendment restores the proper balance between spending and taxes, and forces government officials to prioritize difficult spending choices. It improves the process whereby such decisions are made, forcing Congress to use much greater discipline.

Also, no matter whether the government finances its spending through taxes or borrowing, it's still spending and therefore commanding economic resources. To those who believe in limited government and market systems, the level of federal spending is as much a concern as how that amount is financed. Limiting government borrowing blocks the path of least resistance to government expansion, and so we expect that a Balanced Budget Amendment would act to limit the reach of government into the economy.

Question. Wouldn't Congress just raise taxes to close the deficit?

Answer. In a way, Congress already has. After all, the difference between government borrowing and raising taxes is just a question of taxes today or taxes tomorrow. The important point is that, no matter how it's financed, the government is spending economic resources, and the amount of spending will surely be greater when government is allowed to use deficit spending.

And tax increases to close the deficit gap are being used now anyway--witness the tax increases in 1982, 1983, 1984, 1985, 1988, 1989, 1990, and 1993. In other words, we're already getting the tax increases. By requiring a balanced budget, we expect to place additional pressure on Congress to tackle the spending cuts that should be made.

To answer the question more directly, Congress can't just raise taxes, leave spending intact, and walk away--if it could, it would have done so a decade ago and spared us this long debate on deficit spending. So while it may raise some taxes to close the deficit, Congress will have to confront its voracious spending habit. The end result will be a lower level of government spending, and less government involvement in the economy.

In addition, a couple of provisions in the BBA make it more difficult to raise taxes. Under the amendment, tax increases require both a roll call vote (instead of anonymous voice votes) and a constitutional majority (which means 51 votes would be required in the Senate and 218 votes in the House to raise taxes, instead of a majority of those voting). This may not sound like much of a hurdle, but note that President Clinton's 1993 tax increase would have needed an additional two Senate votes under such a requirement. Instead, it passed after Vice President Gore's vote broke a 49-49 deadlock.

Finally, of course, congressmen and women would have to face the political consequences of raising taxes at the voting booth. Because a roll call vote would identify those who voted to raise taxes, legislators would be held to a higher level of accountability.

Question. What is the primary economic impact of running government deficits?

Answer. The worst thing about government deficit spending is that it distorts the economy's balance between saving and investment, producing adverse long-term productivity growth. The funds the government is borrowing have to come from somewhere, and generally they come from private saving and private investment. Throughout the 1980s and early 1990s, we've seen the saving rate fall from about 8% to consistently below 4% – too low to fuel the kind of investment we need to keep up our high productivity. Since long-term productivity growth is the key to rising standards of living, it's dangerous to be skimping on investment.

Federal borrowing is not inherently wrong or bad for the economy; it depends on how the funds are used. If the funds were being used exclusively to create stronger schools, better highways, safer bridges, and so forth, we would be increasing the productive capacity of the economy. This means that we would be creating the means by which future generations can create the wealth to pay back the borrowed funds. But if we're using those funds to provide ourselves with consumption-oriented short-term benefits that don't improve our long-term productive capacity, then we're raising our standard of living by lowering that of future generations. To quote NationsBank economist Mickey Levy:

"Deficits matter most because they distort the way current national resources are allocated, generally favoring current consumption at the expense of private investment."

Question. Are there other effects of deficit spending that harm the economy?

Answer. In a complex, interlocking, international economy, you can expect sustained deficit spending to cause other distortions as well. First, chronic government borrowing tends to put upward pressure on interest rates. Businesses seeking to raise capital and households applying for mortgages have to compete with the federal government in securing loanable funds. This increase in demand pushes interest rates up. Consequently, fewer loans are made to the private sector, and those that are made carry a higher interest rate. This is known as "crowding out," since government borrowing displaces some private borrowing.

Second, because our economy is increasingly linked to the global market, there are important international impacts related to the budget deficit.\2\ Higher interest rates tend to raise the foreign exchange value of the dollar, meaning that our trading partners face price increases on the goods and services they buy from the U.S. This lowers our exports, pushing up our trade deficit. Many contend that one of the major forces behind the huge trade deficits of the 1980s was the federal budget deficit.

Third, the amount we're paying to service our national debt has grown almost fivefold since 1979--from $43 billion to $203 billion in 1994. As a share of total government outlays, interest payments on the debt have about doubled from 7.4% during the 1970s to over 14% currently. That means that for the same amount of revenue, there's less money for other government programs, whether it's for national defense, our court system, Head Start, or environmental clean-up. No matter what the budget priorities are, fewer funds are available.

To sum up, there are serious economic side-effects of deficit spending that Washington tends to ignore. In addition to restoring discipline to the spending decisions of Congress, the Balanced Budget Amendment seeks to remove the economic distortion caused by chronic deficit spending.

Question. Back to that notion of "crowding out" for a moment. If increased government borrowing leads to higher interest rates, as you claim, then why did interest rates fall during the 1980s just as the budget deficit was expanding?

Answer. The key to this apparent paradox is the behavior of inflation during the 1980s. After starting out the decade in the double-digits, the inflation rate fell sharply due to tighter monetary policy and, in mid-decade, the collapse of oil prices. Since expectations of future inflation are embedded in market interest rates, this decline in inflation pushed interest rates down.

This more than offset the impact of increasing federal deficits, which were working at the same time to push interest rates up.

So while it's true that market interest rates fell significantly during the 1980s, it's correct to say that they would have fallen even further had the federal budget been brought into balance. In fact, later in this document we'll present results from an econometric study that show significantly lower interest rates as a result of moving to a balanced budget.

Question. Doesn't government spending represent an investment in the economy, with highway and transportation construction funds going to education, etc?

Answer. Some government spending can be regarded as "investment spending," meaning that funds spent now will generate stronger economic growth later. Spending on infrastructure–highways, bridges, dams, and mass transit, for example--and other programs such as education, are often thought of that way, since they provide benefits over a long period of time. But the bulk of government spending goes to projects and programs that don't provide much of a return over time, but instead represent "current spending." Such programs include Social Security, Medicare, federal retirement programs, unemployment insurance, agricultural extensions offices, and so forth. While many of these programs are desirable, we need to recognize that we're borrowing vast sums to pay for benefits that are only short-lived.

Because an extra dollar of private investment is generally more efficient than an extra dollar of government investment, our productive capacity generally grows less when funds are diverted away from the private sector. This means that productivity and wage growth will be held back, lowering our standard of living.

Question. Why a Balanced Budget Amendment now? After all, we've gotten along without it for 200 years.

Answer. Until about 1960 or so, running a balanced budget over time was almost an unwritten Constitutional amendment. The U.S. government ran deficits during the War of 1812, the severe recession of 1837-43, the Civil War, and the Spanish American War, to name a few episodes. But in other periods, the federal government ran surpluses to reduce its outstanding debt. On the whole, only emergencies justified running a deficit.

But since 1960, this informal rule apparently has gone by the wayside. In the past 34 years, the U.S. has avoided a deficit only once, when in 1969 there was a surplus of $43 billion. Given the chronic deficits we've come to expect, it's time to make explicit through a Constitutional amendment the old implicit principle of government living within its means.

Question. Will passing a Balanced Budget Amendment really add discipline to the federal government?

Answer. Lawmakers have tried statutory measures to rein in government deficit spending, but they just haven't worked. For example, in 1985 Congress passed the Gramm- Rudman-Hollings deficit reduction bill, which was supposed to reduce the deficit to zero by fiscal year 1991 from the $293 billion deficit projected at the time for fiscal year 1991.\3\ As it turned out, even with passage of GRH, we ended up with a $196 billion deficit in 1991 and a $289 billion deficit in 1992.

That's because hard-won budget rules can be waived or modified by a simple majority vote. The Balanced Budget Amendment, on the other hand, requires a three-fifths vote of each house to enact a budget with a deficit (in times of war, only a simple majority is required).

It's clear that these statutory measures haven't worked, and so it's time to turn to the stronger medicine of a balanced budget amendment.

Question. Didn't we move to balancing the budget with the passage in August 1993 of President Clinton's package, the Omnibus Budget Reconciliation Act (OBRA)?

Answer. Washington made some progress in trimming the deficit last summer when it passed OBRA. The nonpartisan Congressional Budget Office estimated in September 1993 that OBRA will cut $433 billion of debt over the next five years from the projected baseline (i.e., pre-OBRA) level of debt.

But not only is the post-OBRA deficit still at $200 billion in FY 1998, but it's also on the rise. By 2003, according to CBO, the deficit is projected to hit $359 billion. As a percentage of total output, that means the deficit rises from 2.5% of GDP in FY 1998 to 3.6% in FY 2003. \4\ Like the budget deals in the previous decade before it, OBRA clearly does not solve the deficit problem. That's why it's imperative to turn to a constitutional, rather than a statutory, remedy for our chronic deficit problem.

Question. What's the relationship between the federal deficit and federal debt?

Answer. The federal deficit is the difference between the government's outlays and receipts in any one year, while federal debt is the total amount of government debt outstanding. The debt, in other words, is the total accumulation of deficits over the years. In 1993, the federal deficit was $255 billion, and the total deferral debt was $4.5 trillion.

Question. A federal debt of $4.5 trillion sounds like a lot, but is it historically high?

Answer. In absolute terms, it's the highest it's ever been. But because of inflation and the growth of our economy, it's best to answer this question by measuring the federal debt relative to the size of the economy; that is, to look at the ratio of debt to GDP. Today, the total debt held by the public is 52% of current GDP. \5\ While that's less than half of 1946's 114% of GDP, we don't have as much to show for it. The debt then paid for victory in World War II, while the current debt is simply funding higher levels of consumption.

Moreover, this ratio is currently moving in the wrong direction. It's grown from below 30% during the 1970s to just over 40% during the mid-1980s, and now to over 50%. In contrast, the federal debt ratio in the postwar period was pruned from 114% to 68% by 1951, and generally kept falling until the early 1970s.

Question. So the federal debt's higher, and it's been growing for twenty years. But while some continue to feel economic discomfort from structural changes unrelated to the higher federal debt (such as the defense build-down and the commercial real estate overhang), the U.S. seems to be doing fine. What's the crisis?

Answer. The growing federal debt is not a problem that can be characterized as "a wolf at the door," which requires immediate attention. Instead, to use the analogy introduced by President Carter's top economist, Charles Schultze, it's a "colony of termites in the wall." \6\ In other words, it's a serious long-term problem that can be ignored in the short-term. The damage--lower investment, lower productivity, slower wage growth, etc.--may be hard to perceive or even hidden by other economic forces, but that doesn't mean it's not occurring. The termites are still chomping away and must still be dealt with, because the destruction can be massive.

Question. Won't the Balanced Budget Amendment hamper government activity in times of a national emergency, such as a war?

Answer. The Amendment will not compromise America's ability to respond to national emergencies. In general, the Amendment can be suspended for a specific fiscal year whenever three-fifths of both houses of Congress vote to do so. In wartime, this requirement is lowered to a simple majority in both chambers.

Questions. Won't balancing the budget cause a serious disruption of economic growth?

Answer. If the deficit were reduced all at once--from FY 1994's projected $250 billion to zero next year, for example--there indeed would be a severe disruption. Because the removal of so much fiscal stimulus in one year is not advisable, the Balanced Budget Amendment calls for the provision to become law in FY 1999, or two years after the ratification by three-quarters of the states, whichever is later. The Amendment does not provide a specific path for deficit reduction in the meantime, but Congress would have five years to implement the needed changes.

While we should expect some disruption--balancing the budget is not, in the short-term, an economic growth policy--we will see several long-term benefits after the budget is balanced. And the short-term distress can be mitigated, according to economic simulations performed in a 1992 study conducted by Laurence H. Meyer & Associates a nonpartisan and highly regarded macroeconomics consulting firm based in St. Louis, Missouri. If we had started in 1993 and balanced the budget by 1998, using Federal Reserve policy to cushion the economy, the LHM&A model shows that total output would be between 1% to 1.6% higher in 2003.\7\ Even 1% additional output means an economy that's $80 billion larger (measured in today's dollars.)

Question. Does it make any difference whether Congress balances the budget using tax increases or spending cuts?

Answer. It makes a big difference. In the study cited above, LHM&A found that the highest gains from deficit reduction come from expenditure cuts. That is because increases in taxes create disincentives for labor and investment, mitigating some of the beneficial effects of deficit reduction on interest rates.

In the following table we report the results of two policy simulations conducted by LHM&A in which the budget is balanced, and compare it to the baseline case where policy is left as is.

The first column of results shows where the economy would be if no action were taken on balancing the budget (the "Baseline"scenario).

The second column shows where the economy would be if expenditures were cut by the entire amount necessary to balance the budget ("All Spending").

The final column shows the results of balancing the budget by raising spending and cutting expenditures by exactly the same amount ("Mix").

The two balanced budget scenarios assume that the Federal Reserve eases monetary policy enough to maintain the unemployment rate at the baseline level of 5.2%. The following table (on the next page) compares how the economy would look with and without deficit reduction by showing some of the results for the first five years.

Notice how interest rates are significantly lower in the scenarios where the deficit has been reduced. This is the fuel for the higher lever of business investment. In fact, the inflation-adjusted value of the nation's plant and equipment (what economists call the real capital stock) is 2 percent higher after the first five years of deficit reduction, and 6 percent higher after ten years, when comparing the result of the "All Spending" scenario to the baseline. While those figures may sound small, they mean $120 billion worth of additional computers and manufacturing plants within five years, and $390 billion more in ten years.

And it should be noted that the capital stock is almost 2 percent higher when the budget is balanced entirely through spending cuts rather than an equal mix of spending cuts and tax increases. While inflation is a bit higher in the deficit-reduction scenarios (due to the Federal Reserve's cushioning), growth in real GDP (inflation-adjusted output) is stronger, on average, in the five-year period, as the deficit is reduced. Real personal disposable income grows at a slower rate (1.7 percent and 1.5 percent versus 2.3 percent) in the cases where the deficit is lowered. But note that it's stronger in the case where all of the deficit reduction comes from reductions in government spending. This shows that moving to a balanced budget will inflict some economic pain. The short-term pain is unavoidable, but it helps set the stage for stronger growth in the years after the deficit has been balanced.

THE ECONOMIC IMPACT OF BALANCING THE BUDGET
(The first 5 years of deficit reduction)

	No deficit reduction	Deficit reduction scenarios	
	Baseline	All Spending	Mix
Levels in the fifth year:			
Federal deficit ($ bill)............	-251	0	-1
3-month T-bill rate (%).............	5.5	4.7	4.6
30-year Government bond yield (%)...	6.9	5.7	5.8
AAA corp bond yield (%).............	7.1	5.8	5.9
Average annual growth, first five years (96):			
Real GDP............................	2.6	2.8	2.7
Inflation...........................	3.3	3.5	3.4
Real personal disposable income....	2.3	1.7	1.5

Note: U.S. Chamber of Commerce, February 1994.

Of course, the active participation of Federal Reserve is an important component of LHM&A's simulations, and it comes with the price tag of slightly higher inflation. But the important point is that the model suggests a path that the economy can follow to get to a balanced budget without severe economic hardship.

Question. Most of the states have some sort of balanced budget requirement. What has been their experience?

Answer. According to the National Association of State

Budget Officers, the application of the state experience to the federal experience is not clear-cut. The state balanced budget requirements are diverse and written so generally that they're subject to varying interpretations. According to their 1992 statement, the tradition of balanced budgets, rather than the enforcement provisions or the threat of lower bond ratings, plays the most important role in developing balanced budget.\8\

REFERENCES

\1\Mickey D. Levy, "Deficitphobia: Right for the Wrong Reasons," in Economic and Financial Perspectives, CRT Government Securities Ltd., New York, December 1993, pg1.

\2\Benjamin M. Friedman, "U.S. Fiscal Policy in the 1980s: Consequences of Large Budget Deficits at Full Employment," in Debt and the Twin Deficits Debate, James M. Rock, ed., Mayfield Publishing Company, 1991

\3\Laurence H. Meyer & Associates, "Balancing the Budget by 1991: The Gramm-Rudman-Hollings Proposal," November 1985, pg. 5.

\4\Congressional Budget Office, "The Economic and Budget Outlook: An Update," September 1993, pgs. 26-29.

\5\Congressional Budget Office, "Federal Debt and Interest Costs," May 1993, pg. 92.

\6\Charles L. Schultze, "Of Wolves, Termites and Pussycats," The Brookings Review, Summer 1989, pgs. 26-33.

\7\Laurence H. Meyer & Associates, "Balancing the Budget: An Analysis of the Economic Effects of Deficit Reduction," prepared for the Chase Manhattan Bank, December 1992, pg. 1.

\8\National Association of State Budget Officers, "State Balanced Budget Requirements: Provisions and Practices," June 1992, pg. 3.

ETHICS MANUAL FOR MEMBERS, OFFICERS, AND EMPLOYEES OF THE U.S. HOUSE OF REPRESENTATIVES

THE COMMITTEE ON STANDARDS OF OFFICIAL CONDUCT

102d Congress, 2nd Session
U.S. GOVERNMENT PRINTING OFFICE
53-077 WASHINGTON : 1992

COMMITTEE ON STANDARDS OF
OFFICIAL CONDUCT

LOUIS STOKES, Ohio, Chairman
MATTHEW F. McHUGH, New York
JAMES V. HANSEN, Utah
GARY L. ACKERMAN, New York
FRED GRANDY, Iowa
GEORGE (BUDDY) DARDEN, Georgia
NANCY L. JOHNSON, Connecticut
BENJAMIN L. CARDIN, Maryland
JIM BUNNING, Kentucky
NANCY PELOSI, California
JON L. KYL, Arizona
JIM McDERMOTT, Washington
PORTER J. GOSS, Florida
DAVID L. HOBSON, Ohio
Bernard Raimo, Chief Counsel
Mark J. Davis, Director
Office of Advice and Education
Ellen L. Weintraub, Counsel
Ethics Manual Editor-in-Chief
Ronald C. Crump, Counsel
Edward W. Hosken, Jr., Counsel
David J. McCarthy, Counsel
Charles J. Willoughby, Counsel
Linda R. Shealy, Legal Assistant

ETHICS MANUAL
THE CODE OF OFFICIAL CONDUCT
House Rule XLIII

A member, officer, or employee of the House of Representatives shall conduct himself at all times in a manner which shall reflect creditably on the House of Representatives.

A member, officer, or employee of the House of Representatives shall adhere to the spirit and the letter of the Rules of the House of Representatives and to the rules of duly constituted committees thereof.

A member, officer, or employee of the House of Representatives shall receive no compensation nor shall he permit any compensation to accrue to his beneficial interest from any source, the receipt of which would occur by virtue of influence improperly exerted from his position in the Congress.

A member, officer, or employee of the House of Representatives shall not accept gifts (other than personal hospitality of an individual or with a fair market value of $100 or less) in any calendar year aggregating more than $250, directly or indirectly, from any person (other than from a relative) except to the extent permitted by written waiver granted in exceptional circumstances by the Committee on Standards of Official Conduct pursuant to clause 4(e)(1)(E) of rule X.

A member, officer, or employee of the House of Representatives, shall accept no honorarium for a speech, writing for publication, or other similar activity.

A member of the House of Representatives shall keep his campaign funds separate from his personal funds. A Member shall convert no campaign funds to personal use in excess of reimbursement for legitimate and verifiable campaign expenditures and shall expend no funds from his campaign account not attributable to bona fide campaign or political purposes.

A member of the House of Representatives shall treat as campaign contributions all proceeds from testimonial dinners or other fund raising events.

A member or officer of the House of Representatives shall retain no one under his payroll authority who does not perform official duties commensurate with the compensation received in the offices of the employing authority. In the case of committee employees who work under the direct supervision of a member other than a chairman, the chairman may require that such member affirm in writing that the employees have complied with the preceding sentence (subject to clause 6 of rule XI) as evidence of the chairman's compliance with this clause and with clause 6 of rule XI.

A member, officer, or employee of the House of Representatives shall not discharge or refuse to hire any individual, or otherwise discriminate against any individual with respect to compensation, terms, conditions, or privileges of employment, because of such individual's race, color, religion, sex (including marital or parental status), age, or national origin, but may take into consideration the domicile or political affiliation of such individual.

A member of the House of Representatives who has been convicted by a court of record for the commission of a crime for which a sentence of two or more years' imprisonment may be imposed should refrain from participation in the business of each committee of which he is a member and should refrain from voting on any question at a meeting of the House, or of the Committee of the Whole House, unless or until judicial or executive proceedings result in reinstatement of the presumption of his innocence or until he is reelected to the House after the date of such conviction.

A member of the House of Representatives shall not authorize or otherwise allow a non-House individual, group, or organization to use the words "Congress of the

United States", "House of Representatives", or "Official Business," or any combination of words thereof, on any letterhead or envelope.

(a) Except as provided by paragraph (b), any employee of the House of Representatives who is required to file a report pursuant to rule XLIV shall refrain from participating personally and substantially as an employee of the House of Representatives in any contact with any agency of the executive or judicial branch of government with respect to nonlegislative matters affecting any nongovernmental person in which the employee has a significant financial interest.

Paragraph (a) shall not apply if an employee first advises his employing authority of his significant financial interest and obtains from his employing authority a written waiver stating that the participation of the employee is necessary. A copy of each such waiver shall be filed with the Committee on Standards of Official Conduct.

ETHICS MANUAL

CODE OF ETHICS FOR GOVERNMENT SERVICE

Resolved by the House of Representatives (the Senate concurring), that it is the sense of the Congress that the following Code of Ethics should be adhered to by all government employees, including officeholders:

CODE OF ETHICS FOR GOVERNMENT SERVICE

Any person in government service should:

Put loyalty to the highest moral principles and to country above loyalty to government persons, party, or department.

Uphold the Constitution, laws, and legal regulations of the United States and of all governments therein and never be a party to their evasion.

Give a full day's labor for a full day's pay; giving to the performance of his duties his earnest effort and best thought.

Seek to find and employ more efficient and economical ways of getting tasks accomplished.

Never discriminate unfairly by the dispensing of special favors or privileges to anyone, whether for remuneration or not; and never accept for himself or his family favors or benefits under circumstances which might be construed by reasonable persons as influencing the performance of his governmental duties.

Make no private promises of any kind binding upon the duties of office, since a government employee has no private word which can be binding on public duty.

Engage in no business with the government, either directly or indirectly, which is inconsistent with the conscientious performance of his governmental duties. Never use any information coming to him confidentially in the performance of governmental duties as a means for making private profit.

Expose corruption wherever discovered.

Uphold these principles, ever conscious that public office is a public trust.

(Passed July 11, 1958.)

CHART I

This chart shows the total tax revenue the government takes in, the annual spending, the surplus or deficit spending, and the accumulated debt.
(in millions of dollars)

YEAR	TOTAL TAX REVENUE	SPENDING	SURPLUS	ACCUMULATED DEBT
1900				1,263
1901	588	525	63	1,221
1902	562	485	77	1,178
1903	562	517	45	1,159
1904	541	584	(43)	1,137
1905	544	567	(23)	1,132
1906	595	570	25	1,142
1907	666	579	87	1,147
1908	602	659	(57)	1,178
1909	604	694	(89)	1,148
1910	676	694	(18)	1,147
1911	702	691	11	1,153
1912	693	690	3	1,193
1913	714	715	(1)	1,193
1914	725	726	(1)	1,188
1915	683	746	(63)	1,191
1916	761	713	48	1,225
1917	1,101	1,954	(853)	2,976
1918	3,645	12,677	(9,032)	12,455
1919	5,130	18,493	(13,363)	25,485
1920	6,649	6,358	291	24,299
1921	5,571	5,062	509	23,977
1922	4,026	3,289	736	22,963
1923	3,853	3,140	713	22,350
1924	3,871	2,908	963	21,251

YEAR	TOTAL TAX REVENUE	SPENDING	SURPLUS	ACCUMULATED DEBT
1925	3,641	2,924	717	20,516
1926	3,795	2,930	865	19,543
1927	4,013	2,857	1,155	18,512
1928	3,900	2,961	939	17,604
1929	3,862	3,127	734	16,931
1930	4,058	3,320	738	16,185
1931	4,116	3,577	(462)	16,301
1932	1,924	4,659	(2,735)	19,487
1933	1,997	4,598	(2,602)	22,538
1934	2,955	6,541	(3,586)	27,053
1935	3,609	6,412	(2,803)	28,701
1936	3,923	8,228	(4,304)	33,779
1937	5,387	7,580	(2,193)	36,425
1938	6,751	6,840	(89)	37,165
1939	6,295	9,141	(2,846)	40,440
1940	6,548	9,468	(2,920)	42,968
1941	8,712	13,653	(4,941)	48,961
1942	14,634	35,137	(20,503)	72,422
1943	24,001	78,555	(54,554)	126,696
1944	43,747	91,304	(47,557)	201,003
1945	45,159	92,712	(47,553)	258,682
1946	39,296	55,232	(15,936)	269,422
1947	38,514	34,496	4,018	258,286
1948	41,560	29,764	11,796	252,292
1949	39,415	38,835	580	252,370
1950	39,443	42,562	(3,119)	257,357
1951	51,616	45,514	6,102	255,222
1952	66,167	67,686	(1,519)	259,105
1953	69,608	76,101	(6,493)	266,071
1954	69,701	70,855	(1,154)	271,260

YEAR	TOTAL TAX REVENUE	SPENDING	SURPLUS	ACCUMULATED DEBT
1955	65,451	68,444	(2,993)	274,374
1956	74,587	70,640	3,947	272,751
1957	79,990	76,578	3,412	270,527
1958	79,636	82,405	(2,769)	276,843
1959	79,249	92,098	(12,849)	284,706
1960	92,492	92,191	301	286,331
1961	94,388	97,723	(3,335)	288,971
1962	99,676	106,821	(7,146)	298,201
1963	106,560	111,316	(4,756)	305,860
1964	112,613	118,528	(5,915)	311,713
1965	116,817	118,228	(1,411)	317,274
1966	130,835	134,532	(3,698)	319,907
1967	148,822	157,464	(8,643)	326,221
1968	152,973	178,134	(25,161)	347,576
1969	186,882	183,640	3,242	353,720
1970	192,807	195,649	(2,842)	370,919
1971	187,139	210,172	(23,033)	408,176
1972	207,309	230,681	(23,373)	435,936
1973	230,799	245,707	(14,908)	466,291
1974	263,224	269,359	(6,135)	483,893
1975	279,090	332,332	(53,242)	541,925
1976	298,060	371,792	(73,732)	628,970
*TQ	81,232	95,975	(14,744)	643,561
1977	355,559	409,218	(53,659)	706,398
1978	399,561	458,746	(59,186)	776,602
1979	463,302	503,485	(40,183)	829,470
1980	517,112	590,947	(73,835)	909,050
1981	599,272	678,249	(78,976)	994,845
1982	617,766	745,755	(127,989)	1,137,345
1983	600,562	808,380	(207,818)	1,371,710
1984	666,457	851,846	(185,388)	1,564,657

YEAR	TOTAL TAX REVENUE	SPENDING	SURPLUS	ACCUMULATED DEBT
1985	734,057	946,391	(212,334)	1,817,521
1986	769,091	990,336	(221,245)	2,120,629
1987	854,143	1,003,911	(149,769)	2,346,125
1988	908,954	1,064,140	(155,187)	2,601,307
1989	990,691	1,144,169	(153,477)	2,868,039
1990	1,031,308	1,251,778	(220,470)	3,206,564
1991	1,054,262	1,323,011	(268,746)	3,598,498
1992	1,090,453	1,380,856	(290,403)	4,002,136
1993	1,153,535	1,408,675	(255,140)	4,351,416
1994	1,257,745	1,460,914	(203,169)	4,643,711
1995 (est.)	1,346,400	1,538,900	(192,500)	4,964,914

* TQ refers to "Transition Quarter." In 1976, the government shifted its fiscal year to October 1, – September 30, from July 1 – June 30. Thus, July through September 1976 is called the Transition Quarter, and carries its own quarterly records.

NOTE:
The cumulative annual deficit in this table does not exactly equal the national debt. The information from this chart is taken from the historical tables of the Budget of the United States Government, Government Printing Office, and the Historical Statistics of the United States, U.S. Department of Commerce. The deficit numbers do not reflect the money the government pays to trust funds, Social Security, other means of financing assets, gold sales, and government purchases, according to an officer of the Congressional Budget Office.

CHART II

The increase of taxes and government spending relative to the Consumer Price Index

YEAR	CPI	TAX INCREASE	SPENDING INCREASE
1960	1.7	16.7	.1
1961	1.0	2.1	6.0
1962	1.0	5.6	9.3
1963	1.3	6.9	4.2
1964	1.3	5.7	6.5
1965	1.6	3.7	0
1966	2.9	12.0	13.8
1967	3.1	13.7	17.0
1968	4.2	2.8	13.1
1969	5.5	22.2	3.1
1970	5.7	3.2	6.5
1971	4.4	-3.0	7.4
1972	3.2	10.8	9.8
1973	6.2	11.3	6.5
1974	11.0	14.0	9.6
1975	9.1	6.0	23.4
1976	5.8	6.8	11.9
1977	6.5	19.3	10.0
1978	7.6	12.4	12.1
1979	11.3	16.0	9.9
1980	13.5	11.6	17.2
1981	10.3	15.9	14.8
1982	6.2	3.1	10.0
1983	3.2	-2.8	8.4
1984	4.3	11.0	5.4

YEAR	CPI	TAX INCREASE	SPENDING INCREASE
1985	3.6	10.1	11.1
1986	1.9	4.8	4.6
1987	3.6	11.1	1.4
1988	4.1	6.4	6.0
1989	4.8	9.0	7.4
1990	5.4	4.1	9.6
1991	4.2	2.2	5.7
1992	3.0	3.4	4.3
1993	3.0	5.8	1.9
1994	2.6	9.0	3.7
1995	2.7	7.1	5.3

CORRELATION:

Consumer Price Increase 1960–1995 = 410%
Federal Taxes Increase 1960–1995 = 1,356%
Federal Spending Increase 1960–1995 = 1,569%

CHART III

The number of government workers (federal, state and local) there are relative to the population of the United States

YEAR	GOVERNMENT EMPLOYMENT (in thousands)	POPULATION (in thousands)	GOV'T EMPLOYEES PER 1,000 U.S. POPULATION
1940	4,474	132,122	33.86
1945	6,556	139,928	46.85
1950	6,402	151,684	42.21
1955	7,432	165,275	44.97
1960	8,808	180,671	48.75
1965	12,898	194,303	66.38
1970	11,758	204,879	57.39
1975	17,174	215,973	79.52
1980	18,507	226,109	81.85
1981	18,256	230,848	79.08
1982	18,178	231,664	78.47
1983	18,258	233,792	78.10
1984	18,592	235,825	78.84
1985	19,037	237,924	80.01
1986	19,385	240,133	80.73
1987	19,703	242,289	81.32
1988	20,055	244,499	82.02
1989	20,455	248,061	82.46
1990	20,862	248,710	83.88
1991	20,589	253,426	81.24
1992	20,608	256,271	80.41
1993	20,658	257,908	80.10
1994	20,793	260,662	79.77

CHART IV

The annual deficit spending and total debt for each United States citizen

YEAR	POPULATION (in millions)	DEFICIT PER CAPITA (in dollars)	DEBT PER CAPITA (in dollars)
1940	132	22	325
1945	140	340	1,848
1950	152	53	1,693
1955	165	18	1,663
1960	181	---	1,582
1965	194	7	1,635
1970	205	14	1,809
1975	216	246	2,509
1980	226	327	4,022
1981	231	342	4,307
1982	232	552	4,902
1983	234	888	5,862
1984	236	786	6,630
1985	238	892	7,637
1986	240	922	8,836
1987	242	619	9,695
1988	244	636	10,661
1989	246	624	11,659
1990	249	885	12,878
1991	253	1,062	14,223
1992	256	1,134	15,633
1993	258	989	16,866
1994	261	778	17,792
1995	263	732	18,878
1996 (est.)	265	735	19,969

NOTES:

1) The cumulative annual deficit in CHART IV does not exactly equal the national debt. The information from this chart is taken from the historical tables of the Budget of the United States Government, Government Printing Office, and the Historical Statistics of the United States, U.S. Department of Commerce. The deficit numbers do not reflect the money the government pays to trust funds, Social Security, other means of financing assets, gold sales, and government purchases, according to an officer of the Congressional Budget Office.

2) While our population increased by **100%** from 1940–1996, the national debt per person increased by **5,100%**.

CHART V

Government receipts by source from 1934–2000, from the U.S. Printing Office

Fiscal Year	Individual Income Taxes	Corporation Income Taxes [1]	Social Insurance Taxes and Contributions Total	Excise Taxes [2]	Other [3]	Total
1934	420	364	30	1,354	788	2,955
1935	527	529	31	1,439	1,084	3,609
1936	674	719	52	1,631	847	3,923
1937	1,092	1,038	580	1,876	801	5,387
1938	1,286	1,287	1,541	1,863	773	6,751
1939	1,029	1,127	1,593	1,871	675	6,295
1940	892	1,197	1,785	1,977	698	6,548
1941	1,314	2,124	1,940	2,552	781	8,712
1942	3,263	4,719	2,452	3,399	801	14,634
1943	6,505	9,557	3,044	4,096	800	24,001
1944	19,705	14,838	3,473	4,759	972	43,747
1945	18,372	15,988	3,451	6,265	1,083	45,159
1946	16,098	11,883	3,115	6,998	1,202	39,296
1947	17,935	8,615	3,422	7,211	1,331	38,514
1948	19,315	9,678	3,751	7,356	1,461	41,560
1949	15,552	11,192	3,781	7,502	1,388	39,415
1950	15,755	10,449	4,338	7,550	1,351	39,443
1951	21,616	14,101	5,674	8,648	1,578	51,616
1952	27,934	21,226	6,445	8,852	1,710	66,167
1953	29,816	21,238	6,820	9,877	1,857	69,608
1954	29,542	21,101	7,208	9,945	1,905	69,701
1955	28,747	17,861	7,862	9,131	1,850	65,451
1956	32,188	20,880	9,320	9,929	2,270	74,587
1957	35,620	21,167	9,997	10,534	2,672	79,990
1958	34,724	20,074	11,239	10,638	2,961	79,636
1959	36,719	17,309	11,722	10,578	2,921	79,249
1960	40,715	21,494	14,683	11,676	3,923	92,492
1961	41,338	20,954	16,439	11,860	3,796	94,388
1962	45,571	20,523	17,046	12,534	4,001	99,676
1963	47,588	21,579	19,804	13,194	4,395	106,560
1964	48,697	23,493	21,963	13,731	4,731	112,613
1965	48,792	25,461	22,242	14,570	5,753	116,817
1966	55,446	30,073	25,546	13,062	6,708	130,835
1967	61,526	33,971	32,619	13,719	6,987	148,822
1968	68,726	28,665	33,923	14,079	7,580	152,973
1969	87,249	36,678	39,015	15,222	8,718	186,882
1970	90,412	32,829	44,362	15,705	9,499	192,807
1971	86,230	26,785	47,325	16,614	10,185	187,139
1972	94,737	32,166	52,574	15,477	12,355	207,309
1973	103,246	36,153	63,115	16,260	12,026	230,799
1974	118,952	38,620	75,071	16,844	13,737	263,224

CHART V

Government receipts by source from 1934–2000, from the U.S. Printing Office
(continued)

Fiscal Year	Individual Income Taxes	Corporation Income Taxes[1]	Social Insurance Taxes and Contributions Total	Excise Taxes[2]	Other[3]	Total
1975	122,386	40,621	84,534	16,551	14,998	279,090
1976	131,603	41,409	90,769	16,963	17,317	298,060
TQ	38,801	8,460	25,219	4,473	4,279	81,232
1977	157,626	54,892	106,485	17,548	19,008	355,559
1978	180,988	59,952	120,967	18,376	19,278	399,561
1979	217,841	65,677	138,939	18,745	22,101	463,302
1980	244,069	64,600	157,803	24,329	26,311	517,112
1981	285,917	61,137	182,720	40,839	28,659	599,272
1982	297,744	49,207	201,498	36,311	33,006	617,766
1983	288,938	37,022	208,994	35,300	30,309	600,562
1984	298,415	56,893	239,376	37,361	34,412	666,457
1985	334,531	61,331	265,163	35,992	37,040	734,057
1986	348,959	63,143	283,901	32,919	40,168	769,091
1987	392,557	83,926	303,318	32,457	41,884	854,143
1988	401,181	94,508	334,335	35,227	43,702	908,954
1989	445,690	103,291	359,416	34,386	47,908	990,691
1990	466,884	93,507	380,047	35,345	55,538	1,031,321
1991	467,827	98,086	396,016	42,402	49,941	1,054,272
1992	475,964	100,270	413,689	45,569	54,961	1,090,453
1993	509,680	117,520	428,300	48,057	49,978	1,153,535
1994	543,055	140,385	461,475	55,225	57,605	1,257,745
1995 estimate	588,460	150,864	484,409	57,600	65,081	1,346,414
1996 estimate	623,372	157,449	509,315	57,194	68,126	1,415,456
1997 estimate	642,514	166,109	532,685	58,403	71,907	1,471,618
1998 estimate	680,529	173,150	559,175	59,289	76,666	1,548,809
1999 estimate	717,304	179,192	585,923	60,662	81,653	1,624,734
2000 estimate	756,360	190,470	614,324	61,778	87,980	1,710,912

CHART VI

Total government expenditures by major category from 1947–1994, from the U.S. Government Printing Office

Fiscal Year	Total Government	Defense and International	Net Interest	Federal Payments For Individuals		Other Federal	State and Local From Own Sources (Except Net Interest)
				Social Security and Medicare	Other		
1947	45.4	18.6	4.3	0.4	8.6	2.6	10.8
1948	43.6	13.7	4.4	0.5	8.5	2.7	13.8
1949	55.0	19.2	4.6	0.6	9.5	5.0	16.1
1950	61.3	18.4	4.9	0.7	12.9	5.7	18.7
1951	65.7	27.2	4.7	1.5	8.8	3.4	20.1
1952	89.4	48.8	4.7	2.0	8.9	3.4	21.7
1953	98.9	54.9	5.2	2.6	8.3	5.1	22.8
1954	95.9	50.9	4.8	3.3	9.3	2.6	25.0
1955	96.5	45.0	4.9	4.3	10.0	4.3	27.9
1956	100.8	44.9	5.2	5.4	9.8	5.4	30.0
1957	109.6	48.6	5.4	6.5	10.5	5.6	32.9
1958	118.4	50.2	5.7	8.0	12.9	5.7	35.9
1959	130.6	52.2	5.9	9.5	13.2	11.4	38.4
1960	131.8	51.1	7.1	11.4	12.8	10.0	39.5
1961	141.3	52.8	6.8	12.2	15.3	10.7	43.5
1962	153.7	58.0	7.0	14.0	14.9	13.0	46.7
1963	161.1	58.7	7.9	15.5	15.5	13.9	49.6
1964	172.2	59.7	8.2	16.2	16.0	18.4	53.7
1965	176.0	55.9	8.4	17.1	16.0	20.6	58.0
1966	198.4	63.7	9.0	20.3	16.8	24.4	64.3
1967	228.7	77.0	9.5	24.5	18.7	27.0	72.0
1968	256.9	87.2	10.1	28.4	21.4	30.0	79.7
1969	272.7	87.1	11.7	33.0	24.2	26.6	90.1
1970	292.2	86.0	12.8	36.4	28.4	30.4	98.1
1971	319.2	83.0	13.2	42.6	38.0	31.7	110.6
1972	347.4	84.0	14.2	47.7	45.3	38.2	118.1
1973	369.1	80.8	15.3	57.2	47.5	42.8	125.5
1974	409.1	85.1	17.8	65.7	54.7	42.4	143.5
1975	489.6	93.6	18.7	77.7	76.2	61.6	161.9
1976	546.4	96.1	22.5	89.6	91.0	68.4	178.9
TQ	142.7	24.7	6.0	24.0	21.5	18.8	47.7
1977	594.7	103.6	25.6	104.5	92.5	78.7	189.8
1978	655.6	112.0	28.4	116.7	95.0	99.5	203.9
1979	722.3	123.8	30.8	130.8	103.1	103.8	230.1
1980	834.2	146.7	34.6	151.0	127.5	113.2	281.1
1981	945.1	170.6	46.3	179.1	145.5	114.2	289.4
1982	1,038.9	197.6	57.3	203.1	154.8	105.2	320.9
1983	1,120.2	221.8	59.3	224.0	172.5	100.3	342.4
1984	1,185.6	243.3	78.1	237.0	164.2	96.2	366.8
1985	1,311.0	268.9	91.9	256.1	171.2	120.7	402.2
1986	1,387.3	287.5	95.7	270.7	180.5	115.5	437.2
1987	1,445.6	293.6	97.8	285.0	186.3	100.3	482.6
1988	1,538.5	300.8	108.7	302.5	198.1	110.8	517.5
1989	1,651.5	313.1	118.9	324.4	211.6	124.7	558.7
1990	1,809.8	313.1	131.7	353.8	230.3	171.3	609.6
1991	1,928.5	289.1	143.3	380.7	269.6	189.5	656.3
1992	2,020.7	314.5	146.2	414.3	313.4	139.3	693.0
1993	2,081.1	308.3	145.6	444.7	338.0	118.9	725.6
1994	2,168.8	298.6	148.6	476.2	346.0	137.1	762.2

CHART VII

Summary of receipts, outlays, and surpluses or deficits in current dollars, from 1940–2000, constant (FY 1987) dollars, from the U.S. Government Printing Office

Fiscal Year	In Current Dollars			In Constant (FY 1987 Dollars)		
	Receipts	Outlays	Surplus or Deficit (–)	Receipts	Outlays	Surplus or Deficit (–)
1940	6.5	9.5	–2.9	67.0	96.8	–29.9
1941	8.7	13.7	–4.9	86.3	135.3	–49.0
1942	14.6	35.1	–20.5	131.2	315.1	–183.9
1943	24.0	78.6	–54.6	200.2	655.2	–455.0
1944	43.7	91.3	–47.6	377.1	787.1	–410.0
1945	45.2	92.7	–47.6	395.8	812.6	–416.8
1946	39.3	55.2	–15.9	329.4	463.0	–133.6
1947	38.5	34.5	4.0	257.4	230.6	26.9
1948	41.6	29.8	11.8	269.3	192.9	76.4
1949	39.4	38.8	0.6	249.1	245.5	3.7
1950	39.4	42.6	–3.1	241.4	260.5	–19.1
1951	51.6	45.5	6.1	324.2	285.9	38.3
1952	66.2	67.7	–1.5	406.7	416.0	–9.3
1953	69.6	76.1	–6.5	406.6	444.5	–37.9
1954	69.7	70.9	–1.2	394.9	401.4	–6.5
1955	65.5	68.4	–3.0	363.4	380.0	–16.6
1956	74.6	70.6	3.9	391.1	370.4	20.7
1957	80.0	76.6	3.4	396.6	379.7	16.9
1958	79.6	82.4	–2.8	374.9	388.0	–13.0
1959	79.2	92.1	–12.8	352.4	409.5	–57.1
1960	92.5	92.2	0.3	393.4	392.1	1.3
1961	94.4	97.7	–3.3	392.1	406.0	–13.9
1962	99.7	106.8	–7.1	406.8	436.0	–29.2
1963	106.6	111.3	–4.8	418.9	437.6	–18.7
1964	112.6	118.5	–5.9	433.8	456.6	–22.8
1965	116.8	118.2	–1.4	440.8	446.1	–5.3
1966	130.8	134.5	–3.7	478.9	492.4	–13.5
1967	148.8	157.5	–8.6	529.0	559.8	–30.7
1968	153.0	178.1	–25.2	522.6	608.6	–86.0
1969	186.9	183.6	3.2	604.4	593.9	10.5
1970	192.8	195.6	–2.8	587.5	596.1	–8.7
1971	187.1	210.2	–23.0	533.5	599.1	–65.7
1972	207.3	230.7	–23.4	554.9	617.5	–62.6
1973	230.8	245.7	–14.9	582.7	620.3	–37.6
1974	263.2	269.4	–6.1	611.2	625.4	–14.2

CHART VII

Summary of receipts, outlays, and surpluses or deficits in current dollars, from 1940–2000, constant (FY 1987) dollars, from the U.S. Government Printing Office

(continued)

Fiscal Year	In Current Dollars			In Constant (FY 1987 Dollars)		
	Receipts	Outlays	Surplus or Deficit (–)	Receipts	Outlays	Surplus or Deficit (–)
1975	279.1	332.3	–53.2	586.6	698.5	–111.9
1976	298.1	371.8	–73.7	584.7	729.3	–144.6
TQ	81.2	96.0	–14.7	153.6	181.5	–27.9
1977	355.6	409.2	–53.7	643.8	740.9	–97.2
1978	399.6	458.7	–59.2	674.0	773.9	–99.8
1979	463.3	504.0	–40.7	719.2	782.4	–63.2
1980	517.1	590.9	–73.8	728.1	832.1	–104.0
1981	599.3	678.2	–79.0	766.6	867.7	–101.0
1982	617.8	745.8	–128.0	738.2	891.1	–152.9
1983	600.6	808.4	–207.8	684.3	921.1	–236.8
1984	666.5	851.8	–185.4	730.4	933.5	–203.2
1985	734.1	946.4	–212.3	776.6	1,001.3	–224.6
1986	769.1	990.3	–221.2	790.0	1,017.3	–227.3
1987	854.1	1,003.9	–149.8	854.1	1,003.9	–149.8
1988	909.0	1,064.1	–155.2	877.3	1,027.1	–149.8
1989	990.7	1,143.2	–152.5	916.2	1,057.2	–141.0
1990	1,031.3	1,252.7	–221.4	914.1	1,110.4	–196.2
1991	1,054.3	1,323.4	–269.2	894.7	1,123.2	–228.4
1992	1,090.5	1,380.9	–290.4	895.1	1,133.4	–238.4
1993	1,153.5	1,408.7	–255.1	921.9	1,125.8	–203.9
1994	1,257.7	1,460.9	–203.2	981.7	1,140.3	–158.6
1995 estimate	1,346.4	1,538.9	–192.5	1,022.0	1,168.1	–146.1
1996 estimate	1,415.5	1,612.1	–196.7	1,041.3	1,186.0	–144.7
1997 estimate	1,471.6	1,684.7	–213.1	1,048.8	1,200.6	–151.9
1998 estimate	1,548.8	1,745.2	–196.4	1,070.5	1,206.2	–135.7
1999 estimate	1,624.7	1,822.2	–197.4	1,089.4	1,221.8	–132.4
2000 estimate	1,710.9	1,905.3	–194.4	1,112.8	1,239.2	–126.5

MEMBERS OF 104TH CONGRESS

ALABAMA

Senators

Senator Howell T. Heflin (D)
728 Hart Senate
Office Building
Washington, DC 20510
Phone: 202-224-4124
FAX: 202-224-3149

Senator Richard C. Shelby (D)
509 Hart Senate
Office Building
Washington, DC 20510
Phone: 202-224-5744
FAX: 202-224-3416

Representatives

Rep. Sonny Callahan (R) (First District)
2418 Rayburn House
Office Building
Washington, DC 20515
Phone: 202-225-4931
FAX: 202-225-0562

Rep. Terry Everett (R) (Second District)
208 Cannon House
Office Building
Washington, DC 20515
Phone: 202-225-2901
FAX: (Unlisted)

Rep. Glen Browder (D) (Third District)
1221 Longworth House
Office Building
Washington, DC 20515
Phone: 202-225-3261
FAX: 202-225-9020

Rep. Tom Bevill (D) (Fourth District)
2302 Rayburn House
Office Building
Washington, DC 20515
Phone: 202-225-4876
FAX: 202-225-1604

Rep. Robert "Bud" Cramer (D) (Fifth District)
1318 Longworth House
Office Building
Washington, DC 20515
Phone: 202-225-4801
FAX: 202-225-4392

Rep. Spencer Bachus (R) (Sixth District)
216 Cannon House
Office Building
Washington, DC 20515
Phone: 202-225-4921
FAX: 202-225-2082

Rep. Earl F. Hilliard (D) (Seventh District)
1007 Longworth House
Office Building
Washington, DC 20515
Phone: 202-225-2665
FAX: 202-226-0772

ALASKA

Senators

Senator Ted Stevens (R)
522 Hart Senate
Office Building
Washington, DC 20510
Phone: 202-224-3004
FAX: 202-224-2354

Senator Frank H. Murkowski (R)
706 Hart Senate
Office Building
Washington, DC 20510
Phone: 202-224-6665
FAX: 202-224-5301

Representative At Large

Rep. Don Young (R) 2331 Rayburn House
Office Building
Washington, DC 20515
Phone: 202-225-5765
FAX: 202-225-0425

ARIZONA

Senators

Senator John Kyl (R)
328 Hart Senate
Office Building
Washington, DC 20510
Phone: 202-224-4521
FAX: 202-224-2302

Senator John S. McCain (R)
111 Russell Senate
Office Building
Washington, DC 20510
Phone: 202-224-2235
FAX: 202-228-2862

Representatives

Rep. Matt Salmon (R) (First District)
1607 Longworth House
Office Building
Washington, DC 20515
Phone: 202-225-2635
FAX: 202-225-2607

Rep. Ed. Pastor
(D) (Second District)
408 Cannon House
Office Building
Washington, DC 20515
Phone: 202-225-4065
FAX: 202-225-1655

Rep. Bob Stump
(R) (Third District)
211 Cannon House
Office Building
Washington, DC 20515
Phone: 202-225-4576
FAX: 202-225-6328

Rep. John Shadegg
(R) (Fourth District)
2440 Rayburn House
Office Building
Washington, DC 20515
Phone: 202-225-3361
FAX: 202-225-1143

Rep. James Thomas Kolbe (R) (Fifth District)
405 Cannon House
Office Building
Washington, DC 20515
Phone: 202-225-2542
FAX: 202-225-0378

Rep. J. D. Hayworth
(R) (Sixth District)
1024 Longworth House
Office Building
Washington. DC 20515
Phone: 202-225-2190
FAX: 202-225-8819

ARKANSAS

Senators
Senator Dale Bumpers
(D)
229 Dirksen Senate
Office Building
Washington, DC 20510
Phone: 202-224-4843
FAX: 202-224-6435

Senator David H. Pryor
(D)
267 Russell Senate
Office Building
Washington, DC 20510
Phone: 202-224-2353
FAX: 202-224-8261

Representatives
Rep. Blanche Lambert
(D) (First District)
1204 Longworth House
Office Building
Washington, DC 20515
Phone: 202-225-4076
FAX: 202-225-4654

Rep. Ray Thornton
(D) (Second District)
1214 Longworth House
Office Building
Washington, DC 20515
Phone: 202-225-2506
FAX: 202-225-9273

Rep. Tim Hutchinson
(R) (Third District)
1541 Longworth House
Office Building
Washington, DC 20515
Phone: 202-225-4301
FAX: 202-225-7492

Rep. Jay Dickey
(R) (Fourth District)
1338 Longworth House
Office Building
Washington, DC 20515
Phone: 202-225-3772
FAX: 202-225-1314

CALIFORNIA

Senators
Senator Barbara Boxer
(D)
112 Hart Senate
Office Building
Washington, DC 20510
Phone: 202-224-3553
FAX: 202-224-6252

Senator Dianne Feinstein
(D)
331 Hart Senate
Office Building
Washington, DC 20510
Phone: 202-224-3841
FAX: 202-224-0656

Representatives

Rep. Frank Riggs
(D) (First District)
114 Cannon House
Office Building
Washington, DC 20515
Phone: 202-225-3311
FAX: 202-225-7710

Rep. Wally Herger
(R) (Second District)
2433 Longworth House
Office Building
Washington, DC 20515
Phone: 202-225-3076
FAX: 202-225-1609

Rep. Vic Fazio (D)
(Third District)
2113 Rayburn House
Office Building
Washington, DC 20515
Phone: 202-225-5716
FAX: 202-225-0354

Rep. John T. Doolittle
(R) (Fourth District)
1542 Longworth House
Office Building
Washington, DC 20515
Phone: 202-225-2511
FAX: 202-225-5444

Rep. Robert T. Matsui
(D) (Fifth District)
2311 Rayburn House
Office Building
Washington, DC 20515
Phone: 202-225-7163
FAX: 202-225-0566

Rep. Lynn Woolsey
(D) (Sixth District)
439 Cannon House
Office Building
Washington, DC 20515
Phone: 202-225-5161
FAX: 202-225-5163

Rep. George Miller
(D) (Seventh District)
2205 Rayburn House
Office Building
Washington, DC 20515
Phone: 202-225-2095
FAX: 202-225-5609

Rep. Nancy Pelosi
(D) (Eighth District)
240 Cannon House
Office Building
Washington, DC 20515
Phone: 202-225-4965
FAX: 202-225-8259

Rep. Ronald V. Delhums
(D) (Ninth District)
2108 Rayburn House
Office Building
Washington, DC 20515
Phone: 202-225-2661
FAX: 202-225-9817

Rep. Bill Baker
(R) (Tenth District)
1714 Longworth House
Office Building
Washington, DC 20515
Phone: 202-225-1880
FAX: 202-225-2150

Rep. Richard W. Pombo
(R) (Eleventh District)
1519 Longworth House
Office Building
Washington, DC 20515
Phone: 202-225-1947
FAX: 202-226-0861

Rep. Tom Lantos
(D) (Twelfth District)
2182 Rayburn House
Office Building
Washington, DC 20515
Phone: 202-225-3531
FAX: 202-225-3127

Rep. Fortney H. "Pete" Stark (D)
(Thirteenth District)
239 Cannon House
Office Building
Washington, DC 20515
Phone: 202-225-5065
FAX: (Unlisted)

Rep. Anna G. Eshoo
(D) (Fourteenth District)
1505 Longworth House
Office Building
Washington, DC 20515
Phone: 202-225-8104
FAX: 202-225-8890

Rep. Norman Y. Mineta
(D) (Fifteenth District)
2221 Rayburn House
Office Building
Washington, DC 20515
Phone: 202-225-2631
FAX: (Unlisted)

Rep. Zoe Lofgren
(D) (Sixteenth District)
2307 Rayburn House
Office Building
Washington, DC 20515
Phone: 220-225-3072
FAX: 202-225-9460

Rep. Sam Farr
(D) (Seventeenth District)
1216 Longworth House
Office Building
Washington, DC 20515
Phone: 202-225-2861
FAX: 202-225-2861

Rep. Gary Condit
(D) (Eighteenth District)
1123 Longworth House
Office Building
Washington, DC 20515
Phone: 202-225-6131
FAX: 202-225-0819

Rep. George Radanovich
(R) (Nineteenth District)
1226 Longworth House
Office Building
Washington, DC 20515
Phone: 202-225-4540
FAX: 202-225-5274

Rep. Calvin Dooley
(D) (Twentieth District)
1227 Longworth House
Office Building
Washington, DC 20515
Phone: 202-225-3341
FAX: 202-225-9308

Rep. William M. Thomas
(R) (Twenty-First District)
2209 Rayburn House
Office Building
Washington, DC 20515
Phone: 202-225-2915
FAX: 202-225-8798

Rep. Michael Huffington
(R) (Twenty-Second
District)
113 Cannon House
Office Building
Washington, DC 20515
Phone: 202-225-3601
FAX: 202-226-1015

Rep. Elton William
Gallegly (R)
(Twenty-Third District)
2441 Rayburn House
Office Building
Washington, DC 20515
Phone: 202-225-5811
FAX: 202-225-0713

Rep. Anthony C.
Beilenson (D)
(Twenty-Fourth District)
2465 Rayburn House
Office Building
Washington, DC 20515
Phone: 202-225-5911
FAX: (Unlisted)

Rep. Howard P. "Buck"
McKeon (R)
(Twenty-Fifth District)
307 Cannon House
Office Building
Washington, DC 20515
Phone: 202-225-1956
FAX: 202-226-0683

Rep. Howard L. Berman
(D) (Twenty-Sixth
District)
2201 Rayburn House
Office Building
Washington, DC 20515
Phone: 202-225-4695
FAX: 202-225-5279

Rep. Carlos J. Moorhead
(R) (Twenty-Seventh
District)
2346 Rayburn House
Office Building
Washington, DC 20515
Phone: 202-225-4176
FAX: 202-226-1279

Rep. David Timothy
Dreier (R)
(Twenty-Eighth District)
411 Cannon House
Office Building
Washington, DC 20515
Phone: 202-225-2305
FAX: 202-225-4745

Rep. Henry A. Waxman
(D) (Twenty-Ninth
District)
2408 Rayburn House
Office Building
Washington, DC 20515
Phone: 202-225-3976
FAX: 202-225-4099

Rep. Xavier Becerra
(D) (Thirtieth District)
1710 Longworth House
Office Building
Washington, DC 20515
Phone: 202-225-6235
FAX: 202-225-2202

Rep. Matthew G.
Martinez (D) (Thirty-First
District) 2231 Rayburn
House
Office Building
Washington, DC 20515
Phone: 202-225-5464
FAX: 202-225-5467

Rep. Julian Carey Dixon
(D) (Thirty-Second
District)
2400 Rayburn House
Office Building
Washington, DC 20515
Phone: 202-225-7084
FAX: 202-225-4091

Rep. Lucille Roybal-Allard (D)
(Thirty-Third District)
324 Cannon House
Office Building
Washington, DC 20515
Phone: 202-225-1766
FAX: 202-226-0350

Rep. Esteban E. Torres (D) (Thirty-Fourth District)
1740 Longworth House
Office Building
Washington, DC 20515
Phone: 202-225-5256
FAX: 202-225-9711

Rep. Maxine Waters (D)
(Thirty-Fifth District)
1207 Longworth House
Office Building
Washington, DC 20515
Phone: 202-225-2201
FAX: 202-225-7854

Rep. Jane Harman (D)
(Thirty-Sixth District)
325 Cannon House
Office Building
Washington, DC 20515
Phone: 202-225-8220
FAX: 202-226-0684

Rep. Walter R. Tucker, III (D) (Thirty-Seventh District)
419 Cannon House
Office Building
Washington, DC 20515
Phone: 202-225-7924
FAX: 202-225-7926

Rep. Steve Horn (R)
(Thirty-Eighth District)
1023 Longworth House
Office Building
Washington, DC 20515
Phone: 202-225-6676
FAX: 202-226-1012

Rep. Ed Royce (R)
(Thirty-Ninth District)
1404 Longworth House
Office Building
Washington. DC 20515
Phone: 202-225-4111
FAX: 202-226-0335

Rep. Jerry Lewis (R)
(Fortieth District)
2312 Rayburn House
Office Building
Washington, DC 20515
Phone: 202-225-5861
FAX: 202-225-6498

Rep. Jay C. Kim (R)
(Forty-First District)
502 Cannon House
Office Building.
Washington, DC 20515
Phone: 202-225-3201
FAX: 202-226-1485

Rep. George E Brown, Jr. (D)
(Forty-Second District)
2300 Rayburn House
Office Building
Washington, DC 20515
Phone: 202-225-6161
FAX: 202-225-8671

Rep. Ken Calvert (R)
(Forty-Third District)
1523 Longworth House
Office Building
Washington, DC 20515
Phone: 202-225-1986
FAX: (Unavailable)

Rep. Sonny Bono (R)
(Forty-Fourth District)
2422 Longworth House
Office Building
Washington, DC 20515
Phone: 202-225-5330
FAX: 202-226-1040

Rep. Dana Rohrabacher (R) (Forty-Fifth District)
1027 Longworth House
Office Building
Washington, DC 20515
Phone: 202-225-2415
FAX: 202-225-0145

Rep. Robert K. Dornan (R) (Forty-Sixth District)
2402 Rayburn House
Office Building
Washington, DC 20515
Phone: 202-225-2965
FAX: 202-225-3694

Rep. C. Christopher Cox (R) (Forty-Seventh District)
206 Cannon House
Office Building
Washington, DC 20515
Phone: 202-225-5611
FAX: 202-225-9177

Rep. Ronald C. Packard (R) (Forty-Eighth District)
2162 Rayburn House Office Building
Washington, DC 20515
Phone: 202-225-3906
FAX: 202-225-0134

Rep. Brian Bilbray (R)
(Forty-Ninth District)
315 Cannon House Office Building
Washington, DC 20515
Phone: 202-225-2040
FAX: 202-225-2042

Rep. Bob Filner (D)
(Fiftieth District)
504 Cannon House Office Building
Washington, DC 20515
Phone: 202-225-8045
FAX: 202-225-9073

Rep. Randy "Duke" Cunningham (R)
(Fifty-First District)
117 Cannon House Office Building
Washington, DC 20515
Phone: 202-225-5452
FAX: 202-225-2558

Rep. Duncan Lee Hunter (R) (Fifty-Second District)
133 Cannon House Office Building
Washington, DC 20515
Phone: 202-225-5672
FAX: 202-225-0235

COLORADO

Senators

Senator Ben Nighthorse Campbell (D)
380 Russell Senate Office Building
Washington, DC 20510
Phone: 202-224-5852
FAX: 202-2263714

Senator Hank Brown (R)
716 Hart Senate Office Building
Washington, DC 20510
Phone: 202-224-5941
FAX: 202-224-6471

Representatives

Rep. Patricia S. Schroeder (D)
(First District)
2208 Rayburn House Office Building
Washington, DC 20515
Phone: 202-225-4431
FAX: 202-225-5842

Rep. David E. Skaggs (D)
(Second District)
1124 Longworth House Office Building
Washington, DC 20515
Phone: 202-225-2161
FAX: 202-225-9127

Rep. Scott McInnis (R)
(Third District)
512 Cannon House Office Building
Washington, DC 20515
Phone: 202-225-4761
FAX: 202-226-0622

Rep. Wayne Allard (R)
(Fourth District)
422 Cannon House Office Building
Washington, DC 20515
Phone: 202-225-4676
FAX: 202-225-8630

Rep. Joel Hefley (R)
(Fifth District)
2442 Rayburn House Office Building
Washington, DC 20515
Phone: 202-225-4422
FAX: 202-225-1942

Rep. Dan L. Schaefer (R)
(Sixth District)
2448 Rayburn House Office Building
Washington, DC 20515
Phone: 202-225-7882
FAX: 202-225-7885

CONNECTICUT

Senators

Senator Christopher J. Dodd (D)
444 Russell Senate Office Building
Washington, DC 20510
Phone: 202-224-2823
FAX: 202-224-5431

Senator Joseph I. Lieberman (D)
316 Hart Senate Office Building
Washington, DC 20510
Phone: 202-224-4041
FAX: 202-224-9750

Representatives

Rep. Barbara B. Kennedy (D)
(First District)
201 Cannon House
Office Building
Washington, DC 20515
Phone: 202-225-2265
FAX: 202-225-1031

Rep. Samuel Gejdenson (D) (Second District)
2416 Rayburn House
Office Building
Washington, DC 20515
Phone: 202-225-2076
FAX: 202-225-4977

Rep. Rosa DeLauro ID)
(Third District)
327 Cannon House
Office Building
Washington, DC 20515
Phone: 202-225-3661
FAX: 202-225-4890

Rep. Christopher Shays (R) (Fourth District)
1034 Longworth House
Office Building
Washington, DC 20515
Phone: 202-225-5541
FAX: 202-225-9629

Rep. Gary Franks (R)
(Fifth District)
435 Cannon House
Office Building
Washington, DC 20515
Phone: 202-225-3822
FAX: 202-225-5085

Rep. Nancy Lee Johnson (R) (Sixth District)
343 Cannon House
Office Building
Washington, DC 20515
Phone: 202-225-4476
FAX: 202-225-4488

DELAWARE

Senators

Senator William V. Roth, Jr. (R)
104 Hart Senate
Office Building
Washington, DC 20514
Phone: 202-224-2441
FAX: 202-224-2805

Senator Joseph R. Biden, Jr. (D)
221 Russell Senate
Office Building
Washington, DC 20514
Phone: 202-224-5042
FAX: 202-224-0139

Representative At Large

Rep. Michael N. Castle (R) 1205 Longworth
House Office Building
Washington, DC 20515
Phone: 202-225-4165
FAX: 202-225-2291

FLORIDA

Senators

Senator Robert Graham (D)
524 Hart Senate
Office Building
Washington, DC 20510
Phone: 202-224-3041
FAX: 202-224-2237

Senator Connie Mack, III (R)
517 Hart Senate
Office Building
Washington, DC 20510
Phone: 202-224-5274
FAX: 202-224-2237

Representatives

Rep. Joe Scarborough (D) (First District)
2435 Rayburn House
Office Building
Washington, DC 20515
Phone: 202-225-4136
Fax: 202-225-5785

Rep. Pete Peterson (D)
(Second District)
426 Cannon House
Office Building
Washington, DC 20515
Phone: 202-225-5235
Fax: 202-225-1586

Rep. Corrine Brown (D)
(Third District)
1037 Longworth House
Office Building
Washington, DC 20515
Phone: 202-225-0123
FAX: 202-225-2256

Rep. Tillie Fowler (R)
(Fourth District)
413 Cannon House
Office Building
Washington, DC 20515
Phone: 202-225-2501
FAX: 202-226-9318

Rep. Karen L. Thurman (D) (Fifth District)
130 Cannon House
Office Building
Washington, DC 20515
Phone: 202-225-1002
FAX: 202-226-0329

Rep. Cliff Stearns (R)
(Sixth District)
332 Cannon House
Office Building, #2015
Washington, DC 20515
Phone: 202-225-5744
FAX: 202-225-3973

Rep. John L. Mica (R)
(Seventh District)
427 Cannon House
Office Building
Washington, DC 20515
Phone: 202-225-4035
FAX: 202-226-0821

Rep. Bill McCollum (R)
(Eighth District)
2266 Rayburn House
Office Building
Washington, DC 20515
Phone: 202-225-2176
FAX: 202-225-0999

Rep. Michael Bilirakis (R) (Ninth District)
2240 Rayburn House
Office Building
Washington, DC 20515
Phone: 202-225-5755
FAX: 202-225-4085

Rep. C. W. Bill Young (R) (Tenth District)
2407 Rayburn House
Office Building
Washington, DC 20515
Phone: 202-225-5961
FAX: 202-225-9764

Rep. Sam M. Gibbons (D) (Eleventh District)
2204 Rayburn House
Office Building
Washington, DC 20515
Phone: 202-225-3376
FAX: (Unlisted)

Rep. Charles T. Canady (R) (Twelfth District)
1107 Longworth House
Office Building
Washington, DC 20515
Phone: 202-225-1252
FAX: 202-225-2279

Rep. Dan Miller (R)
(Thirteenth District)
510 Cannon House
Office Building
Washington, DC 20515
Phone: 202-225-5015
FAX: 202-226-0828

Rep. Porter Goss (R)
(Fourteenth District)
330 Cannon House
Office Building
Washington, DC 20515
Phone: 202-225-2536
FAX: 202-225-6820

Rep. Dave Weldon (D)
(Fifteenth District)
432 Cannon House
Office Building
Washington, DC 20515
Phone: 202-225-3671
FAX: 202-225-9039

Rep. Mark Foley (R)
(Sixteenth District)
2351 Rayburn House
Office Building
Washington, DC 20515
Phone: 202-225-5792
FAX: 202-225-1860

Rep. Carrie Meek (D)
(Seventeenth District)
404 Cannon House
Office Building
Washington, DC 20515
Phone: 202-225-4506
FAX: 202-226-0777

Rep. Ileana Ros-Lehtinen (R)
(Eighteenth District)
127 Cannon House
Office Building
Washington, DC 20515
Phone: 202-225-3931
FAX 202-225-5620

Rep. Harry A. Johnston, II (D)
(Nineteenth District)
204 Cannon House
Office Building
Washington, DC 20515
Phone: 202-225-3001
FAX: 202-225-8791

Rep. Peter Deustch (D)
(Twentieth District)
425 Cannon House
Office Building
Washington, DC 20515
Phone: 202-225-7931
FAX: 202-225-8456

Rep. Lincoln Diaz-Balart (R)
(Twenty-First District)
509 Cannon House
Office Building
Washington, DC 20515
Phone: 202-225-4211
FAX: 202-225-8576

Rep. E. Clay Shaw, Jr. (R)
(Twenty-Second District)
2267 Rayburn House
Office Building
Washington, DC 20515
Phone: 202-225-3026
FAX: 202-225-8398

Rep. Alcee L. Hastings (D)
(Twenty-Third District)
1039 Longworth House
Office Building
Washington, DC 20515
Phone: 202-225-1313
FAX: 202-226-0690

GEORGIA

Senators
Senator Samuel A. Nunn (D)
303 Dirksen Senate
Office Building
Washington, DC 20510
Phone: 202-224-3521
FAX: 202-224-0072

Senator Paul Coverdell (R)
200 Russell Senate
Office Building
Washington, DC 20510
Phone: 202-224-3643
FAX: 202-224-8227

Representatives
Rep. Jack Kingston (R)
(First District)
1229 Longworth House
Office Building
Washington, DC 20515
Phone: 202-225-5831
FAX: 202-226-2269

Rep. Sanford Bishop (D)
(Second District)
1632 Longworth House
Office Building
Washington, DC 20515
Phone: 202-225-3631
FAX: 202-225-2203

Rep. Mac Collins (R)
(Third District)
1118 Longworth House
Office Building
Washington, DC 20515
Phone: 202-225-5901
FAX: 202-225-2515

Rep. John Linder (R)
(Fourth District)
1605 Longworth House
Office Building
Washington, DC 20515
Phone: 202-225-4272
FAX: 202-225-4696

Rep. John R. Lewis (D)
(Fifth District)
329 Cannon House
Office Building
Washington, DC 20515
Phone: 202-225-3801
FAX: 202-225-0351

Rep. Newton L. Gingrich (R)
(Sixth District)
2428 Rayburn House
Office Building
Washington, DC 20515
Phone: 202-225-4501
FAX: 202-225-4656

Rep. Robert Barr (D)
(Seventh District)
2303 Rayburn House
Office Building
Washington, DC 20515
Phone: 202-225-2931
FAX: 202-225-0473

Rep. Saxby Chambuss (R) (Eighth District)
2134 Rayburn House
Office Building
Washington, DC 20515
Phone: 202-225-6531
FAX: 202-225-7719

Rep. Nathan Deal (D)
(Ninth District)
1406 Longworth House
Office Building
Washington, DC 20515
Phone: 202-225-5211
FAX: 202-225-8272

Rep. Charles Norwood (R) (Tenth District)
226 Cannon House
Office Building
Washington, DC 20515
Phone: 202-225-4101
FAX: 202-226-1466

Rep. Cynthia McKinney (D) (Eleventh District)
124 Cannon House
Office Building
Washington, DC 20515
Phone: 202-225-1605
FAX: 202-226-0691

HAWAII

Senators

Senator Daniel K. Inouye (D)
722 Hart Senate
Office Building
Washington, DC 20510
Phone: 202-224-3934
FAX: 202-224-6747

Senator Daniel K. Akaka (D)
720 Hart Senate
Office Building
Washington, DC 20510
Phone: 202-224-6361
FAX 202-224-2126

Representatives

Rep. Neil Abercrombie (D) (First District)
1440 Longworth House
Office Building
Washington, DC 20515
Phone: 202-225-2726
FAX: 202-225-4580

Rep. Patsy T. Mink (D)
(Second District)
2135 Rayburn House
Office Building
Washington, DC 20515
Phone: 202-225-4906
FAX: 202-225-4987

IDAHO

Senators

Senator Dirk Kempthorne (R)
367 Dirksen Senate
Office Building
Washington, DC 20510
Phone: 202-224-6142
FAX: 202-224-5893

Senator Larry Craig (R)
313 Hart Senate
Office Building
Washington, DC 20510
Phone: 202-224-2752
FAX: 202-224-2573

Representatives

Rep. Helen Chenoweth (R)
(First District)
1117 Longworth House
Office Building
Washington, DC 20515
Phone: 202-225-55
FAX: 202-226-1213

Rep. Michael D. Crapo (R) (Second District)
437 Cannon House
Office Building
Washington, DC 20515
Phone: 202-225-5531
FAX: 202-334-1953

ILLINOIS

Senators

Senator Carol Moseley-Braun (D)
320 Hart Senate
Office Building
Washington, DC 20510
Phone: 202-224-2854
FAX: unlisted

Senator Paul Simon (D)
462 Dirksen Senate
Office Building
Washington, DC 20510
Phone: 202-224-2152
FAX: 202-224-0868

Representatives

Rep. Bobby L. Rush (D)
(First District)
1725 Longworth House
Office Building
Washington, DC 20515
Phone: 202-225-4372
FAX: 202-226-0333

Rep. Melvin J. Reynolds (D) (Second District)
514 Cannon House
Office Building
Washington, DC 20515
Phone: 202-225-0773
FAX: 202-225-0774

Rep. William O. Lipinski (D) (Third District)
1501 Longworth House
Office Building
Washington, DC 20515
Phone: 202-225-5701
FAX: 202-225-1012

Rep. Luis V. Gutierrez (D) (Fourth District)
1208 Longworth House
Office Building
Washington, DC 20515
Phone: 202-225-8203
FAX: 202-225-7810

Rep. Michael Flanaghan (D) (Fifth District)
2111 Rayburn House
Office Building
Washington, DC 20515
Phone: 202-225-4061
FAX: 202-225-4064

Rep. Henry John Hyde (R) (Sixth District)
2110 Rayburn House
Office Building
Washington, DC 20515
Phone: 202-225-4561
FAX: 202-226-1240

Rep. Cardiss Collins (D)
(Seventh District)
2308 Rayburn House
Office Building
Washington, DC 20515
Phone: 202-225-5006
FAX: 202-225-8396

Rep. Philip Miller Crane (R) (Eighth District)
233 Cannon House
Office Building
Washington, DC 20515
Phone: 202-225-3711
FAX: 202-225-7830

Rep. Sidney R Yates (D)
(Ninth District)
2109 Rayburn House
Office Building
Washington, DC 20515
Phone: 202-225-2111
FAX: 202-225-3493

Rep. John E. Porter (R)
(Tenth District)
1026 Longworth House
Office Building, #2015
Washington, DC 20515
Phone: 202-225-4835
FAX: 202-225-0157

Rep. Gerald Weber (R)
(Eleventh District)
1032 Longworth House
Office Building
Washington, DC 20515
Phone: 202-225-3635
FAX: 202-225-4447

Rep. Jerry F. Costello (D)
(Twelfth District)
119 Cannon House
Office Building
Washington, DC 20515
Phone: 202-225-5661
FAX: 202-225-0285

Rep. Harris W. Fawell (R) (Thirteenth District)
2342 Rayburn House
Office Building
Washington, DC 20515
Phone: 202-225-3515
FAX: 202-225-9420

Rep. John D. Hastert (R)
(Fourteenth District)
2453 Rayburn House
Office Building
Washington, DC 20515
Phone: 202-225-2976
FAX: 202-225-0697

Rep. Thomas Ewing (R)
(Fifteenth District)
1317 Longworth House
Office Building
Washington, DC 20515
Phone: 202-225-2371
FAX: 202-225-8071

Rep. Donald Manzullo (R) (Sixteenth District)
506 Cannon House
Office Building
Washington, DC 20515
Phone: 202-225-5676
FAX: 202-225-5284

Rep. Lane Evans (D)
(Seventeenth District)
2335 Rayburn House
Office Building
Washington, DC 20515
Phone: 202-225-5905
FAX: 202-225-5396

Rep. Ray LaHood (R)
(Eighteenth District)
2112 Rayburn House
Office Building
Washington, DC 20515
Phone: 202-225-6201
FAX: 202-225-9249

Rep. Glenn Poshard (D)
(Nineteenth District)
107 Cannon House
Office Building
Washington, DC 20515
Phone: 202-225-5201
FAX: 202-225-1541

Rep. Richard J. Durbin (D)
(Twentieth District)
2463 Rayburn House
Office Building
Washington, DC 20515
Phone: 202-225-5271
FAX: 202-225-0170

INDIANA

__Senators__

Senator Richard Green Lugar (R)
306 Hart Senate
Office Building
Washington, DC 20510
Phone: 202-224-4814
FAX: 202-224-7877

Senator Daniel R. Coats (R)
404 Russell Senate
Office Building
Washington, DC 20510
Phone: 202-224-5623
FAX: 202-224-1966

__Representatives__

Rep. Peter J. Visclosky (D) (First District)
2464 Rayburn House
Office Building
Washington, DC 20515
Phone: 202-225-2461
FAX: 202-225-2493

Rep. David McIntosh (R)
(Second District)
2217 Rayburn House
Office Building
Washington, DC 20515
Phone: 202-225-3021
FAX: 202-225-8140

Rep. Tim Roemer (D)
(Third District)
415 Cannon House
Office Building
Washington, DC 20515
Phone: 202-225-3915
FAX: 202-225-6798

Rep. Mark Souder (R)
(Fourth District)
1513 Longworth House
Office Building
Washington, DC 20515
Phone: 202-225-4436
FAX: 202-225-8810

Rep. Steve Buyer (R)
(Fifth District)
1419 Longworth House
Office Building
Washington, DC 20515
Phone: 202-225-5037
FAX: (Unlisted)

Rep. Dan Burton (R)
(Sixth District)
2411 Rayburn House
Office Building
Washington, DC 20515
Phone: 202-225-2276
FAX: 202-225-0016

Rep. John T. Myers (R)
(Seventh District)
2372 Rayburn House
Office Building
Washington, DC 20515
Phone: 202-225-5805
FAX: 202-225-1649

Rep. John Hostettler (R)
(Eighth District)
306 Cannon House
Office Building
Washington, DC 20515
Phone: 202-225-4636
FAX: 202-225-4688

Rep. Lee H. Hamilton (D)
(Ninth District)
2187 Rayburn House
Office Building
Washington, DC 20515
Phone: 202-225-5315
FAX: 202-225-1101

Rep. Andrew Jacobs, Jr. (D) (Tenth District)
2313 Rayburn House
Office Building
Washington, DC 20515
Phone: 202-225-4011
FAX: 202-226-4093

IOWA

__Senators__

Senator Charles E. Grassley (R)
135 Hart Senate
Office Building
Washington, DC 20510
Phone: 202-224-3744
FAX: 202-224-6020

Senator Thomas R. Harkin (D)
531 Hart Senate
Office Building
Washington, DC 20510
Phone: 202-224-3254
FAX: 202-224-9369

Representatives

Rep. James A. S. Leach (R) (First District)
2186 Longworth House
Office Building
Washington, DC 20515
Phone: 202-225-6576
FAX: 202-226-1278

Rep. Jim Nussle (R)
(Second District)
308 Cannon House
Office Building
Washington, DC 20515
Phone: 202-225-2911
FAX: 202-225-9129

Rep. James R. Lighfoot (R) (Third District)
2444 Rayburn House
Office Building
Washington, DC 20515
Phone: 202-225-3806
FAX: 202-225-6973

Rep. Greg Ganske (R)
(Fourth District)
2373 Rayburn House
Office Building
Washington, DC 20515
Phone: 202-225-4426
FAX: (Unlisted)

Rep. Tom Latham (R)
(Fifth District)
418 Cannon House
Office Building
Washington, DC 20515
Phone: 202-225-5476
FAX: 202-225-5796

KANSAS

Senators

Senator Robert Dole (R)
141 Hart Senate
Office Building
Washington, DC 20510
Phone: 202-224-6521
FAX: 202-224-8952

Senator Nancy Landon Kassebaum (R)
302 Russell Senate
Office Building
Washington, DC 20510
Phone: 202-224-4774
FAX: 202-224-3514

Representatives

Rep. Charles P. Roberts (R) (First District)
1125 Longworth House
Office Building
Washington, DC 20515
Phone: 202-225-2715
FAX: 202-225-5375

Rep. Sam Brownback (R)
(Second District)
2243 Longworth House
Office Building
Washington, DC 20515
Phone: 202-225-6601
FAX: 202-225-1445

Rep. Jan Meyers (R)
(Third District)
2338 Rayburn House
Office Building
Washington, DC 20515
Phone: 202-225-2865
FAX: 202-225-0554

Rep. Todd Tiahrt (R)
(Fourth District)
2371 Rayburn House
Office Building
Washington, DC 20515
Phone: 202-225-6216
FAX: 202-225-5398

KENTUCKY

Senators

Senator Wendell Hampton Ford (D)
173A Russell Senate
Office Building
Washington, DC 20510
Phone: 202-224-4343
FAX: 202-224-1144

Senator Mitch McConnell (R)
120 Russell Senate
Office Building
Washington, DC 20510
Phone: 202-224-2541
FAX: 202-224-2499

Representatives

Rep. Edward Whitfield (R) (First District)
1533 Longworth House
Office Building
Washington, DC 20515
Phone: 202-225-3115
FAX: 202-225-2169

Rep. Ron Lewis (R)
(Second District)
2333 Rayburn House
Office Building
Washington, DC 20515
Phone: 202-225-3501
FAX: (Unlisted)

Rep. Mike Ward (D)
(Third District)
2246 Rayburn House
Office Building
Washington, DC 20515
Phone: 202-225-5401
FAX: (Unlisted)

Rep. Jim Bunning (R)
(Fourth District)
2437 Rayburn House
Office Building
Washington, DC 20515
Phone: 202-225-3465
FAX: 202-225-0003

Rep. Harold D. Rogers (R) (Fifth District)
2468 Cannon House
Office Building
Washington, DC 20515
Phone: 202-225-4601
FAX: 202-225-0940

Rep. Scotty Baesler (D)
(Sixth District)
508 Cannon House
Office Building
Washington, DC 20515
Phone: 202-225-4706
FAX: 202-225-2122

LOUISIANA

Senators

Senator J. Bennett Johnston, Jr. (D)
136 Hart Senate
Office Building
Washington, DC 20510
Phone: 202-224-5824
FAX: 202-224-2952

Senator John B. Breaux (D)
516 Hart Senate
Office Building
Washington, DC 20510
Phone: 202-224-4623
FAX: 202-224-2435

Representatives

Rep. Robert Livingston, Jr. (R) (First District)
2368 Longworth House
Office Building
Washington, DC 20515
Phone: 202-225-3015
FAX: 202-225-0739

Rep. William J. Jefferson (D) (Second District)
428 Cannon House
Office Building
Washington, DC 20515
Phone 202-225-6636
FAX: 202-225-1988

Rep. W.J. "Billy" Tauzin (D) (Third District)
2330 Rayburn House
Office Building
Washington, DC 20515
Phone: 202-225-4031
FAX: 202-225-0563

Rep. Cleo Fields (D)
(Fourth District)
513 Cannon House
Office Building
Washington, DC 20515
Phone: 202-225-8490
FAX: 220-225-8959

Rep. James O. McCrery, III (R) (Fifth District)
225 Cannon House
Office Building
Washington, DC 20515
Phone: 202-225-2777
FAX: 202-225-8039

Rep. Richard H. Baker (R) (Sixth District)
434 Cannon House
Office Building
Washington, DC 20515
Phone: 202-225-3901
FAX: 202-225-7313

Rep. James A. Hayes (D)
(Seventh District)
2432 Rayburn House
Office Building
Washington, DC 20515
Phone: 202-225-2031
FAX: 202-225-1175

MAINE

Senators

Senator William S. Cohen (R)
322 Hart Senate
Office Building
Washington, DC 20510
Phone: 202-224-2523
FAX: 202-224-2693

Senator Olympia Snow (R)
176 Russell Senate
Office Building
Washington, DC 20510
Phone: 202-224-5344
FAX: 202-224-6853

Representatives

Rep. James Longley (R)
(First District)
1530 Longworth House
Office Building
Washington, DC 20515
Phone: 202-225-6116
FAX: 202-225-9065

Rep. John Baldacci (D)
(Second District)
2268 Rayburn House
Office Building
Washington, DC 20515
Phone: 202-225-6306
FAX: 202-225-8297

MARYLAND

Senators

Senator Paul S. Sarbanes (D)
309 Hart Senate
Office Building
Washington, DC 20510
Phone: 202-224-4524
FAX: 202-224-1651

Senator Barbara A. Mikulski (D)
709 Hart Senate
Office Building
Washington, DC 20510
Phone: 202-224-4654
FAX: 202-224-8858

Representatives

Rep. Wayne T. Gilchrest (R) (First District)
412 Cannon House
Office Building
Washington, DC 20515
Phone: 202-225-5311
FAX: 202-225-0254

Rep. Robert Erlich (R)
(Second District)
1610 Longworth House
Office Building
Washington, DC 20515
Phone: 202-225-3061
FAX: 202-225-4251

Rep. Benjamin L. Cardin (D)
(Third District)
227 Cannon House
Office Building
Washington, DC 20515
Phone: 202-225-4016
FAX: 202-225-9219

Rep. Albert R. Wynn (D)
(Fourth District)
423 Cannon House
Office Building
Washington, DC 20515
Phone: 202-225-8699
FAX: 202-225-8714

Rep. Steny H. Hoyer (D)
(Fifth District)
1705 Longworth House
Office Building
Washington, DC 20515
Phone: 202-225-4131
FAX: 202-225-4300

Rep. Roscoe Bartlett (R)
(Sixth District)
312 Cannon House
Office Building
Washington, DC 20515
Phone: 202-225-2721
FAX: 202-225-2193

Rep. Kweisi Mfume (D)
(Seventh District)
2419 Rayburn House
Office Building
Washington, DC 20515
Phone: 202-225-4741
FAX: 202-225-3178

Rep. Constance A. Morella (R)
(Eighth District)
223 Cannon House
Office Building
Washington, DC 20515
Phone: 202-225-5341
FAX: 202-225-1389

MASSACHUSETTS

Senators

Senator Edward M. Kennedy (D)
315 Russell Senate
Office Building
Washington, DC 20510
Phone: 202-224-4543
FAX: 202-224-2417

Senator John Kerry (D)
421 Russell Senate
Office Building
Washington, DC 20510
Phone: 202-224-2742
FAX: 202-224-8525

<u>Representatives</u>

Rep. John W. Olver (D)
(First District)
1323 Longworth House
Office Building
Washington, DC 20515
Phone: 202-225-5335
FAX: 202-226-1224

Rep. Richard E. Neal (D)
(Second District)
131 Cannon House
Office Building
Washington, DC 20515
Phone: 202-225-5601
FAX: 202-225-8112

Rep. Peter I. Blute (R)
(Third District)
1029 Longworth House
Office Building
Washington, DC 20515
Phone: 202-225-6101
FAX: 202-225-2217

Rep. Barney Frank (D)
(Fourth District)
2404 Rayburn House
Office Building
Washington, DC 20515
Phone: 202-225-5931
FAX: 202-225-0182

Rep. Martin T. Meehan (D) (Fifth District)
1223 Longworth House
Office Building
Washington, DC 20515
Phone: 202-225-3411
FAX: 202-225-0771

Rep. Peter G. Torkildsen (R) (Sixth District)
120 Cannon House
Office Building
Washington, DC 20515
Phone: 202-225-8020
FAX: 202-225-8037

Rep. Edward J. Markey (D) (Seventh District)
2133 Rayburn House
Office Building
Washington, DC 20515
Phone: 202-225-2836
FAX: 202-225-8689

Rep. Joseph P. Kennedy, II (D) (Eighth District)
1210 Longworth House
Office Building
Washington, DC 20515
Phone: 202-225-5111
FAX: 202-225-9322

Rep. John J. Moakley (D)
(Ninth District)
235 Cannon House
Office Building
Washington, DC 20515
Phone: 202-225-8273
FAX: 202-225-3984

Rep. Gerry E. Studds (D)
(Tenth District)
237 Cannon House
Office Building
Washington, DC 20515
Phone: 202-225-3111
FAX: 202-225-2212

MICHIGAN

<u>Senators</u>

Senator Spencer Abraham (R)
105 Dirksen Senate
Office Building
Washington, DC 20510
Phone: 202-224-4822
FAX: 202-224-8834

Senator Carl M. Levin (D)
459 Russell Senate
Office Building
Washington, DC 20510
Phone: 202-224-6221
FAX: 202-224-5908

<u>Representatives</u>

Rep. Bart Stupak (D)
(First District)
317 Cannon House
Office Building
Washington, DC 20515
Phone: 202-225-4735
FAX: 202-225-4744

Rep. Peter Hoekstra (R)
(Second District)
1319 Longworth House
Office Building
Washington, DC 20515
Phone: 202-225-4401
FAX: 202-226-0779

Rep. Vernon Ehlers (R)
(Third District)
1526 Longworth House
Office Building
Washington, DC 20515
Phone: 202-225-3831
FAX: (Unlisted)

Rep. David Camp (R)
(Fourth District)
137 Cannon House
Office Building
Washington, DC 20515
Phone: 202-225-3561
FAX: 202-225-9679

Rep. James A. Barcia (D)
(Fifth District)
1717 Longworth House
Office Building
Washington, DC 20515
Phone: 202-225-8171
FAX: 202-225-2168

Rep. Frederick S. Upton (R) (Sixth District)
2439 Longworth House
Office Building
Washington, DC 20515
Phone: 202-225-3761
FAX: 202-225-4986

Rep. Nick Smith (R)
(Seventh District)
1708 Longworth House
Office Building
Washington, DC 20515
Phone: 202-225-6276
FAX: 202-225-6281

Rep. Dick Chrysler (R)
(Eighth District)
2347 Rayburn House
Office Building
Washington, DC 20515
Phone: 202-225-4872
FAX: 202-225-1260

Rep. Dale E. Kildee (D)
(Ninth District)
2239 Rayburn House
Office Building
Washington, DC 20515
Phone: 202-225-3611
FAX: 202-225-6393

Rep. David E. Bonior (D)
(Tenth District)
2207 Rayburn House
Office Building
Washington, DC 20515
Phone: 202-225-2106
FAX: 202-226-1169

Rep. Joe Knollenberg (R)
(Eleventh District)
1218 Longworth House
Office Building
Washington, DC 20515
Phone: 202-225-5802
FAX: 202-226-2356

Rep. Sander Martin Levin (D)
(Twelfth District)
106 Cannon House
Office Building
Washington, DC 20515
Phone: 202-225-4961
FAX: 202-226-1033

Rep. Lynn Rivers (D)
(Thirteenth District)
2107 Rayburn House
Office Building
Washington, DC 20515
Phone: 202-225-6261
FAX: 202-225-0489

Rep. John Conyers, Jr. (D) (Fourteenth District)
Rayburn House
Office Building
Washington, DC 20515
Phone: 202-225-5126
FAX: 202-225-0072

Rep. Barbara-Rose Collins (D)
(Fifteenth District)
1108 Longworth House
Office Building
Washington, DC 20515
Phone: 202-225-2261
FAX: 202-225-6645

Rep. John D. Dingell (D)
(Sixteenth District)
2328 Rayburn House
Office Building
Washington, DC 20515
Phone: 202-225-4071
FAX: 202-225-7426

MINNESOTA

Senators

Senator Rod Grams (R)
154 Russell Senate
Office Building
Washington, DC 20510
Phone: 202-224-3244
FAX: 202-224-9931

Senator Paul Wellstone (DFL)
717 Hart Senate
Office Building
Washington, DC 20510
Phone: 202-224-5641
FAX: 202-224-8438

Representatives

Rep. Gil Gutknecht (DFL) (First District)
436 Cannon House
Office Building
Washington, DC 20515
Phone: 202-225-2472
FAX: 202-225-0051

Rep, David Minge (D)
(Second District)
1508 Longworth House
Office Building
Washington, DC 20515
Phone: 202-225-2331
FAX: 202-226-0836

Rep. James Ramstad (R)
(Third District)
322 Cannon House
Office Building
Washington, DC 20515
Phone: 202-225-2871
FAX: 202-225-6351

Rep. Bruce F. Vento (DFL) (Fourth District)
2304 Rayburn House
Office Building
Washington, DC 20515
Phone: 202-225-6631
FAX: 202-225-1968

Rep. Martin Olav Sabo (DFL) (Fifth District)
2336 Rayburn House
Office Building
Washington, DC 20515
Phone: 202-225-4755
FAX: 202-225-4886

Rep. William Luther (D)
(Sixth District)
1713 Longworth House
Office Building
Washington, DC 20515
Phone: 202-225-2271
FAX: 202-225-9802

Rep. Collin C. Peterson (DFL) (Seventh District)
1133 Longworth House
Office Building
Washington, DC 20515
Phone: 202-225-2165
FAX: 202-225-1593

Rep. James L. Oberstar (DFL) (Eighth District)
2366 Rayburn House
Office Building
Washington, DC 20515
Phone: 202-225-6211
FAX: 202-225-0699

MISSISSIPPI

Senators

Senator Thad Cochran (R)
326 Russell Senate
Office Building
Washington, DC 20510
Phone: 202-224-5054
FAX: 202-224-3576

Senator Trent Lott (R)
487 Russell Senate
Office Building
Washington, DC 20510
Phone: 202-224-6253
FAX: 202-224-2262

Representatives

Rep. Roger Wicker (R)
(First District)
2314 Rayburn House
Office Building
Washington, DC 20515
Phone: 202-225-4306
FAX: 202-225-4328

Rep. Bennie Thompson (D) (Second District)
1408 Longworth House
Office Building
Washington, DC 20515
Phone: 202-225-5876
FAX: 202-225-5898

Rep. G. V. "Sonny" Montgomery (D)
(Third District)
2184 Rayburn House
Office Building
Washington, DC 20515
Phone: 202-225-5031
FAX: 202-225-3375

Rep. Mike Parker (D)
(Fourth District)
1410 Longworth House
Office Building
Washington, DC 20515
Phone: 202-225-5865
FAX: 202-225-5886

Rep. Gene Taylor (D)
(Fifth District)
214 Cannon House
Office Building
Washington, DC 20515
Phone: 202-225-5772
FAX: 202-225-7074

MISSOURI

<u>Senators</u>

Senator John Ashcroft (R)
249 Russell Senate
Office Building
Washington, DC 20510
Phone: 202-224-6154
FAX: 202-224-7615

Senator Christopher Samuel "Kit" Bond (R)
293 Russell Senate
Office Building
Washington, DC 20510
Phone: 202-224-5721
FAX: 202-224-7491

<u>Representatives</u>

Rep. William L. Clay (D)
(First District)
2306 Rayburn House
Office Building
Washington, DC 20515
Phone: 202-225-2406
FAX: 202-225-1725

Rep. James M. Talent (R)
(Second District)
1022 Longworth House
Office Building
Washington, DC 20515
Phone: 202-225-2561
FAX: 202-225-2563

Rep. Richard A. Gephardt (D)
(Third District)
1432 Longworth House
Office Building
Washington, DC 20515
Phone: 202-225-2671
FAX: 202-225-7414

Rep. Isaac "Ike" Skelton, IV (D)
(Fourth District)
2227 Rayburn House
Office Building
Washington, DC 20515
Phone: 202-225-2876
FAX: 202-225-269S

Rep. Karen McCarthy (D) (Fifth District)
2334 Rayburn House
Office Building
Washington, DC 20515
Phone: 202-225-4535
FAX: 202-225-5990

Rep. Pat Danner (D)
(Sixth District)
1217 Longworth House
Office Building
Washington, DC 20515
Phone: 202-225-7041
FAX: 202-225-8221

Rep. Melton D. Hancock (R) (Seventh District)
129 Cannon House
Office Building
Washington, DC 20515
Phone: 202-225-6536
FAX: 202-225-7700

Rep. Bill Emerson (R)
(Eighth District)
2454 Cannon House Office Building
Washington, DC 20515
Phone: 202-225-4404
FAX: 202-225-9621

Rep. Harold L. Volkmer (D) (Ninth District)
2409 Rayburn House
Office Building
Washington, DC 20515
Phone: 202-225-2956
FAX: 202-225-7834

MONTANA

<u>Senators</u>

Senator Max Baucus (D)
511 Hart Senate
Office Building
Washington, DC 20510
Phone: 202-224-2651
FAX: (Unavailable)

Senator Conrad Burns (R)
183 Dirksen Senate
Office Building
Washington, DC 20510
Phone: 202-224-2644
FAX: 202-224-8594

<u>Representative At Large</u>

Rep. Pat Williams (D)
2457 Rayburn House
Office Building
Washington, DC 20515
Phone: 202-225-3211
FAX: 202-226-0244

NEBRASKA

<u>Senators</u>

Senator J. James Exon (D)
528 Hart Senate
Office Building
Washington, DC 20510
Phone: 202-224-4224
FAX: 202-224-5213

Senator Joseph R. Kerrey (D)
303 Hart Senate
Office Building
Washington, DC 20510
Phone: 202-224-6551
FAX: 202-224-7645

__Representatives__
Rep. Douglas K. Bereuter (R)
(First District)
2348 Rayburn House
Office Building
Washington, DC 20515
Phone: 202-225-4806
FAX: 202-226-1148

Rep. Jon Christensen (R)
(Second District)
1113 Longworth House
Office Building
Washington, DC 20515
Phone: 202-225-4155
FAX: 202-225-4684

Rep. William Barrett (R)
(Third District)
1213 Longworth House
Office Building
Washington, DC 20515
Phone: 202-225-6435
FAX: 202-225-0207

NEVADA

__Senators__
Senator Harry M. Reid (D)
324 Hart Senate
Office Building
Washington, DC 20510
Phone: 202-224-3542
FAX: 202-224-7327

Senator Richard H. Bryan (D)
364 Russell Senate
Office Building
Washington, DC 20510
Phone: 202-224-6244
FAX: 202-224-1867

__Representatives__
Rep. John Ensign (D)
(First District)
2431 Rayburn House
Office Building
Washington, DC 20515
Phone: 202-255-5965
FAX: 202-225-8808

Rep. Barbara F. Vucanovich (R)
(Second District)
2202 Rayburn House
Office Building
Washington, DC 20515
Phone: 202-225-6155
FAX: 202-225-2319

NEW HAMPSHIRE

__Senators__
Senator Judd Gregg (R)
393 Russell Senate
Office Building
Washington, DC 20510
Phone: 202-224-3324
FAX: 202-224-4952

Senator Robert C. Smith (R)
332 Dirksen Senate
Office Building
Washington, DC 20510
Phone: 202-224-2841
FAX: 202-224-1353

__Representatives__
Rep. William Zeliff (R)
(First District)
224 Cannon House
Office Building
Washington, DC 20515
Phone: 202-225-5456
FAX: 202-225-4370

Rep. Charles Bass (R)
(Second District)
230 Cannon House
Office Building
Washington, DC 20515
Phone: 202-225-5206
FAX: 202-225-0046

NEW JERSEY

__Senators__
Senator Bill Bradley (D)
731 Hart Senate
Office Building
Washington, DC 20510
Phone: 202-224-3224
FAX: 202-224-8567

Senator Frank R. Lautenberg (D)
506 Hart Senate
Office Building
Washington, DC 20510
Phone: 202-224-4744
FAX: 202-224-9707

__Representatives__
Rep. Robert E. Andrews (D) (First District)
1005 Longworth House
Office Building
Washington, DC 20515
Phone: 202-225-6501
FAX: 202-225-6583

Rep. Frank LoBiondo (R) (Second District)
241 Cannon House
Office Building
Washington, DC 20515
Phone: 202-225-6572
FAX: 202-225-8530

Rep. H. James Saxton (R)
(Third District)
438 Cannon House
Office Building
Washington, DC 20515
Phone: 202-225-4765
FAX: 202-225-0778

Rep. Christopher II. Smith (R)
(Fourth District)
2353 Rayburn House
Office Building
Washington, DC 20515
Phone: 202-225-3765
FAX: 202-225-7768

Rep. Marge S. Roukema (R) (Fifth District)
2244 Rayburn House
Office Building
Washington, DC 20515
Phone: 202-225-4465
FAX: 202-225-9048

Rep. Frank J. Pallone, Jr. (D) (Sixth District)
420 Cannon House
Office Building
Washington, DC 20515
Phone: 202-225-4671
FAX: 202-225-9665

Rep. Bob Franks (R)
(Seventh District)
429 Cannon House
Office Building
Washington, DC 20515
Phone: 202-225-5361
FAX: 202-225-9460

Rep. Bill Martini (R)
(Eighth District)
1728 Longworth House
Office Building
Washington, DC 20515
Phone: 202-225-5751
FAX: 202-226-2273

Rep. Robert G. Torricelli (D)
(Ninth District)
2159 Rayburn House
Office Building
Washington, DC 20515
Phone: 202-225-5061
FAX: 202-225-0843

Rep. Donald M. Payne (D) (Tenth District)
417 Cannon House
Office Building
Washington, DC 20515
Phone: 202-225-3436
FAX: 202-225-4160

Rep. Rodney Frelinghuysen (R)
(Eleventh District)
2447 Rayburn House
Office Building
Washington, DC 20515
Phone: 202-225-5034
FAX: 202-225-0658

Rep. Richard Zimmer (R) (Twelfth District)
228 Cannon House
Office Building
Washington, DC 20515
Phone: 202-225-5801
FAX: 202-226-0792

Rep. Robert Memendez (D) (Thirteenth District)
1531 Longworth House
Office Building
Washington, DC 20515
Phone: 202-225-7919
FAX: 202-22-0792

NEW MEXICO

Senators

Senator Pete V. Domenici (R)
427 Dirksen Senate
Office Building
Washington, DC 20510
Phone: 202-224-6621
FAX: 202-224-7371

Senator Jeff Bingaman (D)
524 Hart Senate
Office Building
Washington, DC 20510
Phone: 202-224-5521
FAX: 202-224-1810

Representatives

Rep. Steven H. Schiff (R)
(First District)
1009 Longworth House
Office Building
Washington, DC 20515
Phone: 202-225-6316
FAX: 202-225-4975

Rep. Joseph R. Skeen (R)
(Second District)
2367 Rayburn House
Office Building
Washington, DC 20515
Phone: 202-225-2365
FAX: 202-225-9599

Rep. Bill Richardson (D)
(Third District)
2349 Rayburn House
Office Building
Washington, DC 20515
Phone: 202-225-6190
FAX: 202-225-1950

NEW YORK

Senators

Senator Daniel Patrick Moynihan (D)
464 Russell Senate
Office Building
Washington, DC 20510
Phone: 202-224-4451
FAX: 202-224-9293

Senator Alfonse M. D'Amato (R)
520 Hart Senate
Office Building
Washington, DC 20510
Phone: 202-224-6542
FAX: 202-224-5871

Representatives

Rep. Michael Forbes (R)
(First District)
229 Cannon House
Office Building
Washington, DC 20515
Phone: 202-225-3826
FAX: 202-225-0776

Rep. Rick Lazio (R)
(Second District)
314 Cannon House
Office Building
Washington, DC 20515
Phone: 202-225-3335
FAX: 202-225-4669

Rep. Peter King (R)
(Third District)
118 Cannon House
Office Building
Washington, DC 20515
Phone: 202-225-7896
FAX: 202-226-2279

Rep. Daniel Frisa (R)
(Fourth District)
116 Cannon House
Office Building
Washington, DC 20515
Phone: 202-225-5516
FAX: 202-225-4672

Rep. Gary L. Ackerman (D) (Fifth District)
2445 Rayburn House
Office Building
Washington, DC 20515
Phone: 202-225-2601
FAX: 202-225-1589

Rep. Floyd H. Flake (D)
(Sixth District)
1035 Longworth House
Office Building
Washington, DC 20515
Phone: 202-225-3461
FAX: 202-225-4169

Rep. Thomas J. Manton (D) (Seventh District)
203 Cannon House
Office Building
Washington, DC 20515
Phone: 202-225-3965
FAX: 202-225-1909

Rep. Jerrold Nadler (D)
(Eighth District)
424 Cannon House
Office Building
Washington, DC 20515
Phone: 202-225-5635
FAX: 202-225-6923

Rep. Charles E. Schumer (D)
(Ninth District)
2412 Longworth House
Office Building
Washington, DC 20515
Phone: 202-225-6616
FAX: 202-225-4183

Rep. Edolphus Towns (D) (Tenth District)
2232 Rayburn House
Office Building
Washington, DC 20515
Phone: 202-225-5936
FAX: 202-225-1018

Rep. Major R. Owens (D)
(Eleventh District)
2305 Rayburn House
Office Building
Washington, DC 20515
Phone: 202-225-6231
FAX: 202-226-0112

Rep. Nydia Velazquez (D) (Twelfth District)
132 Cannon House
Office Building
Washington, DC 20515
Phone: 202-225-2361
FAX: 202-226-0327

Rep. Susan Molinari (R)
(Thirteenth District)
123 Cannon House
Office Building
Washington, DC 20515
Phone: 202-225-3371
FAX: 202-226-1272

Rep. Carolyn Maloney (D) (Fourteenth District)
1504 Longworth House
Office Building
Washington, DC 20515
Phone: 202-225-7944
FAX: 202-225-4709

Rep. Charla Bernard Rangel (D)
(Fifteenth District)
2252 Rayburn House
Office Building
Washington, DC 20515
Phone: 202-225-4365
FAX: 202-225-0816

Rep. Jose E. Serrano (D)
(Sixteenth District)
336 Cannon House
Office Building
Washington, DC 20515
Phone: 202-225-4361
FAX: 202-225-6001

Rep. Eliot L. Engel (D)
(Seventeenth District)
1434 Longworth House
Office Building
Washington, DC 20515
Phone: 202-225-2464
FAX: 202-225-5513

Rep. Nita M. Lowey (D)
(Eighteenth District)
1424 Longworth House
Office Building
Washington, DC 20515
Phone: 202-225-6506
FAX: 202-225-0546

Rep. Sue Kelly (R)
(Nineteenth District)
2354 Rayburn House
Office Building
Washington, DC 20515
Phone: 202-225-5441
FAX: 202-225-0962

Rep. Benjamin A. Gilman (R)
(Twentieth District)
2185 Rayburn House
Office Building
Washington, DC 20515
Phone: 202-225-3776
FAX: 202-225-2541

Rep. Michael R. McNulty (D) (Twenty-First District)
217 Cannon House
Office Building
Washington, DC 20515
Phone: 202-225-5076
FAX: 202-225-5077

Rep. Gerald B. H. Solomon (R)
(Twenty- Second District)
2265 Rayburn House
Office Building
Washington, DC 20515
Phone: 202-225-5614
FAX: 202-225-5234

Rep. Sherwood L. Boehlert (R)
(Twenty-Third District)
1127 Longworth House
Office Building
Washington, DC 20515
Phone: 202-225-3665
FAX: 202-225-1891

Rep. John McHugh (R)
(Twenty-Fourth District)
416 Cannon House
Office Building
Washington, DC 20515
Phone: 202-225-4611
FAX: 202-226-0621

Rep. James T. Walsh (R)
(Twenty-Fifth District)
1330 Longworth House
Office Building
Washington, DC 20515
Phone: 202-225-3701
FAX: 202-225-4042

Rep. Maurice Hinchey (D)
(Twenty-Sixth District)
1313 Longworth House
Office Building
Washington, DC 20515
Phone: 202-225-6335
FAX: 202-226-0774

Rep. L. William Paxon (R)
(Twenty-Seventh District)
1314 Longworth House
Office Building
Washington, DC 20515
Phone: 202-225-5265
FAX: 202-225-5910

Rep. Louise M. Slaughter (D)
(Twenty-Eighth District)
2421 Rayburn House
Office Building
Washington, DC 20515
Phone: 202-225-3615
FAX: 202-225-7822

Rep. John J. LaFalce (D)
(Twenty-Ninth District)
2310 Rayburn House
Office Building
Washington, DC 20515
Phone: 202-225-3231
FAX: 202-225-8693

Rep. Jack Quinn (R)
(Thirtieth District)
331 Cannon House
Office Building
Washington, DC 20515
Phone: 202-225-3306
FAX: 202-226-0347

Rep. Amory "Amo" Houghton, Jr. (R)
(Thirty-First District)
1110 Longworth House
Office Building
Washington, DC 20515
Phone: 202-225-3161
FAX: 202-225-5574

NORTH CAROLINA

Senators

Senator Jesse A. Hehns (R)
403 Dirksen Senate
Office Building
Washington, DC 20510
Phone: 202-224-6342
FAX: 202-224-7588

Senator Lauch Faircloth (R)
702 Hart Senate
Office Building
Washington, DC 20510
Phone: 202-224-3154
FAX: 202-224-7406

Representatives

Rep. Eva Clayton (D)
(First District)
222 Cannon House
Office Building
Washington, DC 20515
Phone: 202-225-3101
FAX: 202-225-3354

Rep. Walter Jones (D)
(Second District)
2229 Rayburn House
Office Building
Washington, DC 20515
Phone: 202-225-4531
FAX: 202-225-1539

Rep. Walter Jones (R)
(Third District)
2436 Rayburn House
Office Building
Washington, DC 20515
Phone: 202-225-3415
FAX: 202-225-0666

Rep. Fred Heineman (D)
(Fourth District)
2458 Rayburn House
Office Building
Washington, DC 20515
Phone: 202-225-1784
FAX: 202-225-6314

Rep. Richard Burr (D)
(Fifth District)
2469 Rayburn House
Office Building
Washington, DC 20515
Phone: 202-225-2071
FAX: 202-225-4060

Rep. John Howard Coble (R)
(Sixth District)
403 Cannon House
Office Building
Washington, DC 20515
Phone: 202-225-3065
FAX: 202-225-8611

Rep. Charles G. Rose, III (D) (Seventh District)
2230 Rayburn House
Office Building
Washington, DC 20515
Phone: 202-225-2731
FAX: 202-225-2470

Rep. W.G. "Bill" Hefner (D) (Eighth District)
2470 Rayburn House
Office Building
Washington, DC 20515
Phone: 202-225-3715
FAX: 202-225-4036

Rep. Sue Myrick (R)
(Ninth District)
401 Cannon House
Office Building
Washington, DC 20515
Phone: 202-225-1976
FAX: 202-225-8995

Rep. David Funderburk (R) (Tenth District)
2238 Rayburn House
Office Building
Washington, DC 20515
Phone: 202-225-2576
FAX: 202-225-0316

Rep. Charles H. Taylor (R) (Eleventh District)
516 Cannon House
Office Building
Washington, DC 20515
Phone: 202-225-6401
FAX: 202-225-0519

Rep. Melvin Watt (D)
(Twelfth District)
1232 Longworth House
Office Building
Washington, DC 20515
Phone: 202-225-1510
FAX: 202-225-1512

NORTH DAKOTA

<u>Senators</u>

Senator Byron L. Dorgan (D)
713 Hart Senate
Office Building
Washington, DC 20510
Phone: 202-224-2551
FAX: 202-224-1193

Senator Kent Conrad (D)
724 Hart Senate
Office Building
Washington, DC 20510
Phone: 202-224-2043
FAX: 202-224-7776

<u>Representative At Large</u>

Rep. Earl Pomeroy (D)
318 Cannon House
Office Building
Washington, DC 20515
Phone: 202-225-2611
FAX: 202-226-0893

OHIO

<u>Senators</u>

Senator John H. Glenn, Jr. (D)
503 Hart Senate
Office Building
Washington, DC 20510
Phone: 202-224-3353
FAX: 202-226-7983

Senator Mike DeWine (R)
140 Russell Senate
Office Building
Washington, DC 20510
Phone: 202-224-2315
FAX: 202-224-6519

<u>Representatives</u>

Rep. Steve Chabot (D)
(First District)
503 Cannon House
Office Building
Washington, DC 20515
Phone: 202-225-2216
FAX: 202-225-4732

Rep. Rob Portman (R)
(Second District)
238 Cannon House
Office Building
Washington, DC 20515
Phone: 202-225-3164
FAX: 202-225-1992

Rep. Tony P. Hall (D)
(Third District)
2264 Rayburn House
Office Building
Washington, DC 20515
Phone: 202-225-6465
FAX: 202-225-6766

Rep. Michael G. Oxley (R) (Fourth District)
2233 Rayburn House
Office Building
Washington, DC 20515
Phone: 202-225-2676
FAX: 202-226- 1160

Rep. Paul E. Gillmor (R)
(Fifth District)
1203 Longworth House
Office Building
Washington, DC 20515
Phone: 202-225-6405
FAX: 202-225-1985

Rep. Frank Cremeans (R) (Sixth District)
1429 Longworth House
Office Building
Washington, DC 20515
Phone: 202-225-5705
FAX: 202-226-0331

Rep. David L. Hobson (R) (Seventh District)
1507 Longworth House
Office Building
Washington, DC 20515
Phone: 202-225-4324
FAX: 202-225-1984

Rep. John A. Boehner (R) (Eighth District)
1020 Longworth House
Office Building
Washington, DC 20515
Phone: 202-225-6205
FAX: 202-225-0704

Rep. Marcy Kaptur (D)
(Ninth District)
2104 Rayburn House
Office Building
Washington, DC 20515
Phone: 202-225-4146
FAX: 202-225-7711

Rep. Martin R. Hoke (R)
(Tenth District)
212 Cannon House
Office Building
Washington, DC 20515
Phone: 202-225-5871
FAX: 202-226-0994

Rep. Louis Stokes (D)
(Eleventh District)
2365 Rayburn House
Office Building
Washington, DC 20515
Phone: 202-225-7032
FAX: 202-225-1339

Rep. John R. Kasich (R)
(Twelfth District)
1131 Longworth House
Office Building
Washington, DC 20515
Phone: 202-225-5355
FAX: (Unlisted)

Rep. Sherrod Brown (D)
(Thirteenth District)
1407 Longworth House
Office Building
Washington, DC 20515
Phone: 202-225-3401
FAX: 202-225-2266

Rep. Thomas C. Sawyer (D) (Fourteenth District)
1414 Longworth House
Office Building
Washington, DC 20515
Phone: 202-225-5231
FAX: 202-225-5278

Rep. Deborah Pryce (R)
(Fifteenth District)
128 Cannon House
Office Building
Washington, DC 20515
Phone: 202-225-2015
FAX: 202-226-0986

Rep. Ralph S. Regula (R)
(Sixteenth District)
2309 Rayburn House
Office Building
Washington, DC 20515
Phone: 202-225-3876
FAX: 202-225-3059

Rep. James A. Traficant, Jr. (D)
(Seventeenth District)
2446 Rayburn House
Office Building
Washington, DC 20515
Phone: 202-225-5261
FAX: 202-225-3719

Rep. E. Bob Ney (R)
(Eighteenth District)
2183 Rayburn House
Office Building
Washington, DC 20515
Phone: 202-225-6265
FAX: 202-225-3087

Rep. Steven LaTourette (D) (Nineteenth District)
431 Cannon House
Office Building
Washington, DC 20515
Phone: 202-225-5731
FAX: 202-225-9114

OKLAHOMA

Senators

Senator James InHofe (R)
453 Russell Senate
Office Building
Washington, DC 20510
Phone: 202-225-4721
FAX: (Unlisted)

Senator Donald Nickles (R)
133 Hart Senate
Office Building
Washington, DC 20510
Phone: 202-224-5754
FAX: 202-224-6008

Representatives

Rep. Steve Largent (R)
(First District)
442 Cannon House
Office Building
Washington, DC 20515
Phone: 202-225-2211
FAX: 202-225-9187

Rep. Tom Coburn (R)
(Second District)
2329 Rayburn House
Office Building
Washington, DC 20515
Phone: 202-225-2701
FAX: 202-225-2796

Rep. William Brewster (D) (Third District)
1727 Longworth House
Office Building
Washington, DC 20515
Phone: 202-225-4565
FAX: 202-225-9029

Rep. J. C. Watts (R)
(Fourth District)
2344 Rayburn House
Office Building
Washington, DC 20515
Phone: 202-225-6165
FAX: 202-225-9746

Rep. Earnest J. Istook (R) (Fifth District)
1116 Longworth House
Office Building
Washington, DC 20515
Phone: 202-225-2132
FAX: 202-226-1463

Rep. Frank Lucas (R)
(Sixth District)
2206 Rayburn House
Office Building
Washington, DC 20515
Phone: 202-225-5565
FAX: 202-225-8698

OREGON

Senators

Senator Mark O. Hatfield **(R)**
711 Hart Senate
Office Building
Washington, DC 20510
Phone: 202-224-3753
FAX: 202-224-0276

Senator Robert William Packwood (R)*
259 Russell Senate
Office Building
Washington, DC 20510
Phone: 202-224-5244
FAX: 202-228-3576

Representatives

Rep. Elizabeth Furse (D)
(First District)
316 Cannon House
Office Building
Washington, DC 20515
Phone: 202-225-0855
FAX: 202-225-9497

Rep. Wes Cooley (R)
(Second District)
118 Cannon House
Office Building
Washington, DC 20515
Phone: 202-225-6730
FAX: 202-225-3129

Rep. Ron Wyden (D)
(Third District)
1111 Longworth House
Office Building
Washington, DC 20515
Phone: 202-225-4811
FAX: 202-225-8941

Rep. Peter A. DeFazio (D) (Fourth District)
1233 Longworth House
Office Building
Washington, DC 20515
Phone: 202-225-6416
FAX: 202-225-0694

Rep. Catherine Webber (D) (Fifth District)
218 Cannon House
Office Building
Washington, DC 20510
Phone: 202-225-5711
FAX: 202-225-9477

PENNSYLVANIA

Senators

Senator Rick Santorum (R)
521 Dirksen Senate
Office Building
Washington, DC 20510
Phone: 202-224-6324
FAX: 202-224-4161

Senator Arlen Specter (R)
530 Hart Senate
Office Building
Washington, DC 20510
Phone: 202-224-4254
FAX: 202-224-1893

*resigned during term

<u>**Representatives**</u>

Rep. Thomas M. Foglietta (D)
(First District)
341 Cannon House Office Building
Washington, DC 20515
Phone: 202-225-4731
FAX: 202-225-0088

Rep. Chaka Fattah (D)
(Second District)
410 Cannon House Office Building
Washington, DC 20515
Phone: 202-225-4001
FAX: 202-225-7362

Rep. Robert A. Borski (D) (Third District)
2161 Rayburn House Office Building
Washington, DC 20515
Phone: 202-225-8251
FAX: 202-225-4628

Rep. Ron Klink (D)
(Fourth District)
1130 Longworth House Office Building
Washington, DC 20515
Phone: 202-225-2565
FAX: 202-226-2274

Rep. William F. Clinger, Jr. (R) (Fifth District)
2160 Rayburn House Office Building
Washington, DC 20515
Phone: 202-225-5121
FAX: 202-225-4681

Rep. Tim Holden (D)
(Sixth District)
1421 Longworth House Office Building
Washington, DC 20515
Phone: 202-225-5546
FAX: 202-226-0996

Rep. Wayne C. Weldon (R) (Seventh District)
2452 Cannon House Office Building
Washington, DC 20515
Phone: 202-225-2011
FAX: 202-225-8137

Rep. Jim Greenwood (R)
(Eighth District)
515 Cannon House Office Building
Washington, DC 20515
Phone: 202-225-4276
FAX: 202-225-9511

Rep. E. G. "Bud" Shuster (R)
(Ninth District)
2188 Rayburn House Office Building
Washington, DC 20515
Phone: 202-225-2431
FAX: 202-225-2486

Rep. Joseph M. McDade (R) (Tenth District)
2370 Rayburn House Office Building
Washington, DC 20515
Phone: 202-225-3731
FAX: 202-225-9594

Rep. Paul E. Kanjorski (D) (Eleventh District)
2429 Cannon House Office Building
Washington, DC 20515
Phone: 202-225-6511
FAX: 202-225-9024

Rep. John P. Murtha (D)
(Twelfth District)
2423 Rayburn House Office Building
Washington, DC 20515
Phone: 202-225-2065
FAIN: 202-225-5709

Rep. Jon Fox (R)
(Thirteenth District)
1516 Rayburn House Office Building
Washington, DC 20515
Phone: 202-225-6111
FAX: 202-226-0798

Rep. William J. Coyne (D) (Fourteenth District)
2455 Rayburn House Office Building
Washington, DC 20515
Phone: 202-225-2301
FAX: 202-225-1844

Rep. Paul McHale (D)
(Fifteenth District)
511 Rayburn House Office Building
Washington, DC 20515
Phone: 202-225-6411
FAX: 202-225-5320

Rep. Robert S. Walker (R) (Sixteenth District)
2369 Rayburn House
Office Building
Washington, DC 20515
Phone: 202-225-2411
FAX: 202-225-2484

Rep. George W. Gekas (R) (Seventeenth District)
2410 Longworth House
Office Building
Washington, DC 20515
Phone: 202-225-4315
FAX: 202-225-8440

Rep. Michael Doyle (D)
(Eighteenth District)
1222 Longworth House
Office Building
Washington, DC 20515
Phone: 202-225-2135
FAX: 202-225-7747

Rep. William F. Goodling (R)
(Nineteenth District)
2263 Rayburn House
Office Building
Washington, DC 20515
Phone: 202-225-5836
FAX: 202-226-1000

Rep. Frank Mascara (D)
(Twentieth District)
2210 Rayburn House
Office Building
Washington, DC 20515
Phone: 202-225-4665
FAX: 202-225-4772

Rep. Philip English (R)
(Twenty-First District)
1714 Longworth House
Office Building
Washington, DC 20515
Phone: 202-225-5406
FAX: 202-225-1081

RHODE ISLAND

Senators

Senator Claiborne Pell (D)
335 Russell Senate
Office Building
Washington, DC 20510
Phone: 202-224-4642
FAX: 202-224-4680

Senator John H. Chafee (R)
567 Dirksen Senate
Office Building
Washington, DC 20510
Phone: 202-224-2921
FAX: 202-224-7472

Representatives

Rep. Patrick Kennedy (D) (First District)
326 Cannon House
Office Building
Washington, DC 20515
Phone: 202-225-4911
FAX: 202-225-4417

Rep. John F. Reed (R)
(Second District)
1510 Longworth House
Office Building
Washington, DC 20515
Phone: 202-225-2735
FAX: 202-225-9580

SOUTH CAROLINA

Senators

Senator James Strom Thurmond (R)
217 Russell Senate
Office Building
Washington, DC 20510
Phone: 202-224-5972
FAX: 202-224-1300

Senator Ernest F. Hollings (D)
125 Russell Senate
Office Building
Washington, DC 20510
Phone: 202-224-6121
FAX: 202-224-3573

Representatives

Rep. Mark Sanford (R)
(First District)
231 Cannon House
Office Building
Washington, DC 20515
Phone: 202-225-3176
FAX: 202-225-4340

Rep. Floyd D. Spence (R)
(Second District)
2405 Rayburn House
Office Building
Washington, DC 20515
Phone: 202-225-2452
FAX: 202-225-2455

Rep. Lindsey Graham (R) (Third District)
221 Cannon House
Office Building
Washington, DC 20515
Phone: 202-225-5301
FAX: 202-225-5383

Rep. Bob Inglis (R)
(Fourth District)
1237 Longworth House
Office Building
Washington, DC 20515
Phone: 202-225-6030
FAX: 202-226-1177

Rep. John M. Spratt, Jr. (D) (Fifth District)
1536 Longworth House
Office Building
Washington, DC 20515
Phone: 202-225-5501
FAX: 202-225-4464

Rep. James E. Clyburn (D) (Sixth District)
319 Cannon House
Office Building
Washington, DC 20515
Phone: 202-225-3315
FAX: 202-225-2313

SOUTH DAKOTA

Senators

Senator Larry Pressler (R)
283 Rayburn House
Office Building
Washington, DC 20510
Phone: 202-224-5842
FAX: 202-224-1630

Senator Thomas Andrew Daschle (D)
317 Hart Senate
Office Building
Washington, DC 20510
Phone: 202-224-2321
FAX: 202-224-2047

Representative At Large

Rep. Timothy P. Johnson (D)
2438 Rayburn House
Office Building
Washington, DC 20515
Phone: 202-225-2801
FAX: 202-225-2427

TENNESSEE

Senators

Senator Fred Thompson (R)
363 Russell Senate
Office Building
Washington, DC 20510
Phone: 202-224-3344
FAX: 202-224-8062

Senator Bill Frist (R)
506 Dirksen Senate
Office Building
Washington, DC 20510
Phone: 202-224-1036
FAX: 202-228-3679

Representatives

Rep. James H. Quillen (R) (First District)
102 Cannon House
Office Building
Washington, DC 20515
Phone: 202-225-6356
FAX: 202-225-7812

Rep. John J. Duncan, Jr. (R) (Second District)
115 Cannon House
Office Building
Washington, DC 20515
Phone: 202-225-5435
FAX: 202-225-6440

Rep. Zach Wamp (R)
(Third District)
2406 Rayburn House
Office Building
Washington, DC 20515
Phone: 202-225-3271
FAX: 202-225-6974

Rep. Van Hilleary (R)
(Fourth District)
125 Cannon House
Office Building
Washington, DC 20515
Phone: 202-225-6831
FAX: 202-225-4520

Rep. Bob Clement (D)
(Fifth District)
1230 Cannon House Office
Building
Washington, DC 20515
Phone: 202-225-4311
FAX: 202-226-1035

Rep. Barton J. Gordon (D) (Sixth District)
103 Cannon House
Office Building
Washington, DC 20515
Phone: 202-225-4231
FAX: 202-225-6887

Rep. Ed Bryant (R)
(Seventh District)
339 Cannon House
Office Building
Washington, DC 20515
Phone: 202-225-2811
FAX: 202-225-2814

Rep. John S. Tanner (D)
(Eighth District)
1427 Longworth House
Office Building
Washington, DC 20515
Phone: 202-225-4714
FAX: 202-225-1765

Rep. Harold Eugene Ford (D) (Ninth District)
2211 Rayburn House
Office Building
Washington, DC 20515
Phone: 202-225-3265
FAX: 202-225-9215

TEXAS

Senators

Senator Phil Gramm (R)
370 Russell Senate
Office Building
Washington, DC 20510
Phone: 202-224-2934
FAX: 202-228-2856

Senator Kathyrn "Kay" Bailey Hutchison (R)
703 Hart Senate
Office Building
Washington, DC 20510
Phone: 202-224-5922
FAX: 202-224-0776

Representatives

Rep. Jim Chapman (D)
(First District)
2417 Rayburn House
Office Building
Washington, DC 20515
Phone: 202-225-3035
FAX: 202-225-7265

Rep. Charles N. Wilson (D) (Second District)
2256 Rayburn House
Office Building
Washington, DC 20515
Phone: 202-225-2401
FAX: 202-225-1764

Rep. Sam Johnson (R)
(Third District)
1030 Longworth House
Office Building
Washington, DC 20515
Phone: 202-225-4201
FAX: 202-225-1485

Rep. Ralph M. Hall (D)
(Fourth District)
2236 Rayburn House
Office Building
Washington, DC 20515
Phone: 202-225-6673
FAX: 202-225-3332

Rep. John Wiley Bryant (D) (Fifth District)
205 Cannon House
Office Building
Washington, DC 20515
Phone: 202-225-2231
FAX: 202-225-9721

Rep. Joe Linus Barton (R) (Sixth District)
1514 Longworth House
Office Building
Washington, DC 20515
Phone: 202-225-2002
FAX 202-225-3052

Rep. Bill Archer (R)
(Seventh District)
1236 Longworth House
Office Building
Washington, DC 20515
Phone: 202-225-2571
FAX: 202-225-4381

Rep. Jack Fields (R)
(Eighth District)
2228 Rayburn House
Office Building
Washington, DC 20515
Phone: 202-225-4901
FAX: 202-225-2772

Rep. Steve Stockman (R)
(Ninth District)
2449 Rayburn House
Office Building
Washington, DC 20515
Phone: 202-225-6565
FAX: 202-225-1584

Rep. Lloyd Doggett (D)
(Tenth District)
242 Cannon House
Office Building
Washington, DC 20515
Phone: 202-225-4865
FAX: 202-225-3018

Rep. Chet Edwards (D)
(Eleventh District)
328 Cannon House
Office Building
Washington, DC 20515
Phone: 202-225-6105
FAX: 202-225-0350

Rep. Preston M. "Pete" Geren (D)
(Twelfth District)
1730 Longworth House
Office Building
Washington, DC 20515
Phone: 202-225-5071
FAX: 202-225-2786

Rep. William Thornberry (R)
(Thirteenth District)
126 Cannon House
Office Building
Washington, DC 20515
Phone: 202-225-3706
FAX: 202-225-6142

Rep. Greg Laughlin (D)
(Fourteenth District)
236 Cannon House
Office Building
Washington, DC 20515
Phone: 202-225-2831
FAX: 202-225-1108

Rep. E. "Kika" de la Garza (D)
(Fifteenth District)
1401 Longworth House
Office Building
Washington, DC 20515
Phone: 202-225-2531
FAX: 202-225-2534

Rep. Ronald D'Emory Coleman (D)
(Sixteenth District)
440 Cannon House
Office Building
Washington, DC 20515
Phone: 202-225-4831
FAX: 202-225-4831

Rep. Charles W. Stenholm (D)
(Seventeenth District)
1211 Longworth House
Office Building
Washington, DC 20515
Phone: 202-225-6605
FAX: 202-225-2234

Rep. Shelia Lee (D)
(Eighteenth District)
1711 Longworth House
Office Building
Washington, DC 20515
Phone: 202-225-3816
FAX: 202-225-6186

Rep. Larry Ed Combest (R) (Nineteenth District)
1511 Longworth House
Office Building
Washington, DC 20515
Phone: 202-225-4005
FAX: 202-225-9615

Rep. Henry B. Gonzalez (D) (Twentieth District)
2413 Rayburn House
Office Building
Washington, DC 20515
Phone: 202-225-3236
FAX 202-225-1915

Rep. Lamar S. Smith (R)
(Twenty-First District)
2443 Rayburn House
Office Building
Washington, DC 20515
Phone: 202-225-4236
FAX: 202-225-8628

Rep. Tom DeLay (R)
(Twenty-Second District)
407 Cannon House
Office Building
Washington, DC 20515
Phone: 202-225-595 1
FAX: 202-225-5241

Rep. Henry Bonilla (R)
(Twenty-Third District)
1529 Longworth House
Office Building
Washington, DC 20515
Phone: 202-225-4511
FAX: 202-225-2237

Rep. Martin Frost (D)
(Twenty-Fourth District)
2459 Rayburn House
Office Building
Washington, DC 20515
Phone: 202-225-3605
FAX: 202-225-4951

Rep. Ken Bentsen (D)
(Twenty-Fifth District)
303 Cannon House
Office Building
Washington, DC 20515
Phone: 202-225-7508
FAX: 202-225-4210

Rep. Richard K. Armey (R)
(Twenty-Sixth District)
301 Cannon House
Office Building
Washington, DC 20515
Phone: 202-225-7772
FAX: 202-225-7614

Rep. Solomon P. Ortiz (D)
(Twenty-Seventh District)
2136 Rayburn House
Office Building
Washington, DC 20515
Phone: 202-225-7742
FAX: 202-226-1134

Rep. Frank Tejeda (D)
(Twenty-Eighth District)
323 Cannon House
Office Building
Washington, DC 20515
Phone: 202-225-1640
FAX: 202-225-1641

Rep. Gene Green (D)
(Twenty-Ninth District)
1004 Longworth House
Office Building
Washington, DC 20515
Phone: 202-225-1688
FAX: 202-225-9903

Rep. Eddie B. Johnson (D) (Thirtieth District)
1721 Longworth House
Office Building
Washington, DC 20515
Phone: 202-225-8885
FAX: 202-226-1477

UTAH

Senators

Senator Robert Bennett (R)
241 Dirksen Senate
Office Building
Washington, DC 20510
Phone: 202-224-5444
FAX: 202-224-6717

Senator Orrin G Hatch (R)
135 Russell Senate
Office Building
Washington, DC 20510
Phone: 202-224-5251
FAX: 202-224-6331

Representatives

Rep. James V. Hansen (R) (First District)
2466 Rayburn House
Office Building
Washington, DC 20515
Phone: 202-225-0453
FAX: 202-225-5857

Rep. Karen Shepherd (D)
(Second District)
414 Cannon House
Office Building
Washington, DC 20515
Phone: 202-225-3011
FAX: 202-226-0354

Rep. William Orton (D)
(Third District)
1122 Longworth House
Office Building
Washington, DC 20515
Phone: 202-225-7751
FAX: 202-226-1223

VERMONT

Senators

Senator Patrick Leahy (D)
433 Russell Senate
Office Building
Washington, DC 20510
Phone: 202-224-4242
FAX: 202-224-3595

Senator James M. Jeffords (R)
513 Hart Senate
Office Building
Washington, DC 20510
Phone: 202-224-5141
FAX: 202-224-8330

Representative At Large

Rep. Bernard Sanders (Soc)
213 Cannon House
Office Building
Washington, DC 20515
Phone: 202-225-4115
FAX: 202-225-6790

VIRGINIA

Senators

Senator John W. Warner (R)
225 Russell Senate
Office Building
Washington, DC 20510
Phone: 202-224-2023
FAX: 202-224-6295

Senator Charles S. Robb (D)
493 Russell Senate
Office Building
Washington, DC 20510
Phone: 202-224-4024
FAX: 202-224-8689

Representatives

Rep. Herbert H. Bateman (R)
(First District)
2350 Rayburn House
Office Building
Washington, DC 20515
Phone: 202-225-4261
FAX: 202-225-4382

Rep. Owen B. Pickett (D)
(Second District)
2430 Rayburn House
Office Building
Washington, DC 20515
Phone: 202-225-4215
FAX: 202-225-4218

Rep. Robert C. Scott (D)
(Third District)
501 Cannon House
Office Building
Washington, DC 20515
Phone: 202-225-8351
FAX: 202-225-8354

Rep. Norman Sisisky (D)
(Fourth District)
2352 Cannon House Office
Building
Washington, DC 20515
Phone: 202-225-6365
FAX: 202-226-1170

Rep. Lewis F. Payne, Jr. (D) (Fifth District)
1119 Longworth House
Office Building
Washington, DC 20515
Phone: 202-225-4711
FAX: 202-226-1147

Rep. Robert W. Goodlatte (R)
(Sixth District)
214 Cannon House
Office Building
Washington, DC 20515
Phone: 202-225-5431
FAX: 202-225-9681

Rep. Thomas J. Bliley, Jr. (R) (Seventh District)
2241 Rayburn House
Office Building
Washington, DC 20515
Phone: 202-225-2815
FAX: 202-225-0011

Rep. James P. Moran, Jr. (D) (Eighth District)
430 Cannon House
Office Building
Washington, DC 20515
Phone: 202-225-4376
FAX: 202-225-0017

Rep. Rick Boucher (D)
(Ninth District)
2245 Rayburn House
Office Building
Washington, DC 20515
Phone: 202-225-3861
FAX: 202-225-0442

Rep. Frank R. Wolf (R)
(Tenth District)
104 Cannon House
Office Building
Washington, DC 20515
Phone: 202-225-5136
FAX: 202-225-0437

Rep. Thomas Davis (R)
(Eleventh District)
1609 Longworth House
Office Building
Washington, DC 20515
Phone: 202-225-1492
FAX: 202-225-2274

WASHINGTON

Senators

Senator Patty Murray (D)
302 Hart Senate
Office Building
Washington, DC 20510
Phone: 202-224-2621
FAX: 202-224-0238

Senator Slade Gorton (R)
730 Hart Senate
Office Building
Washington, DC 20510
Phone: 202-224-3441
FAX: 202-224-9393

Representatives

Rep. Rick White (R)
(First District)
1520 Longworth House
Office Building
Washington, DC 20515
Phone: 202-225-6311
FAX: 202-225-2286

Rep. Jack Metcalf (R)
(Second District)
1502 Longworth House
Office Building
Washington, DC 20515
Phone: 202-225-2605
FAX: 202-225-2608

Rep. Linda Smith (R)
(Third District)
1527 Longworth House
Office Building
Washington, DC 20515
Phone: 202-225-3536
FAX: 202-225-9095

Rep. Doc Hastings (R)
(Fourth District)
1431 Longworth House
Office Building
Washington, DC 20515
Phone: 202-225-5816
FAX: 202-226-1137

Rep. George Nethercutt (R) (Fifth District)
1201 Longworth House
Office Building
Washington, DC 20515
Phone: 202-225-2006
FAX: 202-225-7181

Rep. Norman D. Dicks (D) (Sixth District)
2467 Rayburn House
Office Building
Washington, DC 20515
Phone: 202-225-5916
FAX: 202-226-1176

Rep. James A. McDermott (D)
(Seventh District)
1707 Longworth House
Office Building
Washington, DC 20515
Phone: 202-225-3106
FAX: 202-225-9212

Rep. Jennifer Dunn (R)
(Eighth District)
1641 Longworth House
Office Building
Washington, DC 20515
Phone: 202-225-7761
FAX: 202-225-8673

Rep. Randy Tate (R)
(Ninth District)
1535 Longworth House
Office Building
Washington, DC 20515
Phone: 202-225-8901
FAX: 202-226-2361

WEST VIRGINIA

Senators

Senator Robert C. Byrd (D)
311 Hart Senate
Office Building
Washington, DC 20510
Phone: 202-224-3954
FAX: 202-224-4025

Senator John D. Rockefeller, IV (D)
109 Hart Senate
Office Building
Washington, DC 20510
Phone: 202-224-6472
FAX: 202-224-7665

Representatives

Rep. Alan B. Mollohan (D) (First District)
2242 Rayburn House
Office Building
Washington, DC 20515
Phone: 202-225-4172
FAX: 202-225-7564

Rep. Robert W. Wise (D)
(Second District)
2434 Rayburn House
Office Building
Washington, DC 20515
Phone: 202-225-2711
FAX: 202-225-7856

Rep. Nick Joe Rahall, II (D)
(Third District)
2269 Rayburn House
Office Building
Washington, DC 20515
Phone: 202-225-3452
FAX: 202-225-9061

WISCONSIN

Senators

Senator Russell Feingold (D)
502 Hart Senate
Office Building
Washington, DC 20510
Phone: 202-224-5323
FAX: 202-224-2725

Senator Herb Kohl (D)
330 Hart Senate
Office Building
Washington, DC 20510
Phone: 202-224-5653
FAX: 202-224-9787

Representatives

Rep. Mark Neumann (R)
(First District)
1719 Longworth House
Office Building
Washington, DC 20515
Phone: 202-225-3031
FAX: 202-225-9820

Rep. Scott L. Klug (R)
(Second District)
1224 Longworth House
Office Building
Washington, DC 20515
Phone: 202-225-2906
FAX: 202-225-6942

Rep. Steven C. Gunderson (R)
(Third District)
2235 Rayburn House
Office Building
Washington, DC 20515
Phone: 202-225-5506
FAX: 202-225-6195

Rep. Gerald D. Kleczka (D) (Fourth District)
2301 Rayburn House
Office Building
Washington, DC 20515
Phone: 202-225-4572
FAX: 202-225-0719

Rep. Thomas M. Barrett (D) (Fifth District)
313 Cannon House
Office Building
Washington, DC 20515
Phone: 202-225-3571
FAX: 202-225-2185

Rep. Thomas E. Petri (R)
(Sixth District)
2262 Rayburn House
Office Building
Washington, DC 20515
Phone: 202-225-2476
FAX: 202-225-2356

Rep. David R. Obey (D)
(Seventh District)
2462 Rayburn House
Office Building
Washington, DC 20515
Phone: 202-225-3365
FAX: 202-225-0561

Rep. Toby Roth (R)
(Eighth District)
2234 Rayburn House
Office Building
Washington, DC 20515
Phone: 202-225-5665
FAX: 202-225-0087

Rep. E. James Sensenbrenner, Jr. (R)
(Ninth District)
2332 Rayburn House
Office Building
Washington, DC 20515
Phone: 202-225-5101
FAX: 202-225-3190

WYOMING

Senators

Senator Craig Thomas (R)
237 Russell Senate
Office Building
Washington, DC 20510
Phone: 202-224-6441
FAX: 202-224-3230

Senator Alan K. Simpson (R)
261 Dirksen Senate
Office Building
Washington, DC 20510
Phone: 202-224-3424
FAX: 202-224-1315

Representative At Large

Rep. Barbara Cubin (R)
1019 Longworth House
Office Building
Washington, DC 20505
Phone: 202-225-2311
FAX: 202-225-0726

BIBLIOGRAPHY

Congressional Quarterly
Politics In America - 1996. Congressional Quarterly Inc., 1995.

Congressional Quarterly
Who's Who In Congress. Congressional Quarterly Inc., 1995.

Felten, Eric
The Ruling Class. Regnery Gateway, 1993

Gross, Martin L.
The Government Racket: Washington Waste From A To Z. Bantam Books, 1992.

Gross, Martin L.
A Call For Revolution. Ballantine Books, 1993.

Henry, H. Lon
Congress: America's Privileged Class. Prima Publishing, 1994.

Heritage Foundation
Issues '94 - The Candidate's Briefing Book. The Heritage Foundation, 1994.

Lewis, Charles and the Center for Public Integrity
The Buying of the President. Avon, 1996.

Orenstein, Norman and Mann, Thomas
Vital Statistics on Congress. American Enterprise Institute, 1992.

Schatz, Thomas A.
Speech Before the Joint Economic Committee 2/16/95. Citizens Against Government Waste, 1995.

Snyder, Alan K.
Article re: Government Mismanagement. American Conservative Union, 1994.

Thompson, Dennis F.
Ethics In Congress. The Brookings Institution, 1995.

United States Government Printing Office
Budget of the United States Government - Historical Charts. Fiscal Year 1996.

U.S. Government Printing Office, 1996
United States Chamber of Commerce, 1995
United States Government Congressional Record, 1995.

Will, George F.
Restoration - Congress, Term Limits and the Recovery Of Deliberative Democracy
The Free Press, 1993.

BOOKS FOR FURTHER READING

The Government Racket: Washington Waste From A To Z, Martin L. Gross; Bantam Books, 1992

A Call For Revolution, Martin L. Gross; Ballantine Books, 1993

Contract With America, Gingrich, Armey, and the House Republicans; Random House, 1994

The Ruling Class, Eric Felten; Regnery Gateway, 1993

Cleaning House: America's Campaign for Term Limits, James K. Coyne and John H. Fund; Regnery Gateway, 1992

Congress: America's Privileged Class, H. Lon Henry; Prima Publishing, 1994

The United States of Ambition: Politicians, Power, and the Pursuit of Office, Alan Ehrenhalt; Times Books, 1991

Vital Statistics on Congress, Norman Ornstein and Thomas Mann; American Enterprise Institute, 1992

The Buying of the President, Charles Lewis and the Center for Public Integrity; Avon, 1996

The Way Things Ought To Be, Rush Limbaugh; Pocket Books, 1992

See, I Told You So, Rush Limbaugh, Pocket Books, 1993

Open Secrets, The Encyclopedia of Congressional Money and Politics, Larry Makinson and Joshua Goldstein; Congressional Quarterly, 1992

Honest Graft: Big Money and the American Political Process, Brooks Jackson; Farragut, 1990

The Imperial Congress, Gordon S. Jones and John A. Marini; The Heritage Foundation and Claremont Institute, co-publishers

Ethics In Congress, Dennis F. Thompson; The Brookings Institution, 1995

Rolling Back Government: A Budget Plan to Rebuild America, Scott A. Hodge; The Heritage Foundation

America's Failed $5.4 Trillion War On Poverty, Robert Rector and William F. Lauber; The Heritage Foundation

Still The Best Congress Money Can Buy, Philip M. Stern; Regnery Gateway, 1992

Adventures In Porkland, Brian Kelly; Villard Books, 1992

Hill Rat: Blowing the Lid Off Congress, John Jackley; Regnery Gateway

Unaccountable Congress, Joseph J. DioGuardi, CPA; Regnery Gateway, 1992

Restoration - Congress, Term Limits and the Recovery Of Deliberative Democracy, George F. Will; The Free Press, 1993

Issues '94 - The Candidate's Briefing Book, The Heritage Foundation, 1994

MAGAZINES

Liberty
P.O. Box 1181, Port Townsend, WA 98368 (800)854-6991

National Review
P.O. Box 668, Mount Morris, IL 61054 (815)734-1232

Reason
P.O. Box 526, Mount Morris, IL 61054 (815)734-1102

NEWSLETTERS

Reforming Congress; Heritage Foundation

ORGANIZATIONS OF INTEREST

Advocates for Self-Government (800)932-1776
3955 Pleasantdale Road, Suite 106A, Atlanta, GA 30340
(770)417-1304

American Conservative Union (703)836-8602
1007 Cameron St., Alexandria, VA 22314
A national lobbying organization that rates members of Congress on conservative voting issues. Annual ratings of each member are available for the asking.

Americans for Democratic Action (202)785-5980
1625 K. Street NW, #210, Washington, DC 20006
Liberal domestic and foreign policy, political action and lobbying organization.

Americans for Tax Reform (202)785-0202
1301 Connecticut Ave. NW, Washington, DC 20036
A coalition of individuals and hundreds of state and local taxpayer groups working to oppose increases in taxation at all levels of government. Runs the Taxpayer Protection Pledge, which candidates are asked to sign to commit themselves to opposing higher taxes.

Business-Industry Political Action Committee
1747 Pennsylvania Ave. NW, #250 Washington, DC 20006 (202)833-1880

Cato Institute (202)642-0200
1000 Massachusetts Ave. NW, Washington, DC 20001
Influential think tank on budget reduction and reform.

Center for Public Integrity (202)783-3900
1634 I Street NW, Suite 902, Washington, DC 20006
Created in 1989, leading activist organization promoting better ethical behavior by members of the legislative and executive branches. Wrote *The Buying of the President.*

Citizens Against Government Waste 800-BE-ANGRY
1301 Connecticut Ave. NW #400 , Washington, DC 20036
600,000-member organization which educates the American people about government waste, fraud, and mismanagement, and encourages Congress to implement Grace Commission recommendations, thus making government more accountable to the taxpayer.

Citizens for a Sound Economy (202)783-3870
1250 H Street NW Suite 700, Washington, DC 20005
Organization with over 250,000 members that focuses on policy changes in the areas of taxes, budget policy, trade, legal reform, and government regulation.

Christian Coalition (202)547-3600
227 Massachusetts Ave. NE, Washington, DC 20002

Common Cause (202)633-1200
2030 M Street NW, Washington, DC 20036
Major organization in the fight for cleaner campaign financing for all elections.

Competitive Enterprise Institute (202)331-1010
1001 Connecticut Ave. NW Suite 1250, Washington, DC 20036
Advocates the principles of free enterprise and limited government. Founded on the belief that free markets and competition best serve the public interest. Focuses on pork-barrel spending, tax, and budget issues.

Concord Coalition (202)737-1077
1025 Vermont Ave. NW #810, Washington, DC 20005
Bipartisan grass-roots organization founded by former Senators Paul Tsongas and Warren Rudman, focusing on eliminating the budget deficit and the national debt.

Congressional Accountability Project (202)296-2787
P.O. Box 19446, Washington, DC 20036
Group spearheaded by Ralph Nader to reform Congress's spending. Among other changes, advocates the cutting of congressional pay and perks.

Conservative Index (414)749-3780
P.O. Box 8040, Appleton, WI 45913
Performance evaluations by John Birch Society, a conservative, anti-Communist education group with the goal of less government and more responsibility.

Consumer Federation of America (202)387-6121
1424 16th Street NW, #604, Washington, DC 20036
A federation of 240 organizations who advocate pro-consumer policies before Congress, regulatory agencies, and the courts.

Foundation for Economic Education (914)591-7230
30 S. Broadway Irvington-on-Hudson, New York 10533

Friends Committee on National Legislation
245 Second St. NE, Washington, DC 20002-5795
(202)547-6000

Future of Freedom Foundation (703)934-6101
11350 Random Hills Road, Suite 800 Fairfax, VA 22030

The Heritage Foundation (202)546-4400
214 Massachusetts Ave. NE, Washington, DC 20002
Founded in 1971 as a non-partisan policy research insti-

tute "dedicated to the principles of free competitive enterprise, limited government, individual liberty, and a strong national defense." Has published over 1,500 books and studies, along with magazines, journals, tapes, and newsletters.

League of Conservative Voters (202)785-8683
1707 L St. NW #550, Washington, DC 20036
(202)785-8683

Libertarian Party (800)682-1775 / (202)543-1988
1528 Pennsylvania Ave. SE, Washington, DC 20003
Political party that supports the idea that "each individual has the absolute right to exercise sole dominion over his or her own life, liberty, and property so long as he or she also respects the equal right of all others to live their lives by the same principle."

Liberty Lobby (202)546-5611
300 Independence Ave. SE, Washington, DC 20003
Nationalists and populists interested in political action on behalf of 102 issues which are pro-individual liberty and pro-patriotic. Supports a free gold market, lower taxes, fewer unfair controls, less government spending, and protective immigration laws.

NAACP (202)638-2269
1025 Vermont Ave. NW, #1120, Washington, DC 20005
National Association for the Advancement of Colored People.

National Center on Public Policy Research
(202)543-1286
300 I Street NE Suite 3, Washington, DC 20002
Group that educates grassroots activists on current political issues facing Congress.

National Empowerment Television (202)546-3000
717 Second Street NE, Washington, DC 20002
National grassroots satellite television network linking activists nationwide to discuss how to devolve government by influencing and changing public policy.

National Federation of Independent Business
600 Maryland Ave. SW, #700, Washington, DC 20024
(202)-554-9000

National Tax-Limitation Committee
201 Massachusetts Ave. NW, Suite C-7, Washington, DC 20002 (202)547-4196
Campaigns for federal and state constitutional amendments which would limit government spending and taxation.

National Taxpayers Union (800)TAX-HALT
325 Pennsylvania Ave. SE, Washington, DC 20003
200,000-member organization seeks to reduce government spending, cut taxes, and protect the rights of taxpayers.

Project Vote Smart (800)622-SMART
Provides information to all voters on your representatives, including issue positions, voting records, and evaluations by dozens of special interest groups.

Public Citizen Congress Watch (202)633-3000
215 Pennsylvania Ave. SE, Washington, DC 20003
Congressional lobby representing consumer interests, specifically citizens' access to government decision-making, campaign finance reform, the S&L crisis, consumer class actions, food and product safety, and protection of public health through environmental legislation.

Tax Foundation (202)783-2760
1258 H Street NW Suite 750, Washington, DC 20005
Organization that informs Americans of the cost of government.

U.S. Chamber of Commerce (202)659-6000
1615 H St. NW, Washington, DC 20062-2000
Group which follows business, tax, labor, government regulation, and issues related to business. Promotes business and community development, and conducts institutes covering organizational management and government, and political affairs.

U.S. Term Limits (202)393-6440
1511 K Street NW Suite 540, Washington, DC 20005
National group spearheading the effort to enact term limits for Congress.

United We Stand America (800)925-4000
P.O. Box 516987, Dallas, TX 75251
Nationwide group started by Ross Perot to help empower the citizens, and bring government control back to its owners, instead of its elected officials in Washington.

INDEX

The ten most frightening words in the English language are, "I'm from the government and I'm here to help you."

Steve Forbes

**"I am a firm believer in the people.
If given the truth, they can be depended
upon to meet any national crisis. The great
point is to bring them the real facts."**

Abraham Lincoln